Take & Rea

The Apocalypse

Ian Boxall
edited by Adrian Graffy

Published in 2015 by Alive Publishing Ltd.

Graphic House, 124 City Road, Stoke on Trent, ST4 2PH.

Tel: +44 (0) 1782 745600   Fax: +44 (0) 1782 745500

www.alivepublishing.co.uk

Scripture texts used in this book are taken from the New Revised Standard Version Bible with Apocryphal/Deutero-canonical Books.
Copyrighted ©1965 and 1996. Used with permission.

©2015 Alive Publishing
British Library Catalogue-in-Publication Data.
A catalogue record for this book is available from the British Library.

Quotations from patristic commentaries are from William C. Weinrich (ed.), Ancient Christian Commentary on Scripture: New Testament XII: Revelation (Downers Grove: InterVarsity Press, 2005).

ISBN 978-1-906278-20-5

Front cover: The Adoration of the Mystic Lamb, from the Ghent Altarpiece, lower half of central panel, 1432, Hubert Eyck (c.1370-1426) & Jan van (1390-1441)

Contents

Editor's Foreword

One of the features of the Church of today is the rediscovery of the Bible. In the years since the Second Vatican Council this thirst for the Scriptures has become stronger and stronger. The desire for a deeper engagement with the Bible is clear from the enormous popularity of publications such as *Walk with Me* and *Bible Alive*.

Take and Read is designed to assist people in their need to understand the Bible more deeply. The series has been developed as a follow-up to the document *The Gift of Scripture*, which was produced in 2005 by the Bishops of England and Wales, and of Scotland, to mark the 40th anniversary of the Council document on Divine Revelation, *Dei Verbum*.

The story of the conversion of Saint Augustine to the Catholic faith inspired the title of the series. He recounts in his 'Confessions' how he heard a voice calling to him with the words *Tolle, lege* 'Take and Read'. At that moment he picked up the New Testament and read the first chapter his eyes fell upon, from the Letter to the Romans. His conversion was assured.

These books are a major new resource for prayerful reading of the Scriptures both for groups and for individuals. Passages from the Scriptures are accompanied by commentary, quotations from the Fathers and from Church documents, Christian art and inspiring photographs, as well as suggestions for prayer and reflection.

It is a great pleasure to acknowledge the work of those who helped develop this series. Representatives from dioceses throughout Britain worked on the preparatory stages. Particular thanks should go to Anne White, Anne Dixon and Sister Vicky Hummel. I record my gratitude to the authors who have collaborated with me in working on the series. After the initial books on the four gospels we are now turning our attention to other books of the New Testament. I am particularly grateful for the support of Mike Conway of *Alive Publishing,* who readily agreed to publish the *Take and Read* series.

Take and Read will help you to delve more deeply into the Scriptures, to understand them better, and to pray with the Scriptures. *Take and Read* will assist you in *lectio divina,* that prayerful reading of Scripture which has always been central to the life of the Church.

Fr Adrian Graffy

Introduction to the Apocalypse

The Apocalypse, also known as the *Book of Revelation*, has both fascinated and baffled Christians for centuries. It is a visionary book, in places like a dream, and full of strange characters and symbols. It is therefore very different from the Gospels or the letters of Paul, but similar to other 'apocalypses', such as Daniel and 1 Enoch. It was written, either in the late 60s or mid-90s of the first century, by someone who calls himself simply 'John'.

At times, the Apocalypse can read more like a nightmare, with violent, disturbing images. Yet we should not regard it as primarily about the End of the World. The word 'apocalypse' means not violent destruction, but 'unveiling'. John's book, based on visions received on the island of Patmos, claims to unveil heavenly mysteries, things which humans cannot ordinarily know, in order that they might understand their own world better.

Moreover, John opens his book with a declaration about 'what must soon take place' (*1:1*), and an address to 'the seven churches of Asia' (*1:4*). Thus the main target of his book and its urgent message are first century Christian communities in the Roman province of Asia, which was part of present-day western Turkey.

Yet it also speaks powerfully to Christians of today. It presents us with an alternative vision: where those who appear weak are the truly powerful, where powers that oppress or threaten human freedom are unmasked for what they are and thereby robbed of their power, where the veil separating heaven from earth is very thin, and able to be pierced in the Church's Liturgy.

This book in the *Take and Read* series comprises twelve sessions, each presenting a section of the Apocalypse for study and prayer. The passages chosen aim to give you a good idea of John's visionary narrative, its main themes and its concerns, and to help you understand his book more deeply. However, you will understand the Apocalypse better if you read the intervening sections of the book in your own Bible.

The Apocalypse invites us to use our imaginations so as to see the world, and ourselves, differently, from heaven's perspective. It invites us to enter into an unfamiliar world of angels, monsters and heavenly cities, in order to relearn what it means to follow Christ the Lamb, who died but now lives forever and ever.

Opposite: St John the Evangelist at Patmos, from the Mystic Marriage of St Catherine Triptych, 1479, Hans Memling (c.1433-94)

John sees the Risen Jesus

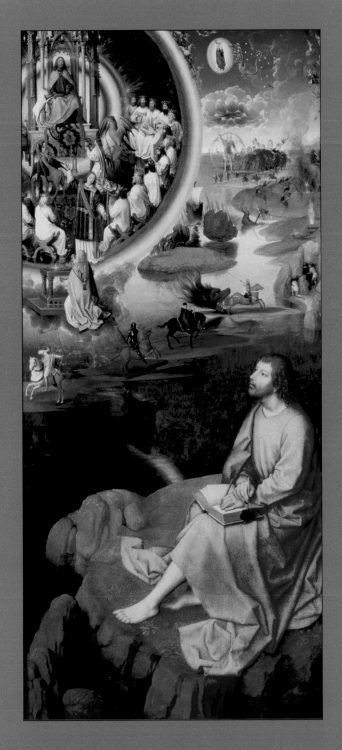

Hear the Word of God

Apocalypse 1:1-20

¹ The revelation of Jesus Christ, which God gave him to show his servants what must soon take place; he made it known by sending his angel to his servant John, ² who testified to the word of God and to the testimony of Jesus Christ, even to all that he saw. ³ Blessed is the one who reads aloud the words of the prophecy, and blessed are those who hear and who keep what is written in it; for the time is near.

⁴ John to the seven churches that are in Asia: Grace to you and peace from him who is and who was and who is to come, and from the seven spirits who are before his throne, ⁵ and from Jesus Christ, the faithful witness, the firstborn of the dead, and the ruler of the kings of the earth.

To him who loves us and freed us from our sins by his blood, ⁶ and made us to be a kingdom, priests serving his God and Father, to him be glory and dominion forever and ever. Amen. ⁷ Look! He is coming with the clouds; every eye will see him, even those who pierced him; and on his account all the tribes of the earth will wail. So it is to be. Amen. ⁸ 'I am the Alpha and the Omega,' says the Lord God, who is and who was and who is to come, the Almighty.

⁹ I, John, your brother who share with you in Jesus the persecution and the kingdom and the patient endurance, was on the island called Patmos because of the word of God and the testimony of Jesus. ¹⁰ I was in the spirit on the Lord's day, and I heard behind me a loud voice like a trumpet ¹¹ saying, 'Write in a book what you see and send it to the seven churches, to Ephesus, to Smyrna, to Pergamum, to Thyatira, to Sardis, to Philadelphia, and to Laodicea.'

¹² Then I turned to see whose voice it was that spoke to me, and on turning I saw seven golden lampstands, ¹³ and in the midst of the lampstands I saw one like the Son of Man, clothed with a long robe and with a golden sash across his chest.

¹⁴ His head and his hair were white as white wool, white as snow; his eyes were like a flame of fire, ¹⁵ his feet were like burnished bronze, refined as in a furnace, and his voice was like the sound of many waters. ¹⁶ In his right hand he held seven stars, and from his mouth came a sharp, two-edged sword, and his face was like the sun shining with full force.

[17] When I saw him, I fell at his feet as though dead. But he placed his right hand on me, saying, 'Do not be afraid; I am the first and the last, 18 and the living one. I was dead, and see, I am alive forever and ever; and I have the keys of Death and of Hades.

[19] 'Now write what you have seen, what is, and what is to take place after this. [20] As for the mystery of the seven stars that you saw in my right hand, and the seven golden lampstands: the seven stars are the angels of the seven churches, and the seven lampstands are the seven churches.'

Cave of the Apocalypse, Patmos

Understand the Word of God

This session will explore:

- ❖ the kind of book the Apocalypse claims to be
- ❖ the purpose of John's opening vision
- ❖ John's description of the risen Christ
- ❖ the message for today

Setting in the Book

This crucial opening section makes clear to us what kind of book the Apocalypse is, and sets the scene for the visions to unfold in its remaining chapters. First, these verses root what John describes in heaven, where God is acknowledged as God. As the book continues, we will be taken back to heaven to reorient ourselves.

However, in an apocalypse heaven and earth are not disconnected. Rather, what a visionary sees in heaven is a revelation of what is true, or what will be the case, on earth. So secondly this opening section roots the heavenly visions of the Apocalypse firmly on earth. Just a few miles across the Aegean Sea from Patmos, seven Christian congregations struggle to live out their Christian faith as small minorities in their respective cities. John's first vision of 'one like the Son of Man' will contain a series of messages to these seven churches, containing words of comfort to the vulnerable, and challenge to the complacent (*Apocalypse 2-3*).

What Kind of Text?

This passage falls neatly into three sections: two complementary introductions to the book as a whole (*verses 1-3 and 4-8*), and an initial vision (*verses 9-20*). The introductions provide important clues as to the kind of book this is, and how we should therefore interpret it. First, it is a 'revelation', 'apocalypse' or 'unveiling' (Greek *apokalupsis*, *verse 1*). An apocalypse is a narrative which describes the revelation of heavenly secrets to a human recipient, through a heavenly journey, a dream, or a heavenly mediator. Second, it is a prophetic book, containing 'words of prophecy' (*verse 3*). In it, God's word is addressed directly to his people, both to comfort and to challenge.

The second section (*verses 4-8*) adds two further dimensions. Verses 4-5 resemble a typical letter opening. Verses 6-8 have echoes of early Christian liturgy, suggesting that it was during the liturgy that the Apocalypse was read to the earliest Christians. In other words, it is a circular letter to be read during worship to seven first-century Christian communities, containing both an account of heavenly mysteries revealed to John the seer, and prophetic words to the churches.

Verses 4-5 can be compared to the openings of Paul's letters.

1 Thessalonians 1:1 reads: Paul, Silvanus and Timothy, to the church of the Thessalonians in God the Father and the Lord Jesus Christ: Grace to you and peace.

The third section (*verses 9-20*) describes the opening vision received by John on the island of Patmos. There are echoes here of visions received by Old Testament prophets, especially Ezekiel 1, Daniel 7 and Daniel 10. John's vision serves as a preface to the 'seven messages' of chapters 2-3, and introduces one of the book's main characters, Jesus Christ.

Commentary: verse by verse reading

The Title

vv.1-2 These verses set up a chain of revelation: God gives the revelation to Jesus, who makes it known to his servant John through his angel. Finally, John passes it on to the churches. This suggests that the phrase 'revelation of Jesus Christ' means not so much the 'revelation about Jesus Christ', but rather the revelation which Jesus received from his Father, which is transmitted to John through a heavenly vision.

The reference to Jesus' angel is interesting. We are familiar with the idea of humans having guardian angels (*Matthew 18:10*), while apocalypses often contain 'interpreting angels' providing a running commentary on what the visionary sees and hears. Less common is the notion that Jesus has his own angel. We shall probably meet this angel again in Apocalypse chapter 10. We are in touch here with the strange world of early Christianity.

The Greek verb translated 'he made it known' literally means 'he signified it' (esēmanen, closely related to sēmeion, 'sign'). The message of the book is to be conveyed symbolically. This is the language of poetry rather than prose, of mystical contemplation rather than intellectual reasoning, of vision rather than factual description.

The double phrase 'the word of God and the testimony (or 'witness') of Jesus' recurs throughout the Apocalypse. God speaks his word to his people, and Jesus bears witness to the truth of this word, both through his words and through his actions. Ultimately, he gives his life for this testimony, and Revelation invites Christian readers to follow him in this path.

v.3 Christians associate the word 'beatitude' with Jesus' Beatitudes in the gospels. Matthew 5:3 reads 'Blessed are the poor in spirit'. But the Apocalypse also contains seven beatitudes (also *14:13, 16:15, 19:9, 20:6, 22:7 and 14*). This first beatitude is a reminder that the Apocalypse was intended to be read aloud, probably during the Eucharist. It distinguishes between 'the one who reads aloud' (the reader) and 'those who hear' (the congregation). Hearing a book can have a very different effect from reading it silently. But reading and hearing are only the first steps: the book calls for a response in the lives of the hearers, to 'keep what is written in it'.

This first section ends with a note of urgency: 'for the time is near'. 'Time' here is the Greek *kairos*, which means a special or opportune time, especially the time of the end when God will act.

The Opening of the Letter

vv.4-5a Like Paul, John adapts the ancient convention for opening letters (x, to y, greetings). This indicates that John had a specific audience in mind for his apocalyptic-prophetic letter: 'the seven churches that are in Asia'. Asia refers to the Roman province of that name, in what is now western Turkey. The names of the cities where these first century Christians live are given in verse 11. Yet numbers also have symbolic meaning in Revelation. Seven is the number of completeness. The seven churches symbolise the whole Church.

Also like Paul, John modifies the traditional formula. He changes the expected Greek *chairein* ('greetings') to the similar-sounding theological term 'grace' (*charis*). This points to the 'free gift' of God's favour for his people. Second, he adds the traditional Jewish greeting 'peace' (*shalom*).

But as in Paul, the greeting comes not from the human sender, but from God himself. The description of the deity uses a threefold designation ('from him who is and who was and who is to come') reminding us that God sustains in the present, God created in the past, and God is coming as judge. It recalls the revelation of God's name to Moses at the burning bush *(Exodus 3:14)*.

Alongside God, John names 'the seven spirits' and Jesus Christ. The former could refer to the Holy Spirit, whose sevenfold gifts are listed in Isaiah 11:1-2, or, in the strange world which the Apocalypse describes, the seven archangels who stand close to God's heavenly throne *(Tobit 12:15)*. The reference to Jesus points to his exalted status even at this early stage in the Church's life.

Daniel 7:22 Then judgment was given for the holy ones of the Most High, and the time arrived when the holy ones gained possession of the kingdom.

Mark 1:15 Jesus said: 'The time is fulfilled, and the kingdom of God has come near.'

The Book of Tobit is one of the books of the Greek collection of Scriptures known as the Septuagint which became part of the Old Testament. In the final chapter Raphael, who has assisted the boy Tobias throughout the story, makes known his identity by saying: I am Raphael, one of the seven angels who stand ready and enter before the glory of the Lord. (Tobit 12:15)

vv.5b-6 John moves on to a hymn. It is important to note that it begins with a reference to Christ's love, because the Apocalypse is often read as a book of gloom and destruction. The preferred reading of the Greek –'and freed us from our sins by his blood' – echoes the liberation of the first Exodus. Christ, the new Paschal Lamb, sets his people free. The hymn also describes our vocation as Christians: we are both a kingdom, reigning with Christ, and priests, offering worship to the Father and interceding on behalf of the world. There are allusions here to Exodus 19:6.

vv.7-8 This section of this prophetic book concludes with a prophetic oracle describing Christ's coming again. It picks up on Daniel 7:13 and Zechariah 12:10-14. When Christ comes at the end, what is now veiled, his power and glory, will be made abundantly clear, and the whole world will experience grief when they see the one whom they pierced, the crucified one, revealed in glory. It is a hopeful promise of the offer of universal salvation to all who repent.

Finally God speaks, revealing himself as 'the Alpha and the Omega', the first and last letters of the Greek alphabet. God is the creator who sustains from the beginning, and the goal towards whom all history is moving.

The famous Advent hymn 'Lo, He comes with clouds descending' by Charles Wesley is based on Apocalypse 1:7:

Ev'ry eye shall now behold Him,

Robed in splendour's majesty.

Those who set at naught and sold Him,

Pierced and nailed Him to the tree,

Deeply wailing, deeply wailing,

Shall the true Messiah see.

Patmos, Greece

John's First Vision

v.9 In this first vision in a book of visions, John moves from the ordinary - a geographical location, at a particular time of the week - to the extraordinary, as heaven breaks into Patmos. He first gives some autobiographical details, although not enough to definitively identify him as John the apostle or any other John. He expresses his closeness as 'brother' of other Christians, echoing the idea which permeates the New Testament that the Church is an 'alternative family'.

Negatively, he shares in suffering: the word translated here 'persecution' might simply mean 'trial' or 'tribulation'. There is little firm evidence for state persecution of Christians in the first century, apart from Nero's persecution in Rome in the 60s. It may reflect less formal hostility and suspicion from non-Christian neighbours and local authorities. Positively, however, even in suffering there is a common sharing in that kingdom where the world's values are turned on their head.

Even John's explanation of why he was on Patmos is ambiguous. It could mean, as tradition has it, that he was exiled there because of preaching God's word. But he might have chosen to go there in order to preach, or been prompted to go there by God's word, perhaps to receive a revelation.

vv.10-11 The phrase 'on the Lord's day' probably means Sunday. John may be participating in the Eucharist with fellow Christians on Patmos, or at least praying in solidarity with the seven churches gathered for worship on the mainland. At this point he is explicitly commanded to write to these congregations, putting in writing what he sees.

vv.12-16 John's description of his vision is like a kaleidoscope of images, drawn from a range of Old Testament texts such as Daniel 7, Daniel 10 and Ezekiel 1, which invites us to use our imaginations. Like Daniel before him (*Daniel 7*), he sees 'one like the Son of Man', a heavenly being in human form. The Son of Man's clothing, and his location in the midst of seven golden lampstands or *menorahs*, identify him as the great high priest standing in his temple. The dazzling white of his head and hair, comparable to the Ancient of Days at Daniel 7:9,

Patmos is certainly an appropriate place for retreat: a small island in the eastern Aegean, only forty miles from the Turkish coast. It is not mentioned elsewhere in the Bible, and hardly ever in classical literature. Yet this insignificant island becomes a sacred place, where heaven and earth meet.

the fiery gaze of his eyes, and the brightness of his face, reveal his divine nature.

The seven stars in his right hand reveal that he sustains the whole creation, including the heavenly world. The double-edged sword is a symbol of his word, which judges as well as heals, cutting to the quick (*Isaiah 11:4* and *Hebrews 4:12*). This is a reminder that John hears as well as sees: the voice of the Son of Man makes a deafening sound, 'like the sound of many waters'.

vv.17-18 Aspects of this imagery may be terrifying, appropriate to encountering the God who takes our breath away. Like many visionaries before him (*Ezekiel 1:28, Daniel 8:18*), John is overwhelmed and falls down as if dead. But this is no unknown God. He has the familiar, human face of Jesus, crucified and risen. The risen Christ, who is 'alive forever and ever', casts out John's fear with words of reassurance.

vv.19-20 John is now commanded a second time to write, underscoring the divine authority of his book. This is one of the rare occasions where the Apocalypse 'decodes' its symbols. The seven stars are identified as the angels of the seven churches, probably their heavenly representatives and guardians, who are answerable for their congregations in the heavenly court. The churches themselves are symbolised by the seven lampstands (Hebrew *menorot*), at the heart of the heavenly temple. Christ the high priest stands in the midst of his people, interceding on their behalf.

Andrew of Caesarea, in his sixth century Greek commentary, writes:

He was clothed with a long robe, as a high priest of those things above 'according to the order of Melchizedek'. (Commentary on the Apocalypse 1.12).

Daniel describes his reaction to the appearance of one 'having the appearance of a man':

As he was speaking to me, I fell into a trance, face to the ground; then he touched me and set me on my feet. (Daniel 8:18)

St John the Evangelist on the Island of Patmos, c.1618 (oil on canvas), Diego Velazquez (1599-1660)

The Word Lives On

The opening section of the Apocalypse is full of phrases and images which have had an impact on Christian culture. The title of God as 'Alpha and Omega' has left its mark on the earliest Christian art. The description of Christians as both a kingdom and priests continues to speak powerfully of the dignity of all the baptised.

Alpha and Omega

John's visionary experience on Patmos has been a particular favourite of artists. Several of them (e.g. Jean Duvet, Diego Velazquez) seem to have painted self-portraits, as if to claim John's authority for their own artistic 'inspirations'. Others have concentrated on depicting what John saw. Memling's famous altarpiece in Bruges has John in the lower right hand corner, while a kaleidoscope of visions are played out in the sky above. Still others have attempted to portray the awe-inspiring character of the Son of Man, most famously Thomas Vathas in his icon of the scene, now in the Cave of the Apocalypse on Patmos.

In the Lectionary

The first Preface for Sundays in Ordinary Time reads:

He has freed us from sin and death and called us to the glory that has made us a chosen race, a royal priesthood, a holy nation, a people set apart.

Apocalypse 1:1-4, together with 2:1-5, is found in the Weekday Lectionary for Monday of Week 33 of the year (Year II). Apocalypse 1:5-8 is the second reading for the Mass of Chrism, and also for Christ the King in Year B. Apocalypse 1:9-13, 17-19 is the second reading for the Second Sunday of Easter in Year C.

Live the Word of God

Listen again to the reading: Apocalypse 1:1-20

Suggestions for reflection and prayer

John writes: 'blessed are those who hear'. What difference does it make when you hear the Apocalypse read aloud rather than reading it silently to yourself?

Listen again to the description of the Son of Man in verses 12-20. How do the different details speak to you? What kind of emotions do they evoke?

Jesus Christ loves us and has freed us from our sins by his blood.

❖ Pray for discernment to recognise those things from which you need setting free.

Christ is coming with the clouds, and every eye will see him.

❖ Pray for those who struggle to see Christ, or long for the gift of faith.

Christ places his right hand on us and says, 'Do not be afraid'.

❖ Pray for a deeper acceptance of that love which casts out fear.

Saint John Paul II wrote in 1990 in his encyclical letter on the missionary activity of the Church:

The witness of a Christian life is the first and irreplaceable form of mission: Christ, whose mission we continue, is the 'witness' par excellence (Rev 1:5; 3:14) and the model of all Christian witness. (Redemptoris Missio 42)

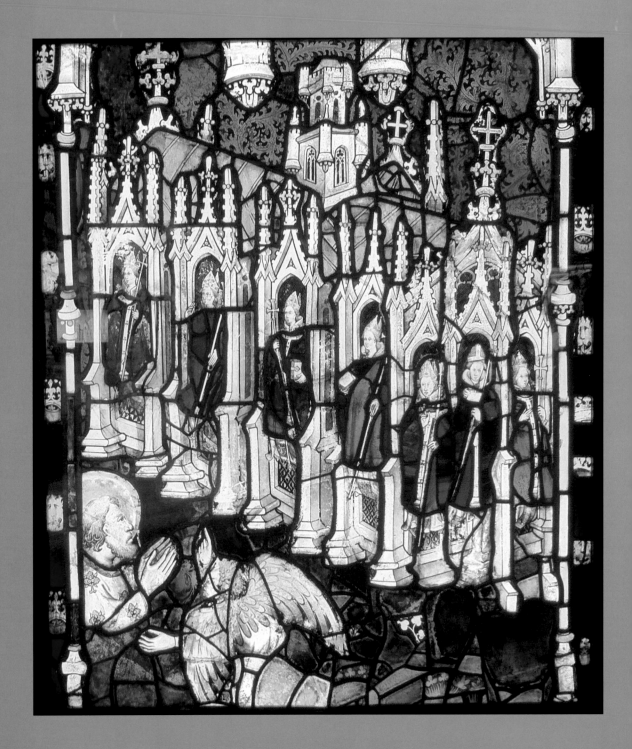

Hear the Word of God

Apocalypse 3:7-22

[7] And to the angel of the church in Philadelphia write: These are the words of the holy one, the true one, who has the key of David, who opens and no one will shut, who shuts and no one opens:

[8] I know your works. Look, I have set before you an open door, which no one is able to shut. I know that you have but little power, and yet you have kept my word and have not denied my name.

[9] I will make those of the synagogue of Satan who say that they are Jews and are not, but are lying - I will make them come and bow down before your feet, and they will learn that I have loved you. [10] Because you have kept my word of patient endurance, I will keep you from the hour of trial that is coming on the whole world to test the inhabitants of the earth.

[11] I am coming soon; hold fast to what you have, so that no one may seize your crown. [12] If you conquer, I will make you a pillar in the temple of my God; you will never go out of it. I will write on you the name of my God, and the name of the city of my God, the new Jerusalem that comes down from my God out of heaven, and my own new name. [13] Let anyone who has an ear listen to what the Spirit is saying to the churches.

[14] And to the angel of the church in Laodicea write: The words of the Amen, the faithful and true witness, the origin of God's creation:

[15] I know your works; you are neither cold nor hot. I wish that you were either cold or hot. [16] So, because you are lukewarm, and neither cold nor hot, I am about to spit you out of my mouth. [17] For you say, 'I am rich, I have prospered, and I need nothing.' You do not realise that you are wretched, pitiable, poor, blind, and naked.

[18] Therefore I counsel you to buy from me gold refined by fire so that you may be rich; and white robes to clothe you and to keep the shame of your nakedness from being seen; and salve to anoint your eyes so that you may see.

[19] I reprove and discipline those whom I love. Be earnest, therefore, and repent. [20] Listen! I am standing at the door, knocking; if you hear my voice and open the door, I will come in to you and eat with you, and you with me.

[21] To the one who conquers I will give a place with me on my throne, just as I myself conquered and sat down with my Father on his throne. [22] Let anyone who has an ear listen to what the Spirit is saying to the churches.

Opposite: Seven churches of Asia in stained glass (East window of York Minster), John Thornton

Understand the Word of God

This session will explore:

- ❖ the purpose of the seven messages
- ❖ the historical background of the seven churches
- ❖ the meaning of the symbols
- ❖ the message for today

Setting in the Book

In the previous passage John described his vision of the risen Christ received on Patmos on the Lord's Day. Christ came to John from heaven in order to give him a heavenly perspective on what is happening on earth. That opening vision provides the setting for this second passage. As John sees and listens, the heavenly Jesus speaks to the angels of the seven churches, and through the angels, to the congregations themselves. Each of the seven messages has a similar format: a greeting to the angel, a 'school report' of the church whom that angel represents, with praise and/or blame in varying degrees, a promise to the one who is victorious, and an exhortation to 'listen to what the Spirit is saying to the churches'. This passage contains the last two of the seven messages.

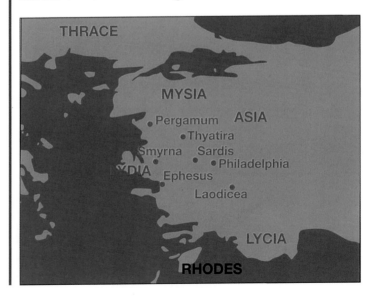

Map of the Seven Churches

What Kind of Text?

Although the contents of Apocalypse 2-3 are often called the 'letters to the seven churches', this title is a misnomer. As we have already seen, the book of Revelation is one great circular letter, addressed to all the churches. These so-called 'letters' within it are better described as 'seven messages'. They sound like the word of the Lord spoken through Israel's prophets such as Amos, Jeremiah and Ezekiel. Christ the Lord speaks through his prophet John. There are also similarities with royal proclamations or Roman imperial edicts, as the true King speaks. Where they differ from both Old Testament prophecy and imperial proclamations is that they are addressed, not directly to God's people, but to their heavenly representatives, the angels.

Nevertheless, these may not be straightforward transcripts of what John heard on Patmos. Visionaries remain rooted in their own culture and religious tradition when they attempt to describe what they have seen and heard. Hence it should not surprise us that John draws upon the language and imagery of the Old Testament and other Jewish traditions as he attempts to express the inexpressible. Moreover, commentators have often detected in the seven messages echoes of the local history and geography of the cities where the seven churches were located. John the visionary is also John the pastor, who knows his congregations intimately.

Commentary: verse by verse reading

The Message to Philadelphia

v.7 The message to Philadelphia is the sixth of the seven messages. It provides a window into a Christian congregation which remains faithful to its Christian calling, even in the face of hostility and suffering. The Philadelphian church serves as a model for faithful Christian churches in every generation.

In Isaiah 22:15-25 Shebna, the master of the palace, is rejected and the office is given to Eliakim, son of Hilkiah. He is given the key of the house of David. He shall open, and no one shall shut. He shall shut, and no one shall open. (verse 22)

In each of the seven messages, Christ introduces himself by a different title. Two of the titles here, 'the holy one, the true one', are used of God at Apocalypse 6:10, underscoring Christ's unity with the Father. That Christ holds the 'key of David' reminds us that he is the royal Messiah of David's line, and has the authority to open and shut the door gaining access to the royal treasures.

v.8 Revelation has a great deal to say about opening and shutting. Its message is that heaven has been opened, so that humans can see the world more clearly. Soon John will see an open door in heaven, enabling him to ascend. Here he exploits the image of 'the open door' to describe the mission of the Christians of Philadelphia. Historically, Philadelphia's geographical location, between the territories of Lydia and Phrygia, made it an excellent centre for disseminating Greek culture into the surrounding area. Perhaps the Christians there are being offered a similar mission for disseminating the 'counter-culture' of the gospel.

Paul describes his missionary work in Asia as an 'open door':

When I came to Troas to proclaim the good news of Christ, a door was opened for me in the Lord. (2 Corinthians 2:12)

From the world's perspective, the Philadelphian Christians were lacking in power: perhaps the church in that city numbered no more than a few dozen. But from heaven's perspective, they are powerful. They follow the Lamb, whose power is revealed in weakness.

v.9 This verse provides one of the few glimpses in the Apocalypse of the situation of first century Asian Christians, albeit couched in symbolic language. As in the earlier message to Smyrna (2:9), this message hints at hostility from a group referred to as 'the synagogue of Satan', probably non-Christian Jews.

Interpreting the phrase 'the synagogue of Satan' calls for sensitivity. We have here the 'name-calling' of a vulnerable minority towards the majority. Such religious polemic becomes destructive when that minority has become the majority, with power to persecute those it demonises. More positively, the term 'Jew' is a term of respect, for John and his fellow Christians claim that title for themselves.

v.10 The 'hour of trial' refers to a time of tribulation which many Jews expected would precede the coming of God's kingdom. The Apocalypse does not promise that Christians will be exempted from it, but that they will come safely through it, even if, as in the case of martyrs, it costs them their lives.

The phrase 'the inhabitants of the earth' is frequent in Revelation. It refers to those who cannot follow the Lamb, because of their attachment to the transitory values of this world rather than the values of God's kingdom. Perhaps a better translation might be 'those who make their home on the earth'.

v.11 The Apocalypse is full of urgency, hence the saying of Christ: 'I am coming soon.' But we should not only associate this with Christ's final coming. If we remember that John sees this vision 'on the Lord's Day' (Sunday), we may also recall that Christ comes to his people repeatedly, especially during the Eucharist.

The 'crown' (Greek *stephanos*) is strictly a 'wreath', like the victory wreath awarded to the winners in Greek athletic games. It is therefore a symbol of victory, or 'conquering', although, for Revelation, victory is achieved through weakness.

v.12 Each of the seven messages ends with a promise to the one who is victorious through remaining faithful. The promises sometimes pick up on elements from the opening vision in Apocalypse 1:9-20, and sometimes, as here, from the final glorious vision of the new Jerusalem in chapters 21-22. That city is also a temple, and the first promise to the victor is to be a pillar in that living temple, an integral part of that holy people built up like living stones.

The final part of the Our Father in Matthew 6:13 reads:

And do not bring us to the time of trial, but rescue us from the evil one .

The second promise is of a set of new names: God's name, marking out God's people as his, the name of the new Jerusalem, which is already descending from heaven, and of which the faithful Christian is a citizen, and finally Christ's new name. After an earthquake in AD 17, Philadelphia was renamed Neocaesarea. Those who belong to Christ have a new name, a new identity, which remains forever.

Mark 4:9 Let anyone with ears to hear listen!

Matthew 13:9 Let anyone with ears listen!

Luke 8:8 Let anyone with ears to hear listen!

v.13 According to the synoptic gospels, Jesus concluded his parables with the following phrase: 'Let anyone with ears to hear listen!' (e.g. *Mark 4:9*). In the Apocalypse, the heavenly Christ speaks with a similar voice, though this time reminding his hearers that he now speaks through his Spirit. However different he may appear in John's visionary imagery, he is the same Jesus who spoke parables to the crowds in Galilee.

Philadelphia in Asia

Laodicea in Asia

The Message to Laodicea

v.14 If the angel of Phildelphia received heartfelt praise, the angel of the church at Laodicea receives a rebuke. Laodicea was an impressive city, strategically located in the middle of the wide valley of the River Lycus, close to other cities with Christian communities, Hierapolis and Colossae. Yet Laodicea's Christians were far from impressive in their commitment to Christ.

Again, Christ introduces himself with titles expressing an aspect of his role. Here he uses the divine title 'the Amen' (*Isaiah 65:16*), meaning the one who is true or trustworthy. He has proved himself such through his faithful witness, which led him to the cross. But Christ has been active from the beginning: as in Paul's letter to the Christians of nearby Colossae, this message to Laodicea describes him as the 'origin' or 'beginning' of God's creation. The whole universe has been created through Christ and for Christ.

Colossians 2:1 I want you to know how much I am struggling for you, and for those in Laodicea, and for all who have not seen me face to face.

Colossians 4:13 Epaphras has worked hard for you (in Colossae) and for those in Laodicea and in Hierapolis.

Colossians 1:15 He is the image of the invisible God, the firstborn of all creation.

Colossians 1:18 He is the head of the body, the church; he is the beginning, the firstborn from the dead.

vv.15-16 The great rebuke for the Laodicean angel, and the Christians he represents, is lukewarmness. But this probably means more than loss of fervour, for Christ's words imply that it is better to be cold than lukewarm. More likely there is a local allusion. Nearby Hierapolis was a thermal spa, the hot waters having healing properties. Colossae to the south had springs of cold water, refreshing to drink. Both extremes of water were beneficial. In contrast, the Laodiceans, lukewarm like the water which reached their city by aqueduct, benefited no-one.

vv.17-19 Unlike the humble but trusting Philadelphian church, the church in Laodicea trusts in its own self-sufficiency. The truth is that it is 'wretched, pitiable, poor, blind and naked'. Metaphorically, it is not able to see clearly.

Even here Christ the healer offers a remedy. He urges them to learn from their surroundings. Laodicea was renowned for its banking, its black wool, and the famous Phrygian eye-salve. Christ promises gifts more satisfying than their proud city's greatest offerings: the refined gold of a tested faith, the white garments of those purified by martyrdom, and the true eye-ointment granted through baptism, whereby the candidate passes from darkness to the light.

Wisdom speaks in this way to her children:

My child, do not despise the Lord's discipline or be weary of his reproof, for the Lord reproves the one he loves, as a father the son in whom he delights. (Proverbs 3:11-12)

This is the offer of a loving Saviour rather than a harsh judge. Those who wish to become mature adults in Christ must learn to grow up, and education may include rebuke as well as instruction. Christ here speaks as did Wisdom in the Old Testament.

v.20 The Philadelphians were promised an 'open door' of missionary activity to their neighbours. In Laodicea there is also a door to be opened, the closed door to the human heart. Christ knocks, but does not impose: the door can only be opened from the inside. The promise if the invitation is accepted is to share in Christ's supper. This is a reminder of the Eucharistic context within which Revelation would have been read.

vv.21-22 The final promise to the victor is a sharing of Christ's reign, symbolised by sitting on his throne. But the reference to Christ's own victory warns us that Christ's rule is not like that of human rulers and human thrones. It is a just and gentle rule which is established through Christ's faithfulness to the Father, gained through the suffering of the cross.

The Light of the World, c.1852,
William Holman Hunt (1827-1910)

The Word Lives On

The messages to the seven churches continue to inspire and challenge countless Christians, and they have become the subject of countless sermons and Bible study courses. In the twelfth century, Geoffrey of Auxerre used them as the basis of a series of sermons to his fellow monks, encouraging them in the monastic calling.

The cities of the seven churches remain on the itinerary of pilgrimages in the steps of St John, although several of them are ruins and few have surviving Christian populations. The words 'Behold, I stand at the door and knock', from the message to Laodicea, most famously inspired Holman Hunt's painting The Light of the World, versions of which hang in the chapel of Keble College, Oxford, and St Paul's Cathedral, London.

In the Lectionary

Apocalypse 3:1-6 and 14-22 occur in the Weekday Lectionary for Tuesday of Week 33 of the year (Year II). Apocalypse 3:14 and 20-22 is an optional first reading for celebrations of Holy Men and Women in the Easter Season.

Live the Word of God

Listen again to the reading: Apocalypse 3:7-22

Suggestions for reflection and prayer

Which church do you most identify with in these two messages: the church in Philadephia or the church in Laodicea?

How should Christians today interpret the 'synagogue of Satan' language in verse 3:9?

Reflect on the words of Oecumenius in the margin.

The Son of Man knows all our works.

❖ Pray for the honesty to acknowledge your failings.

The Son of Man overturns our worldly perceptions of wealth and power.

❖ Pray for the wisdom to see that God's power is made perfect in weakness.

The Son of Man stands at the door and knocks.

❖ Pray for the courage to open the door and welcome him.

The sixth century Greek commentator Oecumenius writes on Apocalypse 3:20:

Here the Lord reveals his own humble and peaceful nature. The devil with axe and hammer smashed the doors of those who do not receive him, as the prophet said, but the Lord even now in the Song of Songs says to the bride, 'Open to me, my sister, my bride.' And should someone open to him, he will come in, but if not, he goes away. That supper which is with the Lord signifies the reception of the holy mysteries. (Commentary on the Apocalypse 3.14-22)

The Lamb on the Throne

Hear the Word of God

Apocalypse 5:1-14

[1] Then I saw in the right hand of the one seated on the throne a scroll written on the inside and on the back, sealed with seven seals; [2] and I saw a mighty angel proclaiming with a loud voice, 'Who is worthy to open the scroll and break its seals?'

[3] And no one in heaven or on earth or under the earth was able to open the scroll or to look into it. [4] And I began to weep bitterly because no one was found worthy to open the scroll or to look into it. [5] Then one of the elders said to me, 'Do not weep. See, the Lion of the tribe of Judah, the Root of David, has conquered, so that he can open the scroll and its seven seals.'

[6] Then I saw between the throne and the four living creatures and among the elders a Lamb standing as if it had been slaughtered, having seven horns and seven eyes, which are the seven spirits of God sent out into all the earth. [7] He went and took the scroll from the right hand of the one who was seated on the throne.

[8] When he had taken the scroll, the four living creatures and the twenty-four elders fell before the Lamb, each holding a harp and golden bowls full of incense, which are the prayers of the saints. [9] They sing a new song:

> 'You are worthy to take the scroll
> and to open its seals,
> for you were slaughtered and by your
> blood you ransomed for God
> saints from every tribe and language
> and people and nation;
> [10] you have made them to be a kingdom
> and priests serving our God,
> and they will reign on earth.'

[11] Then I looked, and I heard the voice of many angels surrounding the throne and the living creatures and the elders; they numbered myriads of myriads and thousands of thousands, [12] singing with full voice,

> 'Worthy is the Lamb that was slaughtered
> to receive power and wealth
> and wisdom and might
> and honour and glory and blessing!'

Polyptych of the Apocalypse, 1343, Jacobello Alberegno

[13] Then I heard every creature in heaven and on earth and under the earth and in the sea, and all that is in them, singing,

     'To the one seated on the throne and to the Lamb

     be blessing and honour and glory

     and might forever and ever!'

[14] And the four living creatures said, 'Amen!' And the elders fell down and worshipped.

Papyrus Scroll

Understand the Word of God

This session will explore:

- ❖ the purpose of the throne vision
- ❖ the understanding of Christ as lion and lamb
- ❖ the importance of canticles in the Apocalypse
- ❖ the message for today

Setting in the Book

The message to the Laodicean church described Christ knocking at a closed door, inviting the hearer to open and let him in. Immediately afterwards, John saw an 'open door' in heaven (*4:1*), giving him access to God's world. In an apocalypse, heaven is the realm where God is acknowledged as God, and from where a true perspective on this world can be viewed. John ascends, and like many visionaries before and after him, he sees God seated on a throne. He attempts to describe the heavenly throne-room, in a manner very similar to the Emperor's court in Rome. Thus he challenges those who place their trust in earthly centres of power to rethink: it is in God that we learn what true power is. The song of the elders in verse 11 sums this up well. John will return to this heavenly throne scene again and again throughout his book.

What Kind of Text?

The two books known as 1 Enoch and the Apocalypse of Abraham are not found in the Catholic canon of Scripture. These writings and others, referred to sometimes as 'apocrypha' and sometimes as 'pseudepigrapha', are nevertheless of great interest when we explore the religious ideas of the late centuries BC and the early centuries AD.

This passage, the second part of John's description of heaven's throne-room which began in chapter 4, is full of features which are unfamiliar to us: strange heavenly characters and symbolic features. But it would have been quite familiar to first century Christians, who knew the Old Testament and other Jewish apocalyptic writings. An account of an ascent by a human being to heaven, described variously as a temple or a palace with its throne-room, is regularly found in such books as the First Book of Enoch chapter 14, and the Apocalypse of Abraham chapter 18. These are influenced by Old Testament descriptions of God on his throne, seen in Isaiah chapter 6, Daniel chapter 7 and 1 Kings 22:19, but especially by Ezekiel's vision of God's throne-chariot (*Ezekiel 1*).

Apocalypse 5 differs from earlier apocalyptic texts in giving the central place to Jesus. In apocalypses, human beings are regularly symbolised as animals. Thus Jesus, in his human nature, is represented by a Lamb. Yet he is no mere human: as the passage progresses, the Lamb becomes the object of worship, alongside the one who sits on the throne.

This is particularly expressed in the canticles sung by the characters in the scene. The twenty-four elders are probably heavenly representatives of God's people of old and new covenants. The four living creatures are rather terrifying beasts who combine the characteristics of Isaiah's seraphim (*Isaiah 6*) and Ezekiel's cherubim (*Ezekiel 1*). The canticles, perhaps little glimpses of early Christian worship, provide a kind of running commentary on the action.

Commentary: verse by verse reading

John Sees the Scroll

v.1 John sees in God's right hand, which in Exodus 15:6 is a symbol of God's power to save, a tightly-sealed scroll or book. There are seven seals, a perfect number, which suggests that the scroll is utterly sealed, so that no-one can tamper with it. The scroll probably contains God's plan to put right the world which has gone so wrong, including overcoming injustice and saving the oppressed and vulnerable. But in order for that plan to be put into action, the tightly-sealed scroll needs to be opened.

Exodus 15:6 Your right hand, O Lord, glorious in power – your right hand, O Lord, shattered the enemy.

vv.2-3 In apocalypses, an interpreting angel often guides the visionary through the heavens, explaining what is seen and heard. Here a 'mighty angel' fulfils that role for John. He poses the question - 'Who is worthy to open the scroll?' - which he will then answer in verse 5. For now, however, John learns that no one was able to do so. We might be surprised that there was no one in heaven able to do so, given the large number of angels and archangels. But, as we shall discover, 'worthiness' is connected with obedience through suffering. The one who is able belongs to earth as well as heaven, and his power is found in weakness.

Primasius, sixth century bishop of Hadrumetum, wrote this in his Latin commentary:

When it says that no one in heaven was found worthy, it indicates that opening the scroll exceeded the capacities of the angels. This was not because they were ignorant of the future mystery of the Lord's incarnation and work, but because this was not to be completed through an angelic creature. For the Son of God, who through the assumption of true humanity was going to redeem humanity, wishes to fulfil all things through himself. (Commentary on the Apocalypse 5.3)

v.4 Books like Revelation move the reader emotionally. No one reading the Apocalypse can fail to be touched by John's grief. He longs for God to act to overcome injustice and suffering. But when he learns that no one can open the scroll, he weeps bitterly.

The dying Jacob blesses his son Judah with these words:

Judah is a lion's whelp; from the prey, my son, you have gone up. He crouches down, he stretches out like a lion, like a lioness – who dares rouse him up? (Genesis 49:9).

The prophet Isaiah speaks thus of a descendant of King David's father Jesse:

A shoot shall come out from the stock of Jesse, and a branch shall grow out of his roots. (Isaiah 11:1)

v.5 The response of the elder breaks the tension. He declares that there is, after all, someone worthy to open the scroll and inaugurate God's plan. He is given two names. First, he is 'the Lion of the tribe of Judah'. When Jacob blessed his sons before his death, he likened Judah to a lion, and promised that he would possess a royal sceptre (*Genesis 49:9-10*). Hence the kingly Messiah was expected to be from the tribe of Judah, the tribe to which King David belonged. The lion is a powerful animal, the 'king of the forest', an appropriate symbol for a warrior king who would overcome the enemy. Second, the one who can open the scroll is 'the Root of David', echoing Isaiah's prophecy that a branch would grow out from the roots of Jesse, David's father (*Isaiah 11:1*). 'The Branch' thus became an alternative title for the Messiah.

The Lion Becomes the Lamb

vv. 6-7 What John sees causes him to rethink what he hears. Instead of a terrifying Lion, he sees a Lamb. The Lamb is powerful in weakness: it is 'standing as if it had been slaughtered'! The Passover Lamb, whose blood marks out God's people in Egypt and rescues them from death (*Exodus 12*), may be behind this. Jesus, the new Passover Lamb, also saves his people through dying. His seven horns, the perfect number, symbolises that he is all-powerful. He has seven eyes, because he is all-seeing and assisted by the 'seven spirits of God' (*Zechariah 4:10* and *Revelation 1:4*). The narrative now changes in a favourable direction as this powerful, omniscient Lamb approaches God's throne and takes the scroll from his right hand.

v.8 The Apocalypse is very clear that only God can be worshipped (*19:10* and *22:9*). But from an early stage, especially in the liturgy, Christians found themselves offering divine worship to Jesus. Here in the heavenly Temple, with the four living creatures and twenty-four elders functioning as priests and ministers, the Lamb is worshipped with prostrations, incense and a hymn of praise, similar to that sung to the one on the throne at 4:11. Both harps and incense bowls were used in the worship of the Jerusalem temple, and so are appropriate for use in its true, heavenly counterpart.

But this liturgical scene is one of intercession as well as adoration. The sweet-smelling incense of worship also represents 'the prayers of the saints'. Here we are reminded that what the Lamb is now about to do – open the scroll to enable God's saving plan to be enacted – is the result of centuries of anguished prayers and petitions, from God's people of both old and new covenants.

vv. 9-10 The accompanying hymn of praise recalls the lamb of the Exodus. Jesus the Paschal Lamb has also acted as a 'ransom' to set free God's enslaved people. But this people is no longer restricted to the twelve tribes of Israel. Rather, they come from 'every tribe and language and people and nation'. God's people is a rich, diverse, multi-ethnic people, in which many cultures co-exist and many different languages are heard praising God.

The Apocalypse also reminds us that it is the whole people which shares in the task of ruling and offering priestly service. But the rules of government are those topsy-turvy rules of the Kingdom of God, and the priestly ministry one which intercedes on behalf of the whole world.

vv. 11-12 The praise of those closest to the throne is now echoed by those encircling them: the many angels who worship God and minister in the heavenly Temple. The sheer intensity of noise as they sing their canticle of praise to the Lamb is expressed by their number: myriads of myriads, or 'ten thousand times ten thousand', and thousands of thousands.

Apocalypse 19:10 Then I fell down at the angel's feet to worship him, but he said to me, 'You must not do that! I am a fellow servant with you and your comrades who hold the testimony of Jesus. Worship God!'

The psalmist exploited the same symbolic potential of incense: Let my prayer be counted as incense before you, and the lifting up of my hands as an evening sacrifice (Psalm 141:2).

Apocalypse 4:11 You are worthy, our Lord and God, to receive glory and honour and power, for you created all things, and by your will they existed and were created.

Some of the qualities attributed to the Lamb, power, honour and glory, are attributes of God (*4:11*), underscoring the closeness between Christ and his Father. In the world of the Apocalypse, where numbers have symbolic significance, it is appropriate that the attributes of the Lamb are sevenfold: the perfect number!

vv. 13-14 As if the volume of the heavenly choirs was not enough, John now describes a choir of ear-splitting intensity, made up of the whole of creation, not only of heaven, but also of earth, the underworld, and the sea. From his privileged vantage-point in heaven, he glimpses a time when every one of God's creatures will acknowledge God as God, and the crucified and risen Lamb as the means by which salvation has been achieved. Both are acclaimed together in a doxology, a concluding hymn of praise. Appropriately, this heavenly liturgy concludes with a Great Amen, from the lips of those closest to God's throne, and an act of profound adoration.

Thurible, Cathedral of Santiago de Compostela

The Four and Twenty Elders Casting their Crowns before the Divine Throne, c.1803-5,
William Blake (1757-1827)

The Word Lives On

John's vision of the heavenly throne room has inspired mystics and visionaries, been replicated in art, and provided raw materials for musicians. The sealed scroll is found in early Christian mosaics, and William Blake's picture of the whole scene ('The Four and Twenty Elders Casting their Crowns before the Divine Throne', ca. 1803-1805, now in Tate Britain) powerfully evokes its mystery and invites adoration.

It is not surprising that a passage which contains within it psalm-like canticles has inspired musical imitation. Most famous perhaps is 'Worthy is the Lamb' from Handel's Messiah.

In the Lectionary

Apocalypse 5:1-10 is found in the Weekday Lectionary for Thursday of Week 33 of the year (Year II). Apocalypse 5:11-14 is the second reading for the Third Sunday of Easter in Year C.

Portrait of German-English composer George Frideric Handel (1685 - 1759), 1726, Attributed to Balthasar Denner

Live the Word of God

Listen again to the reading: Apocalypse 5:1-14

Suggestions for reflection and prayer

Reflect on the different characteristics of a lion and a lamb. How do the two belong together in talking about Christ?

Imagine yourself with John in the heavenly throne room. What do you see, and how do you react to what you see?

Listen to the words of Victorinus of Pettau in the margin.

Victorinus of Pettau, fourth century Latin commentator on the Apocalypse, says the following about verse 9:

The preaching of the Old Testament joined with the New reveals the Christian people singing a new song, that is, the proclaiming of their public confession. It is new that the Son of God became man; it is new that he was given over into death by men; it is new that he rose again on the third day.

John wept bitterly when he heard that no-one could open the scroll.

❖ Pray for all those who weep at the injustices of this world.

John saw the Lamb standing as if slaughtered.

❖ Pray for all those who lose their lives unjustly, and those responsible for their deaths.

John heard a choir made up of every creature in heaven and on earth, under the earth and in the sea.

❖ Pray for the Church's mission to proclaim the Gospel to all creation.

Six Seals Opened

Hear the Word of God

Apocalypse 6:1-17

Then I saw the Lamb open one of the seven seals, and I heard one of the four living creatures call out, as with a voice of thunder, 'Come!' ² I looked, and there was a white horse! Its rider had a bow; a crown was given to him, and he came out conquering and to conquer.

³ When he opened the second seal, I heard the second living creature call out, 'Come!' ⁴ And out came another horse, bright red; its rider was permitted to take peace from the earth, so that people would slaughter one another; and he was given a great sword.

⁵ When he opened the third seal, I heard the third living creature call out, 'Come!' I looked, and there was a black horse! Its rider held a pair of scales in his hand, ⁶ and I heard what seemed to be a voice in the midst of the four living creatures saying, 'A quart of wheat for a day's pay, and three quarts of barley for a day's pay, but do not damage the olive oil and the wine!'

⁷ When he opened the fourth seal, I heard the voice of the fourth living creature call out, 'Come!' ⁸ I looked and there was a pale green horse! Its rider's name was Death, and Hades followed with him; they were given authority over a fourth of the earth, to kill with sword, famine, and pestilence, and by the wild animals of the earth.

⁹ When he opened the fifth seal, I saw under the altar the souls of those who had been slaughtered for the word of God and for the testimony they had given; ¹⁰ they cried out with a loud voice, 'Sovereign Lord, holy and true, how long will it be before you judge and avenge our blood on the inhabitants of the earth?'

¹¹ They were each given a white robe and told to rest a little longer, until the number would be complete both of their fellow servants and of their brothers and sisters, who were soon to be killed as they themselves had been killed.

¹² When he opened the sixth seal, I looked, and there came a great earthquake; the sun became black as sackcloth, the full moon became like blood, ¹³ and the stars of the sky fell to the earth as the fig tree drops its winter fruit when shaken by a gale. ¹⁴ The sky vanished like a scroll rolling itself up, and every mountain and island was removed from its place.

¹⁵ Then the kings of the earth and the magnates and the generals and the rich and the powerful, and everyone, slave and free, hid in the caves and among the rocks of the mountains, ¹⁶ calling to the mountains and rocks, 'Fall on us and hide us from the face of the one seated on the throne and from the wrath of the Lamb; ¹⁷ for the great day of their wrath has come, and who is able to stand?'

Germany: The Four Horsemen of the Apocalypse, Revelation 6:1-8, Ottheinrich Bible, Matthias Gerung

Understand the Word of God

This session will explore:

- ❖ the relationship between the scroll and the seals
- ❖ the four horsemen of the Apocalypse
- ❖ the role of the martyrs
- ❖ the message for today

Setting in the Book

There is an intimate connection between the visions of this section and the scroll given to the Lamb in the previous chapter. As each of the seven seals is opened, John sees a new vision in heaven, including the famous four horsemen of the Apocalypse. What John sees here is the prelude to the final opening of the scroll in Apocalypse 8:1, as the powers of evil and injustice struggle to hold onto the little power they have. This cycle of seven seals, the first six of which we read about in this chapter, is one of four series of seven throughout the book: the seven messages, the seven seals, the seven trumpets and seven bowls.

The Battle of the Somme

What Kind of Text?

Visions such as this stretch our imaginations to breaking point, as they present complex theological ideas in allusive, poetic language. Modern Christians have largely forgotten how to read such apocalyptic imagery. There are particularly strong links between this passage and the synoptic 'Little Apocalypse' found in Matthew 24-25, Mark 13 and Luke 21.

This suggests that it describes, in visual form, the so-called 'messianic woes' expected by many Jews of the first century. Before God's Kingdom was finally established, Satan and his minions would intensify their activity, aware that they were losing their grip on humanity. This would be reflected in intense human suffering, an increase in natural disasters such as earthquakes and famines, and the persecution of God's people.

How we understand the whole passage affects our understanding of the four horsemen. One line of interpretation holds that they are heavenly agents, perhaps angels, carrying out God's will. But this is theologically problematic, suggesting that God desires war, famine and the violent deaths of his creatures. An alternative, emphasising the tradition of the 'messianic woes', reads this section as a kind of nightmare. The four horsemen, along with the fifth and sixth seals, present a terrifying vision of a world without God, hurtling towards collapse.

An echo of this belief is found in the last request of the Lord's Prayer: but deliver us from evil (or the Evil One).

Commentary: verse by verse reading

The Four Horsemen

In the night I saw a man riding on a red horse! He was standing among the myrtle trees in the glen; and behind him were red, sorrel, and white horses. (Zechariah 1:8)

And again I looked up and saw four chariots coming out from between two mountains – mountains of bronze. The first chariot had red horses, the second chariot black horses, the third chariot white horses, and the fourth chariot dappled grey horses. (Zechariah 6:1-2)

Apocalypse 4:6-7 Around the throne, and on each side of the throne, are four living creatures, full of eyes in front and behind: the first living creature like a lion, the second living creature like an ox, the third living creature with a face like a human face, and the fourth living creature like a flying eagle.

Apocalypse 1:16 In his right hand he held seven stars, and from his mouth came a sharp, two-edged sword, and his face was like the sun shining with full force.

Apocalypse 19:15 From his mouth comes a sharp sword with which to strike down the nations.

vv.1-2 The worthy Lamb now begins to break the seven seals, so that God's plan can be put into action. As each seal is opened, John witnesses a new scene. The first four are grouped together, in that each describes a different coloured horse and its rider. The inspiration here is the prophet Zechariah, two of whose visions described coloured horses, symbolising God's ultimate control over his creation (*Zechariah 1:7-17* and *6:1-8*).

The appearance of each of the four riders is heralded by a thunderous cry from one of the four living creatures around the throne. These four, said in 4:7 to be like a lion, an ox, an eagle and a man, symbolise the whole of creation, wild beasts, domestic animals, birds and humans. That they are intimately involved in the calling out of the four horsemen points to the influence of the latter over the whole earth.

There is some ambiguity about the first rider, seated on a white horse. White is a colour associated with heaven, purity and victory. Thus some have identified this horseman as the victorious Christ. Yet an alternative is that this first rider is a parody of Christ, an 'antichrist'. A number of characters in Revelation, from the first beast to Babylon, appear godlike, benevolent rather than beastly, and deceive many.

The clue that this horseman may be falsely claiming Christ's role lies in his weapon, a bow. The true Christ of the Apocalypse has only one weapon: the word which he speaks, symbolised by a sword emerging from his mouth in 1:16 and 19:15. First century readers of Revelation may have been reminded of the Eastern enemies of Rome, the Parthians, whose cavalry carried bows. John then sees a rival to Christ's way, which believes falsely that victory can be achieved through warfare.

vv.3-4 The dark side of the second rider is more obvious. The red of his horse symbolises the bloodshed he heralds, the tragic waste of warfare. He has a great sword, but the Greek word used is different from the sword of Christ's word at 1:16 and 19:15.

The passive word 'was permitted', repeated through this chapter, has theological meaning. It denotes that God permits. We should not understand this, however, as implying that the horsemen are carrying out God's active will. Rather, it is a way of saying that ultimately God holds all things in his hand. The activity of these destructive horsemen is only temporary. Ultimately, it will give way to God's true will, the defeat of the injustice and bloodshed they symbolise and the redemption of God's creation.

vv.5-6 The third horseman, riding a black horse, symbolises another blight on humanity, famine. This brings with it highly inflated prices: a whole day's pay, literally a denarius. This represents about five times the usual price of barley, and eight times that of wheat. But a heavenly voice places a restraining order on this horseman, with the poor in mind. It is a call not to harm olive trees and vines, which would have affected not just one year's harvest, but many years to come.

vv.7-8 The final horseman provides the inspiration for the Grim Reaper. The colour of his horse, often poorly translated as 'pale', is sickly green, the colour of death. In both Jewish and Greek literature, Death was often personified, and here he is accompanied by Hades, the Greek underworld and abode of the dead, roughly equivalent to Sheol in the Old Testament.

Death and Hades are terrifying reminders of the fragility of human life. They come as unwanted visitors, summoned by a variety of causes, military weapons, famine, plagues, the violence of wild animals. They affect the rich and powerful no less than the poor. But even these great levellers are limited in their destructive power. As John describes his horrifying vision of the messianic woes, he sees that they are only granted authority over a fourth of the earth.

Here the Greek word used is machaira, while in 1:16 and 19:15 we find the word romphaia. It has been suggested that the romphaia was originally a large and broad sword, but the two words came to mean the same thing.

The sixth century Christian writer, Caesarius of Arles, gives a sacramental interpretation to the olive oil and the wine:

The wine is to be interpreted as the blood of Christ, and the oil as the unction of chrismation. (Exposition on the Apocalypse)

The Souls under the Altar

vv.9-10 The fifth seal provides a welcome interlude from the nightmare of the horsemen. John catches a glimpse of the martyrs, those who have lost their lives from Abel to the Christian martyrs of Nero's persecution, under God's heavenly altar. In the Jerusalem temple, there were two altars, the altar where animal sacrifices were offered, and the altar of incense. In heaven, there is only one. The martyrs are sacrificial victims, the shedding of whose blood plays a key role in putting the world to right.

Their prayer is also like an incense offering, which rises to God's throne. We should understand their prayer less as a call for vengeance, than as a longing for justice to be done. Their murderers thought that these little people had been silenced. Yet in heaven, their prayer is heard by the ear of God.

Did not the souls of the righteous in their chambers ask about these matters, saying, 'how long are we to remain here? And when will the harvest of our reward come?' And the archangel Jeremiel answered and said, 'When the number of those like yourselves is completed, for he has weighed the age in the balance.' (4 Ezra 4:35-36)

v.11 The white robe they receive is a symbol of the victory they have achieved through sharing with the Lamb in suffering and death. They are among a predetermined number of righteous deaths which needs to be completed. We find references to this in books outside the Catholic canon, 1 Enoch (*47:3-40*) and 4 Ezra (*4:35-37*). The main concern here is that ultimately the deaths of the righteous are not in vain.

Hiding from the Lamb's Wrath

vv.12-14 The sixth seal vision is full of dramatic apocalyptic imagery, drawing upon a variety of Old Testament texts describing the Day of the Lord, such as Isaiah 34 and Joel 2:30-31. It is a terrifying vision of the reversal of creation in Genesis 1. The reference to 'every mountain and every island' betrays John's location on Patmos, from where the world seems made up of mountainous islands like Samos.

vv.15-17 Again we are reminded that God's salvation causes a world built on injustice to crumble. The long list of those affected reveals that power, wealth and political influence cannot shield us from the transforming power of Christ's victory. The vulnerable yet victorious Lamb, despite his apparent weakness, shares completely in God's power to save. There is an interesting reference here to the 'wrath' of God and of the Lamb.

Isaiah 34:8 The Lord has a day of vengeance, a year of vindication by Zion's cause.

Joel 2:30-31 I will show portents in the heavens and on the earth, blood and fire and columns of smoke. The sun shall be turned to darkness, and the moon to blood, before the great and terrible day of the Lord comes.

Hosea 10:8 They shall say to the mountains, 'Cover us', and to the hills, 'Fall on us'.

Luke 23:30 Then they will begin to say to the mountains, 'Fall on us', and to the hills, 'Cover us'.

Mountains of Samos

The Revelation of 'what must soon take place', the Apocalypse, is borne along by the songs of the heavenly liturgy, but also by the intercession of the 'witnesses' (martyrs). The prophets and the saints, all those who were slain on earth for their witness to Jesus, the vast throng of those who, having come through the great tribulation, have gone before us into the Kingdom, all sing the praise and glory of him who sits on the throne and of the Lamb. (Catechism of the Catholic Church 2642)

The Word Lives On

The vision of the four horsemen of the Apocalypse has had a profound influence on Western culture. Numerous images of this scene have been produced. Some, particularly in medieval illuminations, depict each of the horsemen individually, exploring their significance in turn. Other portrayals have all four horsemen side by side. One of the most famous is Albrecht Dürer's woodcut, where the horsemen trample even noblemen and bishops underfoot.

The scene of the martyrs under the altar has inspired those facing martyrdom in every century, and has been painted among others by El Greco.

The cosmic collapse envisaged by the sixth seal is dramatically depicted in John Martin's The Great Day of His Wrath (Tate Britain).

In the Lectionary

This passage does not appear in the Mass lectionary, either on Sundays or on Weekdays.

The Four Horsemen of the Apocalypse: the Rider on the White Horse, c.1878, George Frederick Watts (1817-1904)

Live the Word of God

Listen again to the reading: Apocalypse 6:1-17

Suggestions for reflection and prayer

How do you respond to hearing the descriptions of the four horsemen? What images do they evoke in your mind?

Reflect on the passage from Tertullian in the margin.

John sees Death riding on a green horse.

❖ Pray for the courage to face death, with faith and trust in Christ.

John sees the souls of the martyrs under the altar.

❖ Pray for all those facing persecution and martyrdom for the Faith in our world.

John sees the stars fall from heaven, and every island and mountain removed from its place.

❖ Pray for those whose lives are falling apart, that they may find peace.

Tertullian of Carthage (ca. 160 – ca. 220) made the following link between the prayer of the souls under the altar and the Lord's Prayer:

With indignation the souls of the martyrs beneath the altar cry aloud to the Lord, 'How long, O Lord, will you refrain from avenging our blood on those who dwell on the earth?' For at least from the end of the world vengeance for them is ordained. Indeed, as quickly as possible, O Lord, may your kingdom come! This is the prayer of Christians; this shall bring shame to the heathens; this shall bring joy to the angels; it is for the coming of this kingdom that we are harassed now, or rather, it is for this coming that we pray. (Tertullian, On Prayer 5)

A Series of Trumpets

Hear the Word of God

Apocalypse 8:1-13

[1] When the Lamb opened the seventh seal, there was silence in heaven for about half an hour.

[2] And I saw the seven angels who stand before God, and seven trumpets were given to them. [3] Another angel with a golden censer came and stood at the altar; he was given a great quantity of incense to offer with the prayers of all the saints on the golden altar that is before the throne.

[4] And the smoke of the incense, with the prayers of the saints, rose before God from the hand of the angel. [5] Then the angel took the censer and filled it with fire from the altar and threw it on the earth; and there were peals of thunder, rumblings, flashes of lightning, and an earthquake.

[6] Now the seven angels who had the seven trumpets made ready to blow them. [7] The first angel blew his trumpet, and there came hail and fire, mixed with blood, and they were hurled to the earth; and a third of the earth was burned up, and a third of the trees were burned up, and all green grass was burned up.

[8] The second angel blew his trumpet, and something like a great mountain, burning with fire, was thrown into the sea. [9] A third of the sea became blood, a third of the living creatures in the sea died, and a third of the ships were destroyed.

[10] The third angel blew his trumpet, and a great star fell from heaven, blazing like a torch, and it fell on a third of the rivers and on the springs of water. [11] The name of the star is Wormwood. A third of the waters became wormwood, and many died from the water, because it was made bitter.

[12] The fourth angel blew his trumpet, and a third of the sun was struck, and a third of the moon, and a third of the stars, so that a third of their light was darkened; a third of the day was kept from shining, and likewise the night.

[13] Then I looked, and I heard an eagle crying with a loud voice as it flew in midheaven, 'Woe, woe, woe to the inhabitants of the earth, at the blasts of the other trumpets that the three angels are about to blow!'

Detail of The Last Judgement, 1535 - 1541: Sistine Chapel, by Michelangelo Buonarroti, 16th Century, (1475-1564)

Understand the Word of God

This session will explore:

- ❖ the meaning of the seven trumpets
- ❖ the priestly ministry of the angels
- ❖ the identity of the eagle's three woes
- ❖ the message for today

Setting in the Book

Apocalypse 7:4 And I heard the number of those who were sealed, one hundred and forty-four thousand, sealed out of every tribe of the people of Israel.

Apocalypse 7:9 After this I looked, and there was a great multitude that no one could count from every nation, from all tribes and peoples and languages, standing before the throne and before the Lamb, robed in white, with palm branches in their hands.

After the sixth seal was opened, the Apocalypse described an unexpected delay (*7:1-17*) before the opening of the seventh. The contents of this interlude included both what John heard, that a hundred and forty-four thousand Israelites were sealed, like an army being prepared for war, and what John saw, a great crowd, impossible to count, from every nation and language.

Although many commentators distinguish between these groups, they are probably one and the same. Just as John heard of a Lion and saw a Lamb in chapter 5, so here what he sees redefines what he hears. The number itself, 144,000 – the number of completion (twelve) multiplied by itself, multiplied by a biblical number for a large multitude (a thousand) – symbolises a huge and perfect number of people. The army of the Lamb is no longer restricted to Israel, and embraces the whole world, in its rich cultural diversity. The Lamb's people may face suffering, but ultimately they will gain the victory.

What Kind of Text?

With the opening of the seventh seal, a reader might expect God's plan finally to be put into effect. But, in fact, it simply inaugurates another set of seven visions, associated with the blowing of seven trumpets. In the background may well be the story of the fall of Jericho, around which the Israelites marched seven times, accompanied by the blowing of ram's horns (*Joshua 6*).

There are also echoes of passages from the prophets about God's judgement, such as Amos 5, Amos 7 and Joel 1-2, and of the plagues of Egypt under Moses, in Exodus 7-12 and Wisdom 11-19. Talk of divine judgement may be problematic for liberal Westerners. From the viewpoint of the economically poor and politically oppressed, however, a God who cannot judge injustice and oppression is no God at all.

The echoes of the Exodus plagues may help us here, for the Exodus story is told from the perspective of Israelite slaves. Similarly, Christians retell the story at the Easter Vigil, not to celebrate the bloody slaughter of Egyptians, but rather the liberation of enslaved underdogs through the new Exodus in Christ.

The contents of these visions clearly overlap with some of the seal visions, suggesting that what we have here is not the next stage in a chronological sequence so much as repetition using different imagery, or perhaps a spiral motion, with some overlap with and some development from the seals sequence.

Joshua 6:15-16 On the seventh day they rose early, at dawn, and marched around the city in the same manner seven times. It was only on that day that they marched around the city seven times. And at the seventh time, when the priests had blown the trumpets, Joshua said to the people, 'Shout! For the Lord has given you the city!'

Commentary: verse by verse reading

Silence in Heaven

v.1 Like the calm before the storm, the opening of the seven seals leads to silence in heaven 'for about half an hour', which suggests a limited period of time. John has encountered heaven as a noisy place so far, where huge choirs sing the praises of God. So the breaking-in of silence is a dramatic contrast with what precedes. This temporary silence perhaps allows the prayers of the saints to be heard at God's throne.

Three of the archangels are known from writings included in the Catholic canon:

Daniel 9:21 While I was speaking in prayer, the man Gabriel, whom I had seen before in a vision, came to me in swift flight at the time of the evening sacrifice.

Daniel 12:1 At that time Michael, the great prince, the protector of your people, shall arise.

Tobit 12:15 I am Raphael, one of the seven angels who stand ready and enter before the glory of the Lord.

v.2 Apparently as a direct result of the prayers being heard, the 'seven angels who stand before God' are given trumpets to blow. These are probably the seven archangels, perhaps to be identified with the 'seven spirits' of 1:4. The full list can only be learnt from non-biblical Jewish writings. They are: Uriel, Raphael, Raguel, Michael, Saraquel (or Sariel), Gabriel and Remiel (or Jeremiel). This scene reflects the ancient view that angels minister as priests in the heavenly sanctuary.

Workshop of Andrea del Verrocchio, Tobias and the Angel

The Angel of Incense

vv. 3-5 Along with the seven is an eighth angel who offers incense on the altar. Burning incense before the Lord, on an altar containing burning coals, was an integral part of the morning service in the Temple, a role allotted to John the Baptist's father Zechariah at Luke 1:5-10. Long ago the psalmist recognised the symbolic parallel between incense smoke rising and human prayers ascending to God's throne (*Psalm 141:2*). Here the incense is either a symbol for, or something to be mingled with, the prayers of the saints. The voices of the little ones on earth are taken utterly seriously in the heavenly liturgy.

This ascent of prayer is now answered by the descent of divine response, symbolised by the throwing down to earth of the golden thurible with its burning coals. The accompanying lightning and the shaking of the earth recalls God's descent to Mount Sinai, as the Saviour of the people.

The First Four Trumpets

vv. 6-7 The scene now returns to the seven archangels. The blowing of trumpets was another feature of the temple morning service. But in early Christian thought, the blowing of a heavenly trumpet was also a sign of the Lord's return (*1 Corinthians 15:52* and *1 Thessalonians 4:16*). Thus readers of the Apocalypse should experience excitement at this point that the End is about to break in, bringing salvation.

Instead, the trumpets inaugurate a set of seven judgements, paralleling those of the Exodus. We should perhaps view them, like the plagues of Egypt, as wake-up calls, confronting humanity with the reality of its situation. The first trumpet-plague combines the extremes of temperature, hail and fire, together with blood. There may be a reminder here of the blood of the Lamb, and the blood of the martyrs, which has particularly cried to heaven for vindication (*6:9-11*). The judgement affects the land and its vegetation. However, it is limited to just a third, rather than the whole earth.

Psalm 141:2 Let my prayer be counted as incense before you, and the lifting up of my hands as an evening sacrifice.

Exodus 19:16 On the morning of the third day there was thunder and lightning, as well as a thick cloud on the mountain, and a blast of a trumpet so loud that all the people who were in the camp trembled.

1 Corinthians 15:52 For the trumpet will sound, and the dead will be raised imperishable, and we will be changed.

1 Thessalonians 4:16 For the Lord himself, with a cry of command, with the archangel's call and with the sound of God's trumpet, will descend from heaven, and the dead in Christ will rise first.

Apocalypse 6:10 They cried out with a loud voice, 'Sovereign Lord, holy and true, how long will it be before you judge and avenge our blood on the inhabitants of the earth?'

vv.8-9 The second trumpet-plague which affects the sea has sometimes been interpreted as a reference to a volcanic eruption, whether of Vesuvius or of a volcanic island closer to Patmos, such as Santorini. However, the prime influence may be Jeremiah 51:25, which speaks of Babylon, Jerusalem's great conqueror, as becoming a 'burned-out mountain'. It is then a subtle warning to the present-day Babylon, imperial Rome, that its demise is inevitable. Readers of the Apocalypse would know that Rome, through Pontius Pilate, crucified the Lord Jesus, and that Rome, under Nero, also martyred many Christians. But again, as if hinting at the divine mercy and restraint, judgement is limited to a third.

vv.10-11 The third trumpet heralds the falling of a great star from heaven, echoing the first Exodus plague which affected the rivers and canals of Egypt (*Exodus 7:19*). In Jewish apocalyptic, stars often stand for angels, so that a fallen angel could be viewed as a falling star (e.g. *1 Enoch 86:1-6*). The name of this star, Wormwood (Greek *apsinthos*), reflects its capacity to turn the waters bitter. Here we have an indication that the disaster of the plagues might not be the direct result of God's will, but rather a consequence of the rebellion of fallen angels. In each of these plagues, we are given little glimpses of the reversal of God's creation, in which God brought order out of chaos (*Genesis 1*).

v.12 The disintegration of God's good creation is seen even more horrifically in the fourth trumpet-plague. According to Genesis 1:14, the creative act of God set up the great lights in heaven to distinguish between night and day.

John's description could mean one of two things. First, it could refer to a diminishment of the light's intensity, so that sun, moon and stars only shine with two-thirds of their usual strength. Given the final clause of verse 12, however ('a third of the day was kept from shining'), what is probably meant is a reduction in length, meaning that longer stretches of both day and night were subject to unnatural levels of darkness. The reference to a third of the stars may also be a poetic description of angelic rebellion, given the association of fallen angels with falling stars.

v.13 Before the fifth and sixth trumpets, each of which describes a judgement in greater detail than the first four, there is an interlude. John hears an eagle, or possibly a vulture (Greek uses the same word) screeching overhead. It is possible that we are meant to identify this eagle with one of the four living creatures around God's throne, who is 'like a flying eagle' (*4:7*).

The Greek *ouai, ouai, ouai* may reflect the sound the eagle makes. The threefold 'woe' is another reminder that the purpose of the trumpet-plagues is to warn humanity of the disaster it is creating for itself. It serves to heighten the tension before the three final trumpets are blown. As the book progresses, two of the unfolding 'woes' will be explicitly mentioned, the 'first woe' at 9:12 and the second at 11:14. But we will be left guessing about the precise identification of the third and final woe.

Apocalypse 4:7 The first living creature like a lion, the second living creature like an ox, the third living creature with a face like a human face, and the fourth living creature like a flying eagle.

Apocalypse 9:12 The first woe has passed. There are still two woes to come.

Apocalypse 11:14 The second woe has passed. The third woe is coming very soon.

Volcano at Santorini

The Word Lives On

Passages such as this, with the profound silence in heaven, angelic activity in the heavenly temple, and the mingling of the Church's prayers with incense, have strongly influenced the Church's liturgy.

The sense of cosmic collapse, of the tragic reversal of God's creation, has inspired countless artists. Particularly vivid are the scenes of the trumpet-plagues in the famous fourteenth century Angers Apocalypse Tapestry, now housed in the Château of Angers.

In the Lectionary

Apocalypse 8:3-4 is an optional reading for the feast of the Dedication of a Church in the Easter Season.

Deforestation

Live the Word of God

Listen again to the reading: Apocalypse 8:1-13

Suggestions for reflection and prayer

Read and reflect on the passage from Oecumenius in the margin.

The trumpet visions depict a terrifying nightmare of creation working in reverse. What might this passage have to say to the world's environmental crisis?

John heard silence in heaven for about half an hour.

❖ Commit yourself to a regular period of silent prayer.

John saw the prayers of the saints arising like incense.

❖ Commit yourself to a regular period of intercessory prayer.

John saw in his visions the consequences of human rebellion and sinfulness.

❖ Commit yourself to a regular period of self-examination.

Oecumenius, commenting on the silence in heaven at the opening of the seventh seal, writes:

And what is the loosing of the seventh seal? It is the second coming of Christ and the giving of blessings as rewards. For although some are handed over to the punishment of sinners, nonetheless it is the aim of Christ and the intention of the incarnation that everyone become an heir of his kingdom. Therefore, when the seventh seal was loosed, 'there was,' it says, 'silence for about half an hour,' since the king of creation was coming and every angelic and supernatural power, astounded at the exceeding greatness of the glory of him who was coming, for that reason became silent. (On the Apocalypse 8.1-2).

Hear the Word of God

Apocalypse 10:1-11:6

[1] And I saw another mighty angel coming down from heaven, wrapped in a cloud, with a rainbow over his head; his face was like the sun, and his legs like pillars of fire. [2] He held a little scroll open in his hand. Setting his right foot on the sea and his left foot on the land, [3] he gave a great shout, like a lion roaring. And when he shouted, the seven thunders sounded.

[4] And when the seven thunders had sounded, I was about to write, but I heard a voice from heaven saying, 'Seal up what the seven thunders have said, and do not write it down.'

[5] Then the angel whom I saw standing on the sea and the land raised his right hand to heaven [6] and swore by him who lives forever and ever, who created heaven and what is in it, the earth and what is in it, and the sea and what is in it: 'There will be no more delay, [7] but in the days when the seventh angel is to blow his trumpet, the mystery of God will be fulfilled, as he announced to his servants the prophets.'

[8] Then the voice that I had heard from heaven spoke to me again, saying, 'Go, take the scroll that is open in the hand of the angel who is standing on the sea and on the land.' [9] So I went to the angel and told him to give me the little scroll; and he said to me, 'Take it, and eat; it will be bitter to your stomach, but sweet as honey in your mouth.' [10] So I took the little scroll from the hand of the angel and ate it; it was sweet as honey in my mouth, but when I had eaten it, my stomach was made bitter.

[11] Then they said to me, 'You must prophesy again about many peoples and nations and languages and kings.'

[11:1] Then I was given a measuring rod like a staff, and I was told, 'Come and measure the temple of God and the altar and those who worship there, [2] but do not measure the court outside the temple; leave that out, for it is given over to the nations, and they will trample over the holy city for forty-two months.

[3] And I will grant my two witnesses authority to prophesy for one thousand two hundred and sixty days, wearing sackcloth.' [4] These are the two olive trees and the two lampstands that stand before the Lord of the earth. [5] And if anyone wants to harm them, fire pours from their mouth and consumes their foes; anyone who wants to harm them must be killed in this manner. [6] They have authority to shut the sky, so that no rain may fall during the days of their prophesying, and they have authority over the waters to turn them into blood, and to strike the earth with every kind of plague, as often as they desire.

John the Theologian, Monreale (mosaic in Santa Maria Nuova di Monreale, Sicily)

Understand the Word of God

This session will explore:

❖ the identity of the mighty angel

❖ the meaning of John's little scroll

❖ the role of the two witnesses

❖ the message for today

Setting in the Book

After the triple 'woe' of the flying eagle, the trumpets sequence has continued with two further visions, initiated by the blowing of the fifth and sixth trumpets (9:1-21). These visions have become increasingly surreal, and their demonic character more explicit. The fifth trumpet led to a plague of scorpion-like locusts, emerging from the 'Abyss', that territory under the earth where evil and chaotic forces dwell. With the sixth trumpet a horrifying army of cavalry emerged, capable of killing a third of humanity. But even this nightmare was insufficient to bring the world to its senses.

Apocalypse 11:15 Then the seventh angel blew his trumpet, and there were loud voices in heaven, saying, 'The kingdom of the world has become the kingdom of our Lord and of his Messiah, and he will reign forever and ever.'

This passage is part of a long interlude which delays the seventh trumpet. This is finally blown only at 11:15. In turn, it prepares the way for what will follow the seventh trumpet: a new set of visions, beginning with the woman and the dragon (11:19-12:18), which describes the vocation of the Church in the last days following the resurrection of Christ: to bear faithful witness even in the face of suffering and martyrdom.

What Kind of Text?

This passage falls neatly into three sections. The first (10:1-7) describes the vision of a mighty angel, one of the many accounts of angelic visitations in both Old and New Testaments. One of the closest parallels is of Daniel's visions of a 'man clothed in linen', thought by many to be the archangel Gabriel (*Daniel 10* and *12*). In such 'angelophanies', the veil between heaven and earth is pierced, allowing God to communicate with human beings.

The second section (*10:8-11*) shifts attention from heaven to earth. Here John is commissioned as a prophet. Old Testament prophets saw visions as well as speaking God's word to his people, as is seen in Isaiah 1:1, Isaiah 6:1 and Obadiah 1:1. So it should not surprise us that this New Testament visionary also utters a word of prophecy. There are particular echoes of Ezekiel's commissioning, notably in the scroll which tastes as sweet as honey but which contains bitter words (*Ezekiel 3:1-11*).

Ezekiel 3:3 He said to me, 'Mortal, eat this scroll that I give you and fill your stomach with it.' Then I ate it; and in my mouth it was as sweet as honey.

Finally, in 11:1-6, John models Ezekiel measuring the temple in Ezekiel 40, and we hear a description of God's two prophet-witnesses, who resemble biblical figures such as Moses and Elijah. But neither John nor these witnesses stand simply for themselves. They also symbolise the role of the Church, called to bear witness and speak God's prophetic word, in these turbulent times between Christ's resurrection and the Last Day.

Commentary: verse by verse reading
A Mighty Angel Descends

Genesis 9:12-13 God said, 'This is the sign of the covenant that I make between me and you and every living creature that is with you, for all future generations: I have set my bow in the clouds, and it shall be a sign of the covenant between me and the earth.'

10:1-3 The identity of this 'mighty angel' with a little scroll has long puzzled commentators. It is quite likely that he is the same 'mighty angel' that John encountered in heaven at 5:2, before the sealed scroll was given to the Lamb. The description of his appearance highlights his awe-inspiring presence as one who reveals God. The rainbow around his head reminds us of Noah's rainbow, a promise of God's enduring mercy (*Genesis 9:8-17*). But there are also similarities with the description of the Son of Man in chapter 1. This might lead us to conclude that he is Jesus' angel, who was first referred to at Apocalypse 1:1. This angel now comes to John to reveal to him what God revealed to Jesus.

The little scroll would then be the scroll with seven seals given to the Lamb. It contains God's plan to put the world right, which can be put into effect now that the scroll is open. It has become 'little' so that a mere human like John can eat it.

Hosea 11:10 They shall go after the Lord, who roars like a lion; when he roars, his children shall come trembling from the west.
Amos 3:8 The lion has roared: who shall not fear? The Lord God has spoken: who can but prophesy?

The ability of the angel to span land and sea with his feet, and without sinking into the water, symbolises his God-given authority over the creation. He roars like a lion, another indication that he is the angel of Christ who is the Lion of the tribe of Judah. This roaring provokes seven thunderclaps. It is as if we are about to witness another set of sevens, following the seven messages, the seven seals and the seven trumpets.

v.4 Instead, a heavenly voice brings this set of seven to an abrupt end. John is about to write, suggesting that he heard the seven thunderclaps as words, divine messages. But he is forbidden from doing so, with the result that readers of Revelation are left guessing what the content of these thunders might have been.

This is a very surprising scene to find in an apocalypse. Normally, seers are commanded to write down heavenly revelations, and then seal them up until the time for them to be unveiled, as shown in Daniel 8:26. John himself has already been commanded to 'write' to the seven churches, although in the Apocalypse there is no sealing of the messages 'because the time is near' (Apocalypse 1:3 and 11).

Daniel 8:26 The vision of the evenings and the mornings that has been told is true. As for you, seal up the vision, for it refers to many days from now.

vv.5-7 In biblical thought, the raising of the hand is a gesture which accompanies swearing an oath, as in Deuteronomy 32:40, and the right hand is a symbol of God's power, as in Exodus 15:6. This underscores the solemn character of the angel's oath. God is acclaimed as creator of all the realms in the Apocalypse's tripartite cosmos: heaven, earth and the sea below the earth. If God is creator, then he has concern for his creation and will seek – not to destroy it – but rather to redeem it.

Deuteronomy 32:40 For I lift up my hand to heaven, and swear.

Exodus 15:6 Your right hand, O Lord, glorious in power – your right hand, O Lord, shattered the enemy.

In verse 6 the phrase which the NRSV translates 'There will be no more delay' literally means 'There will no longer be time'. The Greek word used is *chronos*. But the sense of urgency about God's plan being put into effect suggests that the NRSV may have got it right.

A further problem lies in verse 7. It could mean that God's secret or mystery (Greek musterion) will be finished before the seventh trumpet is sounded, which happens at 11:15, or that the seventh trumpet will mark its completion. Either way, the 'mystery' is not something new, revealed for the first time to John, but something already announced to 'his servants the prophets'.

Cardinals at Conclave swearing on the Gospels

Christians hearing the angel's command ('Take it, and eat') read out during the Eucharist, might also recall the Eucharistic invitation made to them by Christ at the Last Supper (Matthew 26:26). Both word and sacrament are to be taken and consumed.

1 Corinthians 3:16-17 Do you not know that you are God's temple and that God's Spirit dwells in you? If anyone destroys God's temple, God will destroy that person. For God's temple is holy, and you are that temple.

John is Commissioned as Prophet

vv.8-10 As noted several times before, John was particularly influenced by the prophet Ezekiel. Here, as in Ezekiel 3, he is offered a scroll containing God's words. For both prophets, God's words are sweet, symbolized by the honey-like taste of the scroll. But for John, the scroll is bitter to his stomach, reflecting the challenging aspect of God's word and the fact that prophets are rejected.

v.11 When Ezekiel eats his scroll, he goes and prophesies to the people of Israel. The prophetic ministry of John, and that of the Church, is a universal one, involving different languages and ethnic groups, and 'kings' as well as ordinary people. The commission he receives here could mean both that he is to prophesy about many peoples, and that he is to prophesy to them.

John Measures the Temple-Church

11:1-2 John continues his Ezekiel-like ministry by being given a measuring rod, though in the opening verses of Ezekiel chapter 40 it is the angel companion, rather than the prophet himself, who does the measuring. It is most likely that the temple, with its altar and worshippers, represents the Church rather than the temple in geographical Jerusalem. Paul describes Christians as God's temple at 1 Corinthians 3:16-17.

The outer court which is not measured reflects the geography of the Jerusalem temple, where the outer court was accessible to Gentiles and separated from those inner courts into which only Jews could enter. In the Apocalypse, this court probably symbolises those Christians who have not remained faithful in their witness before the world.

The trampling of the 'holy city', which represents God's faithful people, by the Gentiles is limited. Forty-two months is a symbolic period of time in Revelation. Given months of thirty days, this is a period of 1,260 days, or 'a time, times and half a time', or three-and-a-half years, half of a perfect period of seven years. In Daniel, this represents the length of time for which God's people will be persecuted. Suffering is a reality, but it is not unlimited.

vv.3-4 The voice which has been speaking with John since verse 1 now begins to describe the role of the two prophet-witnesses, who symbolise the vocation of the faithful Church. Their number reflects the biblical requirement of two or three witnesses for valid testimony (*Deuteronomy 19:15*). The length of their prophesying, in the sackcloth which symbolizes repentance and mourning, coincides with the period of the Church's persecution.

Apocalypse 12:6 And the woman fled into the wilderness, where she has a place prepared by God, so that there she can be nourished for one thousand two hundred and sixty days.

Apocalypse 12:14 But the woman was given the two wings of the great eagle, so that she could fly from the serpent into the wilderness, to her place where she is nourished for a time, and times, and half a time.

Daniel 7:25 He shall speak words against the Most High, shall wear out the holy ones of the Most High, and shall attempt to change the sacred seasons and the law; and they shall be given into his power for a time, two times, and half a time.

Sistine Chapel Ceiling: The Prophet Ezekiel, 1510, Michelangelo Buonarroti (1475-1564)

Zechariah 4:14 Then he said: 'These are the two anointed ones who stand by the Lord of the whole earth.'

Their description as 'two olive trees' echoes the prophet Zechariah's description of Joshua and Zerubbabel, the high priest and governor in Jerusalem following the return from exile (*Zechariah 4:14*). They are also two lampstands. The seven churches were also identified as 'lampstands' (*Apocalypse 1:20*), and their infidelity meant the removal of their lampstand from its place (*2:5*). The two lampstands therefore symbolise the faithful Church.

2 Kings 2:11 As they continued walking and talking, a chariot of fire and horses of fire separated the two of them, and Elijah ascended in a whirlwind into heaven.

Malachi 4:5 Lo, I will send you the prophet Elijah before the great and terrible day of the Lord comes.

Deuteronomy 18:15 The Lord your God will raise up for you a prophet like me from among your own people; you shall heed such a prophet.

vv.5-6 Future hopes for Jews in the first century included the return of Elijah and a Moses-like figure. Elijah had ascended in a whirlwind, and was to return before the Day of the Lord (*2 Kings 2:11, Malachi 4:5*). Some Jews believed that Moses had been assumed into heaven, and Deuteronomy 18:15 looked to the arrival of a prophet like Moses.

John's two prophet-witnesses share some of the characteristics of Elijah and Moses in their control over the elements (*1 Kings 17-18* and *Exodus 7*). They also have the fiery breath of Elijah and Jeremiah (*1 Kings 18:38, Jeremiah 5:14*). The Church's prophetic vocation is a fiery one, for it challenges as well as consoles. It is bitter as well as being sweet as honey.

1 Kings 18:38 Then the fire of the Lord fell and consumed the burnt offering, the wood, the stones, and the dust, and even licked up the water that was in the trench.

Jeremiah 5:14 I am now making my words in your mouth a fire, and this people wood, and the fire shall devour them.

Elijah Novgorod icon

The Word Lives On

The dramatic vision of the mighty angel has been reproduced by numerous artists as diverse as Albrecht Dürer and William Blake. John's role as prophet, and that of the two witnesses, has inspired individuals in their own sense of a prophetic ministry, and the Church more widely as she seeks to be the prophetic, royal and priestly People of God.

During the Reformation, woodcuts of the two witnesses dressed as Evangelical preachers opposing the Beast (wearing the papal triple tiara!) were used effectively in Catholic-Protestant polemics. Musically, this passage inspired the French composer Olivier Messiaen to compose his Quartet for the End of Time while in a German prisoner of war camp during the Second World War.

In the Lectionary

Apocalypse 10:8-11 is set in the Weekday Lectionary for Friday of Week 33 of the year (Year II).

Olivier Messiaen (1908-1992)

Live the Word of God

Listen once more to the reading: Apocalypse 10:1 — 11:6
Suggestions for reflection and prayer

What aspects of the vision of the mighty angel speak to you, and why?

John is commissioned to prophesy again about many peoples and nations and languages and kings. Reflect on what this says about the extent of God's concern, and the vision of the Church it implies.

How does John's ministry as prophet differ from that of Ezekiel in Ezekiel 3?

John devours the scroll of God's word.
- ❖ Commit yourself to regular study of the Scriptures.

John finds the scroll bitter to his stomach.
- ❖ Pray for the courage to bear witness to your faith, even when that makes you unpopular.

John measures the temple which symbolises the priestly people of God.
- ❖ Reflect on your own vocation to be a member of God's holy priesthood, interceding on behalf of the world.

Hear the Word of God

Apocalypse 12:1-17

[1] A great portent appeared in heaven: a woman clothed with the sun, with the moon under her feet, and on her head a crown of twelve stars. [2] She was pregnant and was crying out in birth pangs, in the agony of giving birth.

[3] Then another portent appeared in heaven: a great red dragon, with seven heads and ten horns, and seven diadems on his heads. [4] His tail swept down a third of the stars of heaven and threw them to the earth.

Then the dragon stood before the woman who was about to bear a child, so that he might devour her child as soon as it was born. [5] And she gave birth to a son, a male child, who is to rule all the nations with a rod of iron. But her child was snatched away and taken to God and to his throne; [6] and the woman fled into the wilderness, where she has a place prepared by God, so that there she can be nourished for one thousand two hundred and sixty days.

[7] And war broke out in heaven; Michael and his angels fought against the dragon. The dragon and his angels fought back, [8] but they were defeated, and there was no longer any place for them in heaven. 9 The great dragon was thrown down, that ancient serpent, who is called the Devil and Satan, the deceiver of the whole world, he was thrown down to the earth, and his angels were thrown down with him.

[10] Then I heard a loud voice in heaven, proclaiming, 'Now have come the salvation and the power and the kingdom of our God and the authority of his Messiah, for the accuser of our comrades has been thrown down, who accuses them day and night before our God. [11] But they have conquered him by the blood of the Lamb and by the word of their testimony, for they did not cling to life even in the face of death. [12] Rejoice then, you heavens and those who dwell in them! But woe to the earth and the sea, for the devil has come down to you with great wrath, because he knows that his time is short!'

[13] So when the dragon saw that he had been thrown down to the earth, he pursued the woman who had given birth to the male child. [14] But the woman was given the two wings of the great eagle, so that she could fly from the serpent into the wilderness, to her place where she is nourished for a time, and times, and half a time. [15] Then from his mouth the serpent poured water like a river after the woman, to sweep her away with the flood. [16] But the earth came to the help of the woman; it opened its mouth and swallowed the river that the dragon had poured from his mouth. [17] Then the dragon was angry with the woman, and went off to make war on the rest of her children, those who keep the commandments of God and hold the testimony of Jesus.

Spain: The Woman and the Dragon (verso). From the Beatus of Leon version of the Apocalypse (1047 CE)

Understand the Word of God

This session will explore:

- ❖ the purpose of the vision of the woman and the dragon
- ❖ the meaning of the 'birth' of the male child
- ❖ the underlying story
- ❖ the message for today

Setting in the Book

The passage describing the ministry of the 'two witnesses' (*11:3-6*), and therefore the Church's prophetic vocation, continued in 11:7-13 by relating how Christ's prophets are to follow in his steps. Speaking God's word will lead to unpopularity, and ultimately to martyrdom. Yet the witnesses also share in Christ's resurrection and ascension. After this interlude, of which our previous passage formed the major part, the seventh trumpet is finally blown, and 'loud voices' proclaim: 'The kingdom of the world has become the kingdom of our Lord and of his Messiah.' (*11:15*)

Yet we are still only halfway through the book! Having announced the End, the second part of the Apocalypse now returns to describe again what has already been told through the visions of the first half, using different imagery. There is particular focus in this second half on the role of the Church. The Church is called to faithful witness, but faithfulness brings persecution and even martyrdom.

What Kind of Text?

Although our Bibles make a break at the beginning of chapter 12, this vision probably begins at 11:19, a division followed by the lectionary reading for the Solemnity of the Assumption of Our Lady. This marks another opening of heaven, a typical feature of an apocalypse which has already been met at 4:1. John sees the Ark of Covenant, the symbol of God's presence among his people, in the heavenly temple.

The main part of this passage is a symbolic vision, in which the individual characters need decoding. A battle between a pregnant woman and a dragon or other monster is a common story to symbolise the struggle between order and chaos, found not only in the Bible but also in the mythologies of the nations around Israel, and in the Graeco-Roman world around Patmos. It also has nightmarish qualities, though these are resolved, as in children's fairy tales, through the reassurance of the defeat of the dragon. However, there is a distinctively Christian focus: the defeat is only won through the death of the ultimate victor and his followers.

Interwoven with the symbolic vision in 12:7-9 is an echo of a story which was originally connected to primeval times. It is about the fall of wicked angels, which offered one explanation as to why there was disorder in God's creation. Also, as elsewhere in the book of Revelation, a canticle or hymn in 12:10-12 provides a running commentary on the action.

Apocalypse 11:19 Then God's temple in heaven was opened, and the ark of his covenant was seen within his temple; and there were flashes of lightning, rumblings, peals of thunder, an earthquake, and heavy hail.

Commentary: verse by verse reading

The Two Portents in Heaven

vv.1-2 The first character in the new vision is a pregnant woman, dazzling with the light of the sun with which she is clothed, standing on the moon. She does not symbolise one thing, but several at once. From the Hebrew Scriptures the woman reflects Eve, the mother of all the living, as described in Genesis 3:15 and 20, but also Israel who is led into the wilderness in Exodus 14, and Jerusalem, personified as a pregnant mother in Isaiah 66:7-9 and Micah 4:10. She also reflects Mary, the mother of the Messiah, and the Church, whose children are reborn as children of God. The twelve stars probably symbolize the twelve tribes of Israel, seen in the dream of Joseph in Genesis 37:9.

vv.3-4 The second character, who introduces an element of danger into the story, is a fiery red dragon-serpent, a symbol of evil and chaos. In verse 9 this dragon will be explicitly identified as the Devil and Satan. The colour red in the case of the red horse in 6:4 symbolized bloodshed and slaughter. This is a warning that the dragon is not all it appears to be, even though it has seven heads (the perfect number!), and its seven diadems suggest that it has royal power. The Apocalypse 'unveils' the terrifying fact that what might appear to be perfect or powerful is in fact evil and to be resisted.

Chaos reverses God's creation. In the Bible's first account of creation, God places the stars in the heavens as part of bringing order out of chaos (*Genesis 1:16*). The threat posed by the dragon is shown by its dragging a third of the stars from heaven. John may have in mind here the fallen angels, angels being symbolized as stars in the Jewish tradition.

v.5 The birth of the male child could refer to the birth of Jesus the Messiah at Bethlehem. However, given that he is immediately 'snatched away' to God's throne in heaven, the 'birth' is probably his death and resurrection. In Apocalypse 1:5 Jesus was called 'the firstborn of the dead'. The 'snatching' would be his ascension into heaven. The dragon has failed in its attempt to devour the child.

There may also be an echo of first century politics here. In the first century several emperors, such as Nero, exploited a version of the woman and dragon story which was associated with Leto, the pregnant mother of the god Apollo, and the dragon Python who tried to destroy her unborn son. Leto was rescued, Apollo was delivered safely, and he grew up to destroy the dragon. Nero saw himself as the Apollo figure. In the Apocalypse we have a shocking reversal of the imperial propaganda, whereby the emperor is revealed as on the side of the evil dragon, and it is Christ who brings order out of chaos.

v.6 The flight of the woman into the wilderness begins a story which will be interrupted, and picked up again in verse 13. The story of a new Exodus in Christ has been running throughout the book of Revelation, starting with the symbolic description of Christ as Passover Lamb in chapter 5.

The woman-as-the-Church now experiences a new time of testing in the desert. On the one hand, this foresees that God's people will face persecution, as the dragon turns its attention to Christ's brothers and sisters. On the other, there is reassurance that this will only be for a limited period: 1,260 days, or three and a half years, half of the complete period of seven, as already seen in 11:1-2.

Pope Benedict XVI says this of the woman of Apocalypse 12:

This Woman represents Mary the Mother of the Redeemer, but at the same time she also represents the whole Church, the People of God of all times, the Church which in all ages, with great suffering, brings forth Christ ever anew. And she is always threatened by the dragon's power. She appears defenceless and weak. But while she is threatened, persecuted by the dragon, she is also protected by God's comfort. And in the end this Woman wins. The dragon does not win. (General Audience, 23 August 2006)

The Woman Receiving Wings to Flee the Dragon, no.37 from 'The Apocalypse of Angers', 1373-87 (tapestry), Nicolas Bataille (fl. 1363-1400)

The Heavenly Battle and the Lamb's Victory

vv.7-9 The action is temporarily interrupted by a flashback to the 'myth' of the fall of Satan and the rebellious angels, a pictorial explanation of the presence of evil in our world. It is phrased in term of a military battle between Michael and Satan, because, like Tolkein's Lord of the Rings or J.K. Rowling's Harry Potter novels, the Apocalypse takes evil utterly seriously. Indeed, it threatens even God's heaven. Yet for John, this is not an evenly-pitched battle between two equal forces of light and darkness. The armies of the Devil are no match for the superior angelic armies of God.

vv.10-12 Moreover, this flashback to the fall of Satan needs to be reinterpreted by this heavenly canticle. What the heavenly voice announces is that the real defeat of evil took place, not at the beginning, but in the death and resurrection of Christ. The 'blood of the Lamb', shed on Calvary, has led to the dragon being conquered.

But Christ's people also have a role in defeating the devil (Greek *diabolos*, a word which literally means 'slanderer' or 'accuser'). This hymn speaks also of the martyrs or faithful witnesses who 'did not cling to life even in the face of death'. They may be slandered on earth by unjust authorities who do Satan's bidding. They may even be falsely accused in courts of law. But ultimately, though weak in the world's eyes, they will be victorious.

God's People in the Wilderness of Persecution

vv.13-14 Christ's death may mean that the dragon no longer has a foothold in God's heaven. But, cast down to the earth, it can still wreak havoc among humans, however temporarily. We return to the story of the Church in the wilderness. Just as Israel was carried by God 'on eagles' wings' at the Exodus (*Exodus 19:4*), so now the Church is given the 'two wings of the great eagle'.

vv.15-17 If Christ is the woman's first child, Christians are also her offspring. The dragon is unsuccessful in its attempts to destroy the woman, through a river of water from its mouth. It therefore turns its attention to persecuting her children. However, in the threat of the dragon's river of death, now swallowed up by the earth, there is the promise of another river which will not destroy but save. In his vision of the new Jerusalem, John will see emerging from the earth another river, the River of Life (*22:1*).

Exodus 19:4 You have seen what I did to the Egyptians, and how I bore you on eagles' wings and brought you to myself.

Primasius, a sixth century commentator of the Apocalypse, writes:

As though they were wings, the church uses the two Testaments, for taught by them and instructed in their precepts, she strives to avoid the snares of the enemy, and, being fashioned to follow their examples, she overcomes. (Commentary on the Apocalypse 12.14)

Apocalypse 22:1-2 Then the angel showed me the river of the water of life, bright as crystal, flowing from the throne of God and of the Lamb through the middle of the street of the city. On either side of the river is the tree of life with its twelve kinds of fruit, producing its fruit each month; and the leaves of the tree are for the healing of the nations.

The Archangel Michael defeating Satan, Guido Reni (1575-1642)

The Word Lives On

This passage is one of the most influential visions from the Apocalypse for later Christian art and devotion. The Marian dimensions of the woman have influenced statues and paintings of Our Lady, who is often portrayed trampling on the dragon or snake, or clothed with the sun.

One potent example is Diego Velazquez's *Immaculate Conception* (National Gallery, London). The battle between Michael and the Devil is also a favourite image for artists and sculptors (as in St Michael's Victory over the Devil on the façade of Coventry Cathedral), and a vision of the victorious St Michael inspired the building of Mont Saint Michel in France.

In some medieval illuminated manuscripts of the Apocalypse, there is an appreciation that the woman symbolizes the Church as well as Mary. In the thirteenth-century Trinity Apocalypse, for example, the woman in the wilderness is fed by an angel holding the host and a chalice.

In his encyclical letter on the Blessed Virgin Mary, Redemptoris Mater, issued in 1987, Saint John Paul II wrote:

The victory of the woman's Son will not take place without a hard struggle, a struggle that is to extend through the whole of human history. The 'enmity' foretold at the beginning (Genesis 3:15) is confirmed in the Apocalypse, the book of the final events of the Church and the world, in which there recurs the sign of the 'woman', this time 'clothed with the sun'. (11)

In the Lectionary

Apocalypse 11:19, 12:1-6, 10 is the first reading for the Assumption (15th August), and an option for the Common of the Blessed Virgin Mary in the Easter Season. Apocalypse 12:7-12 is the alternative first reading for the Feast of the Archangels Michael, Gabriel and Raphael (29th September).

Apocalypse 12:10-12 is the first reading for the Feast of St George (23rd April), and an optional first reading for the Common of Martyrs in the Easter Season.

Live the Word of God

Listen again to the reading: Apocalypse 12:1-17

Suggestions for reflection and prayer

Reflect on the various dimensions of the image of the pregnant woman (Eve, Israel, Jerusalem, Mary, the Church). How does each of them help in understanding this passage and its meaning for today?

Reflect on the passage from the Catechism of the Catholic Church in the margin.

The Catechism of the Catholic Church on the final petition of the Lord's Prayer ('deliver us from evil'):

When we ask to be delivered from the Evil One, we pray as well to be freed from all evils, present, past and future, of which he is the author and instigator. In this final petition, the Church brings before the Father all the distress of the world. Along with deliverance from the evils that overwhelm humanity, the Church implores the precious gift of peace and the grace of perseverance in expectation of Christ's return. (CCC 2854)

The dragon threatens to destroy the woman's male child.

❖ Pray for a deeper respect for life, and for the protection of the vulnerable.

God nourishes his Church in the wilderness for 1,260 days.

❖ Pray for a deeper appreciation of the Scriptures and the Eucharist.

Our persecuted brothers and sisters overcome the dragon by their witness to the truth.

❖ Pray for greater courage to speak the truth when keeping silent is the easier option.

Our Lady of Guadalupe

Hear the Word of God

Apocalypse 13:1-18

[1] And I saw a beast rising out of the sea, having ten horns and seven heads; and on its horns were ten diadems, and on its heads were blasphemous names. [2] And the beast that I saw was like a leopard, its feet were like a bear's, and its mouth was like a lion's mouth. And the dragon gave it his power and his throne and great authority.

[3] One of its heads seemed to have received a death-blow, but its mortal wound had been healed. In amazement the whole earth followed the beast. [4] They worshipped the dragon, for he had given his authority to the beast, and they worshipped the beast, saying, 'Who is like the beast, and who can fight against it?'

[5] The beast was given a mouth uttering haughty and blasphemous words, and it was allowed to exercise authority for forty-two months. [6] It opened its mouth to utter blasphemies against God, blaspheming his name and his dwelling, that is, those who dwell in heaven. [7] Also it was allowed to make war on the saints and to conquer them. It was given authority over every tribe and people and language and nation, [8] and all the inhabitants of the earth will worship it, everyone whose name has not been written from the foundation of the world in the book of life of the Lamb that was slaughtered.

[9] Let anyone who has an ear listen. [10] If you are to be taken captive, into captivity you go; if you kill with the sword, with the sword you must be killed. Here is a call for the endurance and faith of the saints.

[11] Then I saw another beast that rose out of the earth; it had two horns like a lamb and it spoke like a dragon. [12] It exercises all the authority of the first beast on its behalf, and it makes the earth and its inhabitants worship the first beast, whose mortal wound had been healed.

[13] It performs great signs, even making fire come down from heaven to earth in the sight of all; [14] and by the signs that it is allowed to perform on behalf of the beast, it deceives the inhabitants of earth, telling them to make an image for the beast that had been wounded by the sword and yet lived; [15] and it was allowed to give breath to the image of the beast so that the image of the beast could even speak and cause those who would not worship the image of the beast to be killed.

[16] Also it causes all, both small and great, both rich and poor, both free and slave, to be marked on the right hand or the forehead, [17] so that no one can buy or sell who does not have the mark, that is, the name of the beast or the number of its name.

[18] This calls for wisdom: let anyone with understanding calculate the number of the beast, for it is the number of a person. Its number is six hundred and sixty-six.

Germany: The beast with ten horns and the beast with lamb's horns, Ottheinrich Bible, Matthias Gerung

Understand the Word of God

This session will explore:

❖ the purpose of the two visions

❖ the identity of the two monsters

❖ the number of the beast

❖ the message for today

Setting in the Book

The two visions juxtaposed in this passage have been carefully prepared for in the previous chapter. The dragon's pursuit of the woman's children on earth (*12:17*), is now played out in concrete terms through two monsters, who in John's visionary world act as the dragon's earthly minions.

It is a salutary reminder that evil can manifest itself in our world not only through political dictators and exploitative regimes, but also through more mundane political, economic and social institutions and networks. The link between this passage and the last is provided by 12:18, where the dragon stands on the shore of the sea, from which the first monster will emerge.

Apocalypse 12:18 Then the dragon took his stand on the sand of the seashore.

Ruins of Rome

What Kind of Text?

This passage presents us with a further two symbolic visions, in which the main characters require some careful identification. Like the dragon, they shock the reader through their monstrous appearance, in this case the hideous appearance of hybrid creatures on the wrong side of the boundary separating order from chaos.

John's first century audiences would have recognised in them echoes of contemporary politics in the Roman empire of which they were part. But we should beware of decoding the visions so that they simply refer to the ancient past. As scripture, Revelation continues to confront us with the possibility that the world in which we live and participate has its own political and economic monsters.

The Apocalypse then functions as a lens or pair of spectacles through which we are invited to see our own world differently. But it calls for wisdom, not least because human beings are very good at pointing the finger at the failures of others, but less able to see where they themselves might be implicated in what is evil or unjust, or merely guilty of remaining silent.

Interwoven into these two symbolic visions are two other types of text. The first is an oracle (*verses 9-10*), like that spoken by a prophet, though here uttered by a heavenly voice, possibly that of Jesus. The second (*verse 18*) is an invitation, whether from heaven or from John himself, to calculate the number of the beast.

Job 41:1 Can you draw out Leviathan with a fishhook, or press down its tongue with a cord?

Psalm 74:14 You crushed the heads of Leviathan; you gave him as food for the creatures of the wilderness.

Isaiah 27:1 On that day the Lord with his cruel and great and strong sword will punish Leviathan the fleeing serpent, Leviathan the twisting serpent, and he will kill the dragon that is in the sea.

Daniel 7:2-3 I, Daniel, saw in my vision by night the four winds of heaven stirring up the great sea, and four great beasts came up out of the sea, different from one another.

Victorinus of Pettau wrote in his third century commentary:

'One of its heads was mortally wounded, but its mortal wound was healed.' He is referring here to Nero. For it is a well-known fact that when the army sent by the Senate was following him, he cut his own throat. (Commentary on the Apocalypse 13:3)

Commentary: verse by verse reading

The Monster from the Sea

vv.1-2 John's location on the Aegean island of Patmos would have made him especially conscious of the importance of the sea. The sea was crucial for the cohesion of the Roman empire, and Rome would have ruled the waves of the Mediterranean.

Even more significant was the Old Testament's association of the sea with evil, and with chaos monsters like Leviathan (*Job 41:1*, *Psalm 74:14* and *Isaiah 27:1*). Thus it is not surprising that John's first monster emerges from the watery abyss.

Moreover, Daniel describes a similar vision of four monsters from the sea (*Daniel 7:1-8*), each one symbolizing a king or an empire which oppressed God's people, probably Babylonia, Media, Persia and Greece. The one monster that John sees has features of all Daniel's four, and can be understood as a symbol of an empire or ruler more monstrous than all four.

Like the dragon whose purposes it will serve, this monster also has the perfect number of seven heads. Thus it too requires divine revelation in order for its beastly character to be unveiled. It also has ten horns, a biblical symbol of power. Its ten diadems, signifying royal authority, are clues that John understands this beast to be closely connected with the emperors of his own day. This is confirmed by the reference to 'blasphemous names'. Some of the cities to which John writes contained temples of the imperial cult, in which divine titles, such as Lord, Divine or Worthy of Reverence, were ascribed to Roman emperors.

vv.3-4 The specific reference to the death-wound on one of the seven heads is probably to the emperor Nero, who committed suicide in 68. After his death, some people refused to believe that he had died. Others claimed that he would return from the grave, and hence 'its mortal wound had been healed'. We can also see here the suggestion that the monstrous Nero, with his divine pretensions, parodies Christ who died but now lives for ever.

The monster represented in John's day by Rome, and by individual emperors, can be experienced not only as impressive but also as beneficent, bringing economic prosperity as well as political stability to its provinces. Thus it becomes the object of worship. But this is idolatry, for the Apocalypse the greatest sin, not least because worshipping what is less than God results in the impoverishment of the worshipper.

vv.5-8 Just as in heaven the dragon battled against Michael and his angels (*12:7*), so on earth its monster battles against the Church. Revelation presents the world in black-and-white terms, not because it is impossible to cross the boundary, from worshippers of the beast to worshippers of God, or indeed vice versa, but because the stakes are so high that shock tactics are required. Yet there is encouragement: the monster 'was allowed' or 'permitted' to act temporarily, but only for the symbolic limited period of forty-two months (equivalent to 1,260 days).

The reference to 'the book of life of the Lamb', a kind of heavenly ledger to be used at the last judgement, has often been read as suggesting that some are predetermined to be lost through not being written in it. Yet that is less than clear. It could suggest divine omniscience rather than divine predestination. God knows from the beginning those who will ultimately refuse his friendship.

vv.9-10 The vision is interrupted by an oracle, perhaps spoken by Christ, who in the gospels regularly urges those with an ear to listen, as in Mark 4:9. The first part of the oracle, echoing Jeremiah 15:2, is an encouragement to the Church in the face of suffering and even martyrdom. The second part could be an echo of Jesus' words in Gethsemane in Matthew 26:52.

Apocalypse 12:6 And the woman fled into the wilderness, where she has a place prepared by God, so that there she can be nourished for one thousand two hundred and sixty days.

Apocalypse 12:14 But the woman was given the two wings of the great eagle, so that she could fly from the serpent into the wilderness, to her place where she is nourished for a time, and times, and half a time.

Jeremiah 15:2 Those destined for pestilence, to pestilence, and those destined for the sword, to the sword; those destined for famine, to famine, and those destined for captivity, to captivity.

Matthew 26:52 Then Jesus said to him, 'Put your sword back into its place; for all who take the sword will perish by the sword.'

The Monster from the Land

vv.11-12 A second monster now appears, coming either from 'the earth' or from 'the land' (the same word in Greek). The second translation may be preferred on the grounds that John probably interprets this beast as a symbol of those who promote Roman imperial interests in the province of Asia. These may include priests of the imperial cult, and other local officials eager to promote Roman interests locally. But the symbol is imprecise enough, like that of the first beast, to apply to other contexts and subsequent generations beyond John's.

Whereas the first monster had ten horns, this one has only two, suggesting its limited authority, and dependence on the first. That these are horns 'like a lamb' suggests a parody of the true Lamb that was slain. Thankfully, its voice gives it away, for it speaks like the Satanic dragon whose purposes it serves.

vv.13-15 The Satanic deception continues with its miracle-working powers. Its capacity to bring down fire from heaven emulates God's great prophet Elijah (*1 Kings 18:38*). Other abilities are more sinister, such as the power to make cult statues speak. Talking statues were known in ancient temples, although often they were connected with sophisticated mechanical devices and ventriloquism.

Signs and wonders may indeed be signs of divine activity. However, God's people need other criteria also for judging: does such activity promote true worship? Does it liberate or exploit the vulnerable? Is it in accord with the spirit of Jesus, who conquers through self-sacrifice?

vv.16-17 The activity of the second monster also has an economic dimension. Buying and selling is now bound up in worship of the empire. Slaves were branded with the mark of their owners, and so participation in Rome's economic system is revealed to John as a form of slavery. Indeed, this slave 'mark' might include the Roman coins necessary for trade, which bore the emperor's image.

1 Kings describes heaven's response to Elijah's prayer on Mount Carmel, when he defeats the priests of Baal:

Then the fire of the Lord fell and consumed the burnt offering, the wood, the stones, and the dust, and even licked up the water that was in the trench. When all the people saw it, they fell on their faces and said, 'The Lord indeed is God; the Lord indeed is God.' (1 Kings 18:38-39)

Hear the Word of God

Read Apocalypse 17:1-14

[1] Then one of the seven angels who had the seven bowls came and said to me, 'Come, I will show you the judgment of the great whore who is seated on many waters, [2] with whom the kings of the earth have committed fornication, and with the wine of whose fornication the inhabitants of the earth have become drunk.'

[3] So he carried me away in the spirit into a wilderness, and I saw a woman sitting on a scarlet beast that was full of blasphemous names, and it had seven heads and ten horns. [4] The woman was clothed in purple and scarlet, and adorned with gold and jewels and pearls, holding in her hand a golden cup full of abominations and the impurities of her fornication; [5] and on her forehead was written a name, a mystery: 'Babylon the great, mother of whores and of earth's abominations'. [6] And I saw that the woman was drunk with the blood of the saints and the blood of the witnesses to Jesus.

When I saw her, I was greatly amazed. [7] But the angel said to me, 'Why are you so amazed? I will tell you the mystery of the woman, and of the beast with seven heads and ten horns that carries her. [8] The beast that you saw was, and is not, and is about to ascend from the bottomless pit and go to destruction. And the inhabitants of the earth, whose names have not been written in the book of life from the foundation of the world, will be amazed when they see the beast, because it was and is not and is to come.

[9] 'This calls for a mind that has wisdom: the seven heads are seven mountains on which the woman is seated; also, they are seven kings, [10] of whom five have fallen, one is living, and the other has not yet come; and when he comes, he must remain only a little while. [11] As for the beast that was and is not, it is an eighth but it belongs to the seven, and it goes to destruction. [12] And the ten horns that you saw are ten kings who have not yet received a kingdom, but they are to receive authority as kings for one hour, together with the beast. [13] These are united in yielding their power and authority to the beast; [14] they will make war on the Lamb, and the Lamb will conquer them, for he is Lord of lords and King of kings, and those with him are called and chosen and faithful.'

The Whore of Babylon, from the Luther Bible, c.1530

Understand the Word of God

This session will explore:

❖ the purpose of the vision

❖ the identity of Babylon

❖ the clue for dating the Apocalypse

❖ the message for today

Setting in the Book

The dual vision of the two monsters is followed by its mirror image, in which the true Lamb is seen with his followers, standing on Mount Zion, the place of true worship (*14:1-5*). They are presented symbolically as an army ready for battle. The narrative tension rises as three angels proclaim in turn the eternal gospel, the anticipated fall of Babylon, and the fate of those who worship the first beast (*14:6-13*).

A further sequence of seven, in which seven angels pour out the seven bowls of incense, inaugurating plagues like the plagues of Egypt (*15:5—16:21*), culminates in the destruction of Babylon. Thus the proclamation made by the second angel in chapter 14 is fulfilled in the story. This present passage is as it were a telescopic view of the seventh bowl, enabling us to see close up and in greater detail the demise of Babylon the great city.

What Kind of Text?

The vision of Babylon is another symbolic vision, in which clues are provided as to how John has interpreted its meaning for his first century context. It functions rather like a political cartoon in a newspaper, in which political institutions and individual politicians are critiqued and ridiculed, through a potent combination of irony, sarcasm and humour.

But like the visions of the two monsters, this description of Babylon also has wider application. It picks up on the memory that, centuries earlier, ancient Babylon had destroyed the southern kingdom of Judah and its temple in Jerusalem, and subsequently became a place of exile for God's people. 'Babylon' thus becomes an evocative symbol of any subsequent nation or power which oppresses, or destroys, or takes into exile. For John, the new 'Babylon' was the Rome of the emperors. That, however, does not exhaust the power of this image to speak to Christians threatened by, or too closely associated with, subsequent 'Babylons'.

Feminist scholars have reminded us that this feminine imagery for Babylon is problematic. The female is depicted here as an alluring prostitute, portrayed in terms of how she is seen by men, and ultimately destroyed. It is crucial to remember that John is using conventional biblical language, whereby cities and nations are traditionally depicted as female figures. Thus what is being described here in visionary terms is the destruction, not of a woman, but of a city and the empire it sustains.

Caricature gillray plumpudding, 'Pitt and Napoleon',1805, James Gillray

Commentary: verse by verse reading

Seeing the Great Prostitute

vv.1-2 Jewish apocalypses often describe visionary journeys in which the seer is taken by a heavenly interpreter, normally an angel, to see things in a visionary world, allowing them to return to their own world with fresh insight. John's guide here and also for the vision of the New Jerusalem at the end of the book is one of the seven bowl angels from chapter 16.

At this point, John is merely told that he will be shown 'the great prostitute' who 'sits on many waters'. The prostitute's name will not be revealed until verse 5.

v.3 That John's is no ordinary journey is signified by his being carried away 'in the spirit' like the prophet Ezekiel. John's first vision on Patmos on the Lord's Day had occurred while he was 'in the spirit' or 'in ecstasy' (*1:10*), and it was also 'in the spirit' that he was caught up to heaven at 4:2.

The angel takes him to a 'wilderness', perhaps in imitation of Christ's post-baptismal journey into the wilderness to achieve spiritual insight through temptation. There he receives a vision of a woman seated on a scarlet monster. Given its description, it may be the same monster which emerged from the sea in 13:1. Thus it is, at least for John, a symbol of the empire of Rome. If the Roman empire and its rulers are currently the monster, then the woman seated on the beast is the city of Rome. John's description of a seated woman echoes images of the goddess Roma found on some Roman coins. A similar example would be the familiar depiction of Britannia as a woman.

Britannia on a 50 pence piece

vv.4-5 Further details of the woman are provided. The purple and scarlet of her clothing parody the extravagance of imperial Rome, as well as reminding us of the red dragon who is the power behind the throne (*Apocalypse 12:3*). Her fine jewellery probably symbolizes the precious stones and metals adorning the city's buildings, as in Nero's famous *Domus Aurea* or 'Golden House' in Rome. The cup in her hand echoes Jeremiah's description of Babylon as a cup in the Lord's hand in Jeremiah 51:7.

But this apparently great city is unveiled as a prostitute. Moreover, her true identity is now revealed, written on her forehead: Babylon the great. Some have claimed that Roman prostitutes wore their names on their headbands. This would make the revelation of Babylon's name all the more shocking.

v.6a One further detail is revealed to John: Babylon is a persecutor of God's people. She is shockingly portrayed as a vampire as well as a prostitute, drunk on blood. Two groups are mentioned in this connection. The first, 'the saints', probably means God's people of both Old and New Testaments, thus including those killed by Babylon in the past. The second group are specifically 'the witnesses to Jesus', Christian martyrs, not least those who died in Rome during Nero's persecution.

Jeremiah 51:7 Babylon was a golden cup in the Lord's hand, making all the earth drunken; the nations drank of her wine, and so the nations went mad.

The Roman historian Tacitus describes the treatment given by Nero to Christians:

Mockery of every sort was added to their deaths. Covered with the skins of beasts, they were torn by dogs and perished, or were nailed to crosses, or were doomed to the flames and burnt, to serve as a nightly illumination when daylight had expired. Hence, even for criminals who deserved extreme and exemplary punishment, there arose a feeling of compassion; for it was not, as it seemed, for the public good but rather to glut the cruelty of one man that they were being destroyed. (Annals 15)

Domus Aurea

Interpreting the Vision

vv.6b-7 The shocking character of Babylon is only available through divine revelation. Without this special insight, one might view Babylon, understood in the present 'incarnation' of Rome, as beautiful, powerful, magnanimous, and good. Even John is 'greatly amazed' when he sees her. He needs his interpreting angel to put him back on the right track, by revealing the 'mystery' or 'secret' of the woman and the monster on which she sits.

v.8 The angel begins with the monster. The interpretation is complicated by the fact that individual Roman emperors might be symbolized both by the individual heads of the beast and by the beast as a whole. The claim that the monster 'was, and is not, and is about to ascend from the bottomless pit' appears to be another reference to the dead-and-now-returning Nero. As persecutor of the Church, Nero was an especially monstrous emperor. Thus he is both beast and one of the heads of the beast.

vv.9-10 Some tasks, like calculating the number of the beast, can only be achieved by the exercise of wisdom (*13:18*). Understanding the meaning of the seven heads is another difficult task. The angel's interpretation plays on the fact that the city of Rome was built on seven hills.

The Latin poet Virgil describes the city of Rome:

Rome became the fair world's fairest, and with circling wall

clasped to her single breast the sevenfold hills. (Virgil, Georgics 2.534-535)

Palatine Vergil
(5th to 6th century manuscript of Georgics and Bucolics)

But the seven heads have a second meaning also: they signify seven kings or emperors. This passage has been crucial to dating the book of Revelation. It suggests that John is writing in the reign of a sixth emperor in a sequence of seven, five having 'fallen'.

If one includes Julius Caesar among the emperors, this 'sixth' is Nero (54—68). If one begins with Augustus, then John writes in the short reign of Galba (68—69). Other scholars, however, start later in the sequence, or miss out some of the short-lived emperors, on the grounds that St Irenaeus in the second century dates the Apocalypse to the later reign of Domitian (81—96).

v.11 Again, we probably have an allusion to myths relating to Nero's demise. He is both the beast, because of his monstrous persecution of the Church, and one of the seven heads representing kings. Because it is believed he will come again, like a shocking parody of Christ, he is also an eighth king who will return after the seventh.

v.12-14 Nor does Rome operate alone. The empire can only flourish with the support of local aristocracies and client rulers. These are symbolized by the 'ten horns' of the beast, who receive derived authority which is only temporary, 'for one hour'. By association, and perhaps also through promotion of the imperial cult, they are on the side of the beast in the 'war' with the Lamb.

vv.15-18 But cities can so easily crumble when allies withdraw support. John sees how the 'ten horns' ultimately bring Rome down. As a vision of a prostitute, this is particularly shocking, highlighting the victim status of prostitutes as both used and abused by those who pay for their services.

Yet this is the destruction, not of a woman, but of a city. It is a harsh reminder of how evil can flourish as a consequence of political expediency and compromise between allies, and also of how such alliances bear the seeds of their own collapse. The great city may currently rule 'over the kings of the earth', but ultimately only the true King of heaven is reliable, and its kingdom peaceable and just.

List of Roman Emperors:
[Julius Caesar (d. 44 BC)]
Augustus (27 BC—14 AD)
Tiberius (14—37)
Gaius Caligula (37—41)
Claudius (41—54)
Nero (54—68)
Galba (68—69)
Otho (69)
Vitellius (69)
Vespasian (69—79)
Titus (79—81)
Domitian (81—96)

The Venerable Bede writes:
For in the world there are two cities, one that arises from the abyss and the other that comes down from heaven. And so now he compares the same ungodliness, which he had described in the form of a harlot made naked and burned up, with the ruins of a deserted city. (Bede, Explanation of the Apocalypse 17:18).

The Word Lives On

Like so many of Revelation's images, that of Babylon continues to influence human culture. Within the Church, St Augustine's concept of two co-existing cities, the City of God and the City of the Devil, remains important. In wider political discourse, 'Babylon' has been used recently both against Saddam's Iraq, where historical Babylon is located, and paradoxically also against the United States perceived as a modern-day 'Babylon'. This is a reminder of both how fluid and how dangerous some language can be.

In art, Albrecht Dürer's woodcut of Babylon has become iconic, while illustrations of Babylon in German Lutheran Bibles, starting with Luther's New Testament of September 1522, exploited the potential of linking past imperial Rome with present papal Rome by depicting Babylon wearing the Pope's triple tiara.

In the Lectionary

The passage does not feature in the Mass lectionary.

Tiara of Pope Paul VI
(last pope to be crowned with
the papal tiara)

Live the Word of God

Listen again to the reading: Apocalypse 17:1-14

Suggestions for reflection and prayer

Reflect on the pros and cons of the feminine imagery in this vision from the Apocalypse.

Reflect on the words from Primasius given in the margin.

John is taken into a wilderness to see his vision.

❖ Pray in union with Christ, who goes into the wilderness to prepare for his mission.

John marvels when he sees Babylon.

❖ Pray for a deeper desire for the values of the Gospel than for the values of this world.

John sees the beast which goes to destruction.

❖ Pray for a greater appreciation of that which endures over that which is transitory.

Primasius writes in his sixth century commentary:

The holy Scriptures teach that from the beginning of the world there has been the rise and advance to the present time of two cities. Of these, one is of God and the other is of the devil, and in this passage the city of the devil is indicated by the beast as representing altogether the whole body of the wicked. And so it says that it was and is not, because in the passing away of generations that succeed one another, it is built up and supplemented. And, therefore, it follows that it is going to ascend from the abyss as well as to go to destruction. For by the hidden yet just judgment of God, it is brought to its end. (Commentary on the Apocalypse 17:8)

Christ as Bridegroom and Soldier

Hear the Word of God

Read Apocalypse 19:6-21

⁶ Then I heard what seemed to be the voice of a great multitude, like the sound of many waters and like the sound of mighty thunder-peals, crying out, 'Hallelujah! For the Lord our God the Almighty reigns. ⁷ Let us rejoice and exult and give him the glory, for the marriage of the Lamb has come, and his bride has made herself ready; ⁸ to her it has been granted to be clothed with fine linen, bright and pure' - for the fine linen is the righteous deeds of the saints.

⁹ And the angel said to me, 'Write this: Blessed are those who are invited to the marriage supper of the Lamb.' And he said to me, 'These are true words of God.' ¹⁰ Then I fell down at his feet to worship him, but he said to me, 'You must not do that! I am a fellow servant with you and your brothers who hold the testimony of Jesus. Worship God! For the testimony of Jesus is the spirit of prophecy.'

¹¹ Then I saw heaven opened, and there was a white horse! Its rider is called Faithful and True, and in righteousness he judges and makes war. ¹² His eyes are like a flame of fire, and on his head are many diadems; and he has a name inscribed that no one knows but himself. ¹³ He is clothed in a robe dipped in blood, and his name is called 'The Word of God'. ¹⁴ And the armies of heaven, wearing fine linen, white and pure, were following him on white horses.

¹⁵ From his mouth comes a sharp sword with which to strike down the nations, and he will rule them with a rod of iron; he will tread the wine press of the fury of the wrath of God the Almighty. ¹⁶ On his robe and on his thigh he has a name inscribed, 'King of kings and Lord of lords'.

¹⁷ Then I saw an angel standing in the sun, and with a loud voice he called to all the birds that fly in mid-heaven, 'Come, gather for the great supper of God, ¹⁸ to eat the flesh of kings, the flesh of captains, the flesh of the mighty, the flesh of horses and their riders – the flesh of all, both free and slave, both small and great.'

¹⁹ Then I saw the beast and the kings of the earth with their armies gathered to make war against the rider on the horse and against his army. ²⁰ And the beast was captured, and with it the false prophet who had performed in its presence the signs by which he deceived those who had received the mark of the beast and those who worshipped its image. These two were thrown alive into the lake of fire that burns with sulphur. ²¹ And the rest were killed by the sword of the rider on the horse, the sword that came from his mouth; and all the birds were gorged with their flesh.

The Angel Standing in the Sun, exhibited 1846, Joseph Mallord William Turner (1775-1851)

Understand the Word of God

This session will explore:

- ❖ the meaning of Christ's victory
- ❖ the imagery of Christ the warrior
- ❖ the 'dark side' of the great supper
- ❖ the message for today

Setting in the Book

The announcement of Babylon's demise at the end of chapter 17 is followed by an extended dirge or lament (*Apocalypse 18*). There is sadness as well as joy at Babylon's fall. In particular, those whose livelihoods have depended on the great city - client kings, merchants, seafarers - join in an expression of grief and regret. One cannot help being moved by the pathos of the passage. The city has become a shadow of its former self, and its streets are now silent and dark, lacking even the sound of music and the voice of bride and bridegroom (*18:22-23*).

However, there is another side to the story. For the silent millions who have been exploited by 'Babylon', whether Rome or any other city, and been enslaved by her or even killed, this fall is a cause for rejoicing. Heaven provides a voice for the voiceless, with a canticle of praise to the God whose judgements are 'true and just' (*19:1-5*). Our passage begins halfway through this heavenly song.

What Kind of Text?

Several different genres are mixed together in this passage. We begin in verses 6-8 with a piece of liturgy or a hymn, sung by a great multitude. What has happened to Babylon is an outworking of Christ's victory at Easter. Indeed, Apocalypse 19 is the only place in the whole New Testament where the Easter acclamation 'Alleluia' occurs (*verses 1, 3, 4, 6*). This hymn is followed by one of two passages in which John attempts, unsuccessfully, to worship an angel (*verses 9-10*).

The remainder of the chapter is another symbolic vision in two parts. Part one, verses 11-16, is inaugurated by another 'opening of heaven' which promises divine revelation, as in 4:1 and 11:19. Christ appears under the guise of a heavenly warrior, drawing on a wide variety of Old Testament passages. This unusual image for Jesus, which some Christians might find disturbing, is a reminder that the battle against evil and injustice is only too real. Yet the violence may be more symbolic than literal.

The second part of the vision, in verses 17-21, describes the completion of Christ's victory, including a rather gruesome supper, where the flesh of humans and horses is eaten by the birds of heaven. It is interwoven with a description of a battle, during which the earthly associates of the dragon, the beast and the false prophet, are rounded up and destroyed.

Apocalypse 22:8-9 I, John, am the one who heard and saw these things. And when I heard and saw them, I fell down to worship at the feet of the angel who showed them to me; but he said to me, 'You must not do that! I am a fellow servant with you and your brothers the prophets, and with those who keep the words of this book. Worship God!'

Commentary: verse by verse reading
Celebrating the Lamb's Wedding

v.6 Revelation has moments of ear-splitting intensity. This is one of them, as 'a great multitude' sings its Hallelujah chorus. This is presented to us as like the noise made by a vast waterfall, or the terrifying rumbling of a powerful thunderstorm. Yet the content of the singing describes good news, not news of woe. The Lord God reigns, not those rival 'lords' who govern through bloodshed, manipulation and exploitation.

In Mark 2:19 Jesus says:

The wedding guests cannot fast while the bridegroom is with them, can they? As long as they have the bridegroom with them, they cannot fast.

In John 3:29 John the Baptist says of Jesus:

He who has the bride is the bridegroom. The friend of the bridegroom, who stands and hears him, rejoices greatly at the bridegroom's voice. For this reason my joy has been fulfilled.

In 2 Corinthians 11:2 Paul writes:

I feel a divine jealousy for you, for I promised you in marriage to one husband, to present you as a chaste virgin to Christ.

vv.7-8 A common motif for describing the relationship between Christ and his people is that of bridegroom and bride, which is found, for example, in Mark 2:19-20 and John 3:29, as well as in 2 Corinthians 11:2 and Ephesians 5:22-33. It builds on an Old Testament metaphor for God's covenant with Israel, found famously in Hosea 1—3. There is a contrast here with the prostitute Babylon, for prostitution is a metaphor for idolatry, investing what is less than God with ultimate significance. The Church as Bride, which includes male Christians no less than female, is called to be single-minded in attachment to Christ, and joyfully expectant for the bridegroom's return.

As if to underscore the intimate relationship between Church and members, the wedding dress of the bride, made of fine white linen, symbolizes the 'righteous deeds of the saints'. This is in sharp contrast with the purple and scarlet clothing of Babylon, produced from the blood, sweat and tears of the recipients of Babylon's 'unrighteous deeds.'

The Apocalypse shares the New Testament tension between what is already the case and what is still to come in the future. The heavenly choir proclaims that 'the marriage of the Lamb has come'. The future breaks into the present, as it does every time Mass is celebrated.

vv.9-10 Indeed, we are probably meant to hear a reference to the Eucharist. Every Mass is an anticipation of the Lamb's wedding banquet. This is reiterated by the angel, who in another of Revelation's seven beatitudes declares an invitation to the Lamb's marriage supper a cause of blessing.

John's attempt to worship the angel at this point is perhaps not surprising, given the exalted status of interpreting angels in many apocalypses. Yet the Apocalypse draws a very clear line between the Creator and the creature, including the created angelic world. However exalted, this angel is simply a 'fellow servant' with John and with us. This is in contrast to the Graeco-Roman world, within which the early church found itself, where even deceased emperors, and occasionally living ones, could be offered worship. The only exception is the Lamb, who is worshipped because Christ is divine as well as human.

The Divine Warrior

vv.11-12 The opening of heaven enables us to see the Lamb again, although he now appears in unfamiliar guise. What John describes is influenced by Old Testament passages such as Isaiah 11 and 63, and Wisdom 18, but we should allow the overall impact of the imagery to work on us. This is the terrifying divine warrior, who is victorious in battle, but there are indications that that this is no ordinary warrior, and no ordinary battle.

First, as 'faithful and true', the first of four names in this passage, which express different aspects of Christ's character, he wages war in 'righteousness'. He is the true Son of David, whose rule is one which establishes justice, and defends the poor and meek, as suggested in Isaiah 11:4. Second, his dazzling gaze 'like a flame of fire' (*1:14*) identifies him as Jesus Christ, whose look pierces us to the heart, yet is tinged with love and compassion. His 'many diadems' mean that his power to rule is greater than that of the monster from the sea, which had only ten diadems (*13:1*).

Verse 9 of course inspires the words of the priest at Mass as the moment of communion approaches: 'Behold the Lamb of God, who takes away the sins of the world. Blessed are those called to the supper of the Lamb.'

Isaiah 11:3-4 He shall not judge by what his eyes see,
or decide by what his ears hear;
but with righteousness he shall judge the poor,
and decide with equity for the meek of the earth;
he shall strike the earth with the rod of his mouth,
and with the breath of his lips he shall kill the wicked.

Wisdom 18:14-16

*For while gentle silence enveloped all things,
and night in its swift course was now half gone,
your all-powerful word leaped down from heaven,
from the royal throne,
into the midst of the land that was doomed,
a stern warrior, carrying the sharp sword of your authentic command,
and stood and filled all things with death,
and touched heaven while standing on the earth.*

His second name is unknown to others, probably because to know someone's name is to have power over them. If one wanted to speculate, one might conclude that this 'secret name' is the unpronounceable name of God, YHWH, given to Jesus according to Philippians 2:9.

vv.13-14 Another indication that this is no ordinary battle is that the warrior's robe is 'dipped in blood' even before he engages the enemy, which only occurs in verse 19. Thus it may be his own blood, and that of the martyrs, who follow him like an army on white horses. John sees a warrior who is victorious, not through killing, but through the sacrifice of the Cross.

His third name, 'the Word of God', emphasizes Christ's role as revealer of the Father and echoes John's Prologue (*1:1* and *1:14*). It also alludes to the redemptive role of the Word at the Exodus (*Wisdom 18:14-16*), now relived in the death and resurrection of Christ.

Christ mosaic, 6th century,
Archbishop's Chapel,
Ravenna, Italy

vv.15-16 As Word of God, he speaks the word of truth, which cuts more finely than any double-edged sword (*Hebrews 4:12*). This ability to speak the truth is symbolized by the sword coming out of his mouth (*Isaiah 11:4*). Finally, his fourth name reveals his supremacy over all rival powers: 'King of kings and Lord of lords.'

The Great Supper of God

vv.17-18 The second part of the vision describes the horrific antithesis of the 'marriage feast of the Lamb'. Birds of prey are invited by an angel 'standing in the sun' to gather for the great supper of God. The inspiration here is Ezekiel 39:17-20, another indication that John possibly meditated on the text of Ezekiel in preparation for his visionary experience. It presents in shocking dream-like terms the consequences of refusing the invitation to the Lamb's wedding. Acceptance of the invitation promises life, whereas rejecting it can only mean death.

vv.19-21 What John sees is the 'last battle', which is described only briefly, with no voyeuristic interest in the details. Battle is engaged by the beast from the sea, together with its allies 'the kings of the earth'. The beast is captured, along with the 'false prophet', an alternative name for the 'beast from the land' of 13:11-18. Both monsters are cast into the 'lake of fire', because all that stands in the way of God's Kingdom of peace and justice must be finally defeated, if the Kingdom is truly to come.

Apocalypse 1:16 In his right hand he held seven stars, and from his mouth came a sharp, two-edged sword, and his face was like the sun shining with full force.

In Ezekiel 39:19-20 the Lord God addresses the birds and wild animals with these words:
You shall eat fat until you are filled, and drink blood until you are drunk, at the sacrificial feast that I am preparing for you. And you shall be filled at my table with horses and charioteers, with warriors and all kinds of soldiers.

The Word Lives On

The opening canticle of this passage is perhaps most famously preserved in the *Hallelujah Chorus* from Handel's *Messiah*.

The vision of the rider on the white horse is a favourite image in medieval Apocalypse cycles, both in illuminated manuscripts and sculpted in stone on medieval cathedrals.

The vision has also inspired authors like William Blake, John Bunyan and John Milton, and left its mark on Christopher Wordsworth's Ascension hymn: '*See, the conqueror mounts in triumph.*'

The '*angel standing in the sun*' has been painted by a number of artists, including William Turner (Tate Britain, London).

In the Lectionary

The reading for Thursday of the Last Week of the Year (Year II), mainly taken from Apocalypse 18, includes 19:9. Apocalypse 19:1 and 19:5-9 is an optional first reading for Holy Men and Women in the Easter Season.

The End of Borodino Battle, 1899-1900, Vasily Vereshchagin

Live the Word of God

Listen again to the reading: Apocalypse 19:6-21

Suggestions for reflection and prayer

Which images of Christ in this vision speak most powerfully to you? Are there any which you find difficult or problematic, and why?

Reflect on the words of Primasius in the margin.

The marriage of the Lamb has come.
- ❖ Pray for single-minded devotion to Christ and to Christ's Kingdom.

The angel urges John to worship God.
- ❖ Pray for a greater sense of reverence and awe in God's presence.

The rider judges and makes war in righteousness.
- ❖ Pray for the strength to act justly, and to challenge injustice.

The sixth century commentator Primasius writes:

He judges as the King of all ages. He makes war as one who always suffers in his members. When he fights, he conquers; he crowns himself; he offers himself as strength to those who struggle; he promises himself as the prize for those who overcome. (Commentary on the Apocalypse 19:11)

XVI

Hear the Word of God

Read Apocalypse 20:1-15

[1] Then I saw an angel coming down from heaven, holding in his hand the key to the bottomless pit and a great chain. [2] He seized the dragon, that ancient serpent, who is the Devil and Satan, and bound him for a thousand years, [3] and threw him into the pit, and locked and sealed it over him, so that he would deceive the nations no more, until the thousand years were ended. After that he must be let out for a little while.

[4] Then I saw thrones, and those seated on them were given authority to judge. I also saw the souls of those who had been beheaded for their testimony to Jesus and for the word of God. They had not worshipped the beast or its image and had not received its mark on their foreheads or their hands. They came to life and reigned with Christ a thousand years. [5] (The rest of the dead did not come to life until the thousand years were ended.) This is the first resurrection. [6] Blessed and holy are those who share in the first resurrection. Over these the second death has no power, but they will be priests of God and of Christ, and they will reign with him a thousand years.

[7] When the thousand years are ended, Satan will be released from his prison [8] and will come out to deceive the nations at the four corners of the earth, Gog and Magog, in order to gather them for battle; they are as numerous as the sands of the sea. [9] They marched up over the breadth of the earth and surrounded the camp of the saints and the beloved city. And fire came down from heaven and consumed them. [10] And the devil who had deceived them was thrown into the lake of fire and sulphur, where the beast and the false prophet were, and they will be tormented day and night forever and ever.

[11] Then I saw a great white throne and the one who sat on it; the earth and the heaven fled from his presence, and no place was found for them. [12] And I saw the dead, great and small, standing before the throne, and books were opened. Also another book was opened, the book of life. And the dead were judged according to their works, as recorded in the books.

[13] And the sea gave up the dead that were in it, Death and Hades gave up the dead that were in them, and all were judged according to what they had done. [14] Then Death and Hades were thrown into the lake of fire. This is the second death, the lake of fire; [15] and anyone whose name was not found written in the book of life was thrown into the lake of fire.

The Revelation of St John: 15. The Angel with the Key to the Bottomless Pit, Albrecht Dürer, (1471-1528)

Understand the Word of God

This session will explore:

- ❖ the purpose of the visions of the End
- ❖ the meaning of the Millennium
- ❖ the description of the Last Judgment
- ❖ the message for today

Setting in the Book

1 Corinthians 15:24-26 Then comes the end, when Christ hands over the kingdom to God the Father, after he has destroyed every ruler and every authority and power. For he must reign until he has put all his enemies under his feet. The last enemy to be destroyed is death.

The last battle described at the end of chapter 19 is a crucial stage in the final defeat of evil. It is not the beginning of the end: that privilege belongs to the death and resurrection of Christ, and the emergence of the Church. Since the Cross, Satan has been in retreat. A crucial moment is indeed reached when the dragon's earthly minions, the monster from the sea and the false prophet, are thrown into the lake of fire (*19:20*), unable to wreak any more havoc among humans. But Satan himself now needs to be defeated, along with the consequences of his rule, including the last enemy, death (*1 Corinthians 15:26*). The events described in this passage present the binding and final destruction of the power of evil, along with Death and Hades.

What Kind of Text?

What theologians call the 'eschatological' events, the events of the 'last times' or the 'last things', can only be described allusively, poetically, and using traditional imagery. Scripture and tradition provide a broad map to find our way, though not all the details of what has still to take place.

John is indebted to Old Testament antecedents and other Jewish traditions as he struggles to describe what he has seen in visionary ecstasy on Patmos. In fact, the 'last things' began in the previous passage with the two visions of the divine warrior and the great supper. A final vision will occur at 21:1-8. Together with chapter 20, these 'visions of the end' form another set of seven visions, a recurring feature of the Apocalypse.

The present passage falls into four interconnected parts. The first vision (*20:1-3*) prepares the ground for the second by removing Satan, at least temporarily, from the scene. Verses 4-6 seem to grant a special role to the martyrs, by virtue of their total commitment to Christ. The release of the devil leads to his ultimate defeat in verses 7-10. Finally, death itself is overcome by the resurrection and judgment of humanity before God's throne (*20:11-15*). The way is now open for the full restoration of God's plan for creation.

Commentary: verse by verse reading

Satan is Imprisoned

v.1 Throughout Revelation, John has described a host of angels performing specific tasks of worship, judgment, or revelation. One now descends like a celestial prison warder, with a key and a chain. His task is to put a lid on 'the bottomless pit' or Abyss, the watery chaos below the earth from where demonic forces were able to emerge at 9:1-2. Some early commentators even suggested that this 'angel' was Christ himself, whose coming 'binds' the strong man Satan, as in Matthew 12:29. Although John seems to be speaking of what is still to come, Christ's incarnation and saving death puts it in perspective.

In chapter 12, the dragon lost its foothold in heaven, and intensified its activity against God's people on earth. Now it is confined further to the Abyss, as the Kingdom of God continues to progress and makes evil retreat. The angel acts as the devil's prison warder, seizing, binding and locking him up.

The sixth century commentator Primasius wrote:

We understand the angel coming down from heaven to be our Lord, Jesus Christ, who is called the angel of great counsel. He visited the region of those who are mortal, for as one who is stronger he wished to bind the strong man. (Commentary on the Apocalypse 20:1-2)

Apocalypse 12:9 The great dragon was thrown down, that ancient serpent, who is called the Devil and Satan, the deceiver of the whole world – he was thrown down to the earth, and his angels were thrown down with him.

In the Roman world, prisons were not for long-term prisoners, but provisional holding-places prior to sentencing and probable execution. Hence the binding of Satan is only a temporary measure, for 'a thousand years', the same period of Christ's reign in verses 4-6. We are probably to think of these two periods as simultaneous. Like other numbers in the Apocalypse, 'a thousand' is a symbolic number: a long period of time, yet not one which is indefinite.

The Millennium

This is the essence of the hotly contested concept of 'the millennium', from the Latin word for 'a thousand years'. Many Evangelical Christians today take it literally, as an actual future thousand-year reign of Christ on earth, and they consider it to be central to the Christian faith. Yet for much of the Church's life, it has been understood symbolically. Moreover, given that it is mentioned in just three out of Revelation's 405 verses, its importance may have been exaggerated.

v.4 The scene now shifts to 'thrones', seats of judgement and royal authority. John's Greek is rather unclear at this point. Perhaps the best interpretation is that there are not two groups, judges on thrones and the souls of beheaded martyrs, as in the NRSV translation, but one. In other words, it is those who have witnessed to Christ to the point of death, who now sit in judgement and reign with Christ 'for a thousand years'.

The key to John's vision may be this: what might the world look like if the victims rather than the victors ruled? How might our world be transformed if the Kingdom of God held sway, unrestricted by evil, sin and injustice? What if a human community were to live according to the values of Christ, acknowledging Christ as King? It is not surprising that St Augustine believed the millennium to be a symbol of the life of the Church, that 'alternative society' in the time between the first coming of Christ and his coming again.

Apocalypse 14:4 They have been redeemed from humankind as first fruits for God and the Lamb.

1 Corinthians 15:20 But in fact Christ has been raised from the dead, the first fruits of those who have died.

1 Corinthians 15:23 But each in his own order: Christ the first fruits, then at his coming those who belong to Christ.

vv.5-6 The Apocalypse makes a distinction between 'the first resurrection', of the beheaded martyrs, and by implication all who have witnessed faithfully to Christ, and the general resurrection on the last day in verses 11-15. Because of their closeness to Christ, the martyrs share his privilege of being 'first fruits' of the resurrection (*14:4 and 1 Corinthians 15:20 and 23*). Like the 'first fruits' of the harvest, offered to God as assurance of more to come, as seen in Leviticus 23:9-14, they anticipate the last day when, according to Jewish eschatology, all the dead would be raised.

The 'second death', from which they are exempt, is a Jewish expression denoting not literal but spiritual death, 'exclusion from the world to come', separation from the life of God.

The Release and Defeat of Satan

vv.7-8 The reign of the martyrs shows what our destiny is, but evil still lurks. John's next vision deals will the final obliteration of evil, or perhaps its own self-destruction. The Apocalypse understands Satan to be the great deceiver, who convinces humans to put their trust in that which is not God. This deception is symbolized by the attractive qualities of the monster from the sea and Babylon, only revealed as demonic by divine revelation. Once released, the dragon is up to its old tricks again.

Thus the deceived nations gather again for battle. The mythical figures of Gog and Magog, derived from the reference to the prince 'Gog of the land of Magog' at Ezekiel 38:1, come to symbolize evil nations who need to be defeated in order for good to flourish.

vv.9-10 The 'breadth of the earth' over which they march, although symbolic geography rather than literal, is inspired by Harmagedon, 'the mountain of Megiddo' (16:16). Many of Israel's greatest battles had been fought in the broad plain overlooked by the city of Megiddo, described by Napoleon as probably the finest battle-ground in the world. This made it an appropriate symbolic location for the last great battle between good and evil.

The result of the battle is the confinement of the devil to the lake of fire and sulphur. Unlike the imprisonment in the Abyss, this is no temporary confinement, but the ultimate defeat of evil.

1 Kings 9:15 King Solomon conscripted forced labour to build the house of the Lord and his own house, the Millo and the wall of Jerusalem, Hazor, Megiddo and Gezer.

2 Kings 23:29 Pharaoh Neco king of Egypt went up to the king of Assyria to the river Euphrates. King Josiah went to meet him, but when Pharaoh Neco met him at Megiddo, he killed him.

The Last Judgment

v.11 The many thrones of the martyrs now give way to one 'great white throne', echoing the white figure of God at Daniel 7:9, as John sees a vision of the Last Judgement. It is a reminder that all humans, even the mighty and powerful, must ultimately give account for their lives. That the dead are judged together reminds us that sin has a corporate as well as an individual character.

vv.12-13 All the places holding the dead, Death, Hades or the underworld, the sea, now give them back, and books are opened. These are the books or scrolls which in Jewish tradition contained the deeds of human lives, from the greatest atrocity to the smallest act of kindness. God remembers, even when human beings forget. We are reminded of the martyrs, the voiceless and the disappeared, whose memory might otherwise have been erased. What has been done to them is included in the books.

Great White Throne, Zion National Park, Utah

There is also another book, the 'book of life'. This seems to be a heavenly ledger containing the names of God's people (see *Exodus 32:32-33*), redeemed by God's free choice and not because of what they have done. There is a tension here between the first books, which take human responsibility very seriously, and the one book of life, which is a reminder that eternal life is God's free gift, which cannot be earned.

vv.14-15 The final act of the 'mopping-up operation' is to destroy the 'last enemy'. Personified throughout Revelation as the grim reaper, Death is now thrown into the lake of fire, accompanied by its side-kick Hades. In vivid imagery, John shows death swallowed up in victory (*1 Corinthians 15:54*).

Exodus 32:32-33 Moses said: 'But now, if you will only forgive their sin – but if not, blot me out of the book that you have written.' But the Lord said to Moses, 'Whoever has sinned against me I will blot out of my book.'

1 Corinthians 15:54 When this perishable body puts on imperishability, and this mortal body puts on immortality, then the saying that is written will be fulfilled: 'Death has been swallowed up in victory.'

Christian Martyrs of Nagasaki

The Word Lives On

Images from this chapter have influenced literature such as Milton's *Paradise Lost* and Shelley's poem '*The Serpent Is Shut Out from Paradise.*' Theologians throughout Christian history have attempted to understand the precise meaning of the millennium. Is it an earthly or a heavenly reign? Does it precede or follow the final coming of Christ? Is it something that only God can bring about, or can Christians work to hasten its coming? Is it already present, or still in the future?

The Last Judgement is a theme particularly explored by artists, most famously Michelangelo in his fresco for the Sistine Chapel. The Apocalypse, however, is remarkably restrained about details. Thus images of the scene often resort to other biblical passages, especially Matthew 25, to fill in the details.

In the Lectionary

Apocalypse 20:1-4 and 20:11-21:2 is the reading set in the Weekday Lectionary for Friday of the Last Week of the Year (Year II).

Depiction of Satan, c.1866, Gustave Doré

Live the Word of God

Listen again to the reading: Apocalypse 20:1-15

Suggestions for reflection and prayer

How might Revelation's language of a last great battle and final judgement help us to understand the presence and nature of evil in the world?

Reflect on the words of St Augustine in the margin.

John sees Satan justly seized and bound in prison.
* Pray for those who are unjustly imprisoned or have disappeared without trace.

John sees the dead being judged according to their works.
* Pray for a deeper spirit of penitence.

John sees the opening of the Lamb's book of life.
* Pray for a stronger sense of gratitude for God's free gift of life.

St Augustine writes this concerning the 'millennium':

During the 'thousand years' when the devil is bound, the saints also reign for a 'thousand years' and, doubtless, the two periods are identical and mean the span between Christ's first and second coming. For not only in that future kingdom to which Christ referred in the words, 'Come, blessed of my Father, take possession of the kingdom prepared for you,' but even now those saints reign with him in some authentic though vastly inferior fashion. To them he said, 'Behold, I am with you all days, even to the consummation of the world'. (City of God 20:9)

The New Jerusalem

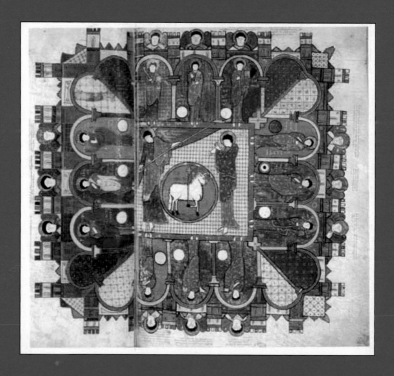

Hear the Word of God

Read Apocalypse 21:9-27

[9] Then one of the seven angels who had the seven bowls full of the seven last plagues came and said to me, 'Come, I will show you the bride, the wife of the Lamb.' [10] And in the spirit he carried me away to a great, high mountain and showed me the holy city Jerusalem coming down out of heaven from God. [11] It has the glory of God and a radiance like a very rare jewel, like jasper, clear as crystal.

[12] It has a great, high wall with twelve gates, and at the gates twelve angels, and on the gates are inscribed the names of the twelve tribes of the Israelites; [13] on the east three gates, on the north three gates, on the south three gates, and on the west three gates. [14] And the wall of the city has twelve foundations, and on them are the twelve names of the twelve apostles of the Lamb.

[15] The angel who talked to me had a measuring rod of gold to measure the city and its gates and walls. [16] The city lies foursquare, its length the same as its width; and he measured the city with his rod, fifteen hundred miles; its length and width and height are equal.

[17] He also measured its wall, one hundred and forty-four cubits by human measurement, which the angel was using. [18] The wall is built of jasper, while the city is pure gold, clear as glass. [19] The foundations of the wall of the city are adorned with every jewel; the first was jasper, the second sapphire, the third agate, the fourth emerald, [20] the fifth onyx, the sixth carnelian, the seventh chrysolite, the eighth beryl, the ninth topaz, the tenth chrysoprase, the eleventh jacinth, the twelfth amethyst. [21] And the twelve gates are twelve pearls, each of the gates is a single pearl, and the street of the city is pure gold, transparent as glass.

[22] I saw no temple in the city, for its temple is the Lord God the Almighty and the Lamb. [23] And the city has no need of sun or moon to shine on it, for the glory of God is its light, and its lamp is the Lamb. [24] The nations will walk by its light, and the kings of the earth will bring their glory into it. [25] Its gates will never be shut by day - and there will be no night there. [26] People will bring into it the glory and the honour of the nations. [27] But nothing unclean will enter it, nor anyone who practises abomination or falsehood, but only those who are written in the Lamb's book of life.

Heavenly Jerusalem, Apocalypse of Saint-Sever (11th century)

Understand the Word of God

This session will explore:

❖ the purpose of the vision

❖ the city's dimensions and architecture

❖ the relationship to the old Jerusalem

❖ the message for today

Apocalypse 21:1-2 Then I saw a new heaven and a new earth; for the first heaven and the first earth had passed away, and the sea was no more. And I saw the holy city, the new Jerusalem, coming down out of heaven from God, prepared as a bride adorned for her husband.

Setting in the Book

The four visions in the previous passage were part of a sequence of seven visions of the end which began in chapter 19.

The seventh and final vision of this sequence (*21:1-8*) describes what can now come about with the final defeat of evil and death. In the old world, where the dragon held sway, there was a separation between God and humanity, heaven and earth, with a third realm also under the earth, the watery sea of the Abyss, from which the first monster came. In the final vision heaven and earth are brought together as the new Jerusalem descends. The third realm where evil lurked has also gone. Apocalypse 21:1 reads: 'and the sea was no more'. With it, death, mourning and crying are also things of the past.

What Kind of Text?

This passage, like the long description of Babylon in chapter 17, is part of another 'telescopic' vision. It enables us to see what is described in 21:1-8 in greater detail. Unlike many of the symbolic visions in the Apocalypse, John does not simply see this vision, but actually participates in it, much as he did in Revelation 10 when he ate the little scroll. He is taken on a tour of the heavenly city, which has now descended to earth, walking its streets, and watching the angel measure its walls. The biblical antecedent is Ezekiel's journey through the ideal Jerusalem and holy land in Ezekiel 40-48.

One way of reading the Apocalypse is as a 'Tale of Two Cities', one holy and one unholy. This city is the antithesis of the immoral, exploitative Babylon, founded on bloodshed and the plundering of the earth's resources. While the New Jerusalem only descends at the very end of this book, it represents a city which has already been breaking in throughout. Wherever faithful witness is given, wherever the values of God's Kingdom persist, there the New Jerusalem breaks in. However, until this final climactic scene, most of us belong to both cities simultaneously.

Commentary: verse by verse reading

The Descent of the City

vv.9-10 John's journey to the New Jerusalem is a journey 'in the spirit', as was his vision of Babylon (*17:3*). Again, one of the seven bowl angels, perhaps the same one who had showed him the great prostitute, acts as interpreter of what he sees.

In contrast to the 'wilderness' from where he saw Babylon (*17:3*), John is taken to a 'great, high mountain', as in Ezekiel 40:2. This exalted mountain-top is probably not simply John's vantage-point but the place to which the holy city descends, emphasizing its superiority over the earthly Jerusalem which was built on a fairly modest hill. Several Jewish writers, moved by the failure of the earthly capital and its temple priests, also envisaged that God had prepared an alternative heavenly Jerusalem, or a temple 'not built by human hands'.

v.11 Earlier we saw the New Jerusalem as Christ's bride, dressed in white linen. Now we see the bride as a city, with architectural rather than sartorial imagery. But because it is a heavenly vision, John again falls back on similes. Its dazzling appearance is 'like a very rare jewel', or 'like jasper', which for the ancients was transparent, and 'clear as crystal'.

vv.12-14 The massive size of this city – the city to replace all cities – is reflected in its 'great, high wall' to match the 'great, high mountain' upon which it descends. But it is also a perfectly ordered city, with twelve gates, three at each compass-point. The number twelve symbolizes completion, for three, the number of God, times four, the number of the created world, makes twelve.

Just as the cherubim guard the gates of the Garden of Eden in Genesis 3:24, so twelve angels guard the gates of this new city, which contains Eden's tree and river of life (*22:1-2*). The need for guards to prevent unworthy people from entering is odd, given the defeat of evil in the previous chapter. But in the dream-like, haphazard Book of Revelation, things do not always work in a straightforward, linear way. At least the angels' presence is a reassurance that this city cannot be corrupted.

Names are inscribed on the city, as marks of ownership. Each of the gates bears the name of one of the twelve tribes; on the twelve foundation stones are the names of 'the twelve apostles of the Lamb.' These are a reminder that Old and New Testaments belong together, and there is continuity from one to the other.

The names on the foundations are a reminder that the Church is 'built upon the foundations of the apostles and prophets' (*Ephesians 2:20*) as the first generation.

Sistine Chapel Ceiling (1508-12): The Fall of Man, 1510, Michelangelo Buonarroti, (1475-1564)

The Measuring of the City

vv.15-17 In 11:1-2 John was allowed to measure the temple for himself. But the enormous size of the heavenly city means that measuring is now the task of the angel, as it was for Ezekiel's angel in Ezekiel 40:3.

The first measurement reveals that the city is 'foursquare' (with equal length, width and height), appropriate to a perfectly proportioned city. This means that the New Jerusalem is a cube, as was the Holy of Holies in Solomon's Temple (*1 Kings 6:20*). The whole city is a temple, a holy place.

The precise dimensions are enormous. The NRSV translation gives them literally as 'fifteen hundred miles', roughly the distance from London to Athens. Yet although we are certainly meant to be impressed by its huge size, the original Greek gives a symbolic number: 'twelve thousand stadia', related to the perfect number twelve. A similar symbolic dimension is given for the city wall, probably its width: one hundred and forty-four cubits, the square of the number twelve.

vv.18-19 Attention now turns from dimensions to building materials. The translucent jasper of the wall enables the dazzling, crystal-like quality of the city's gold to shine through. Twelve precious stones give splendour as well as vivid colour to the city's foundations.

The inspiration may be Isaiah 54:11-12, which envisaged Jerusalem adorned with jewels. Because the city is also a temple, John may also be thinking of the twelve jewels on the breastplate of the High Priest, described in Exodus 28:17-20. These symbolized the twelve tribes, which meant that the High Priest interceded before God with the people 'on his heart'. In John's greater visionary city, the 'names' are those of the apostles, and thus of people 'from every tribe, language, people and nation' who heard the apostolic message.

Finally, we hear that each of the city's gates comprises a single gleaming-white pearl, which gives rise to the common phrase 'the pearly gates' to describe the gates of heaven. The city street is made of the same dazzling gold as the rest of the city.

Ezekiel 40:3 When he brought me there, a man was there, whose appearance shone like bronze, with a linen cord and a measuring reed in his hand; and he was standing in the gateway.

Isaiah 54:11-12 I am about to set your stones in antimony, and lay your foundations with sapphires.

I will make your pinnacles of rubies, your gates of jewels, and all your wall of precious stones.

Tobit 13:16 The gates of Jerusalem will be built with sapphire and emerald, and all your walls with precious stones. The towers of Jerusalem will be built with gold, and their battlements with pure gold. The streets of Jerusalem will be paved with ruby and with stones of Ophir.

The City and the Temple

vv.22-23 John sees one thing missing from the New Jerusalem, which was absolutely crucial to the old Jerusalem, and indeed to every other city in the ancient world: a temple. We have already seen one reason for this: the whole city is a temple, as a perfect cube. However, there is another reason: heaven has become united to earth. The direct presence of God is found in it, thus there is no need for it to be mediated by a temple and a cult. Indeed, the dazzling glory of God, the uncreated light, provides all the light necessary for the city. Together with God is the Lamb, the divine Son who is worshipped alongside the Father in the city-temple.

vv.24-26 Perhaps most surprising, however, is the statement that the 'kings of the earth' bring their glory into the city. The last time we met the 'kings of the earth' they were engaged in warfare with the beast against Christ (*19:19*), and should have been devoured by the birds of heaven (*19:21*). Yet here they are again, as if purged from any attachment to the beast, and able to enter the holy city bringing their good things with them. This is the expected pilgrimage of the Gentiles to Jerusalem in the last days (*Isaiah 60*), one of the Bible's more universalist strands.

This is permanent openness, symbolized by the fact that the city gates remain open (unheard of in any other city). Yet, because it is a temple, rules of ritual purity determining who could and couldn't enter still apply. Thus those characteristics associated with Babylon – uncleanness, abominations, lies – cannot be allowed to threaten the purity of the holy city.

Isaiah 60:11 Your gates shall always be open;
day and night they shall not be shut,
so that nations shall bring you their wealth,
with their kings led in procession.

Germany: New Jerusalem. From the Bamberg Apocalypse, 1000-1200

The Word Lives On

The vision of the New Jerusalem has been a strong influence on liturgy, hymnody, and Christian art. Medieval cathedrals with their colourful stained glass were built as visual reminders of the holy city. Hymns inspired by the vision include Peter Abelard's 'O what their joy and their glory must be,' and Bernard of Cluny's 'Jerusalem the Golden'. William Blake's 'Jerusalem' understands this passage not as some distant future hope, but as a vision to be realized already in this present world: 'I will not cease from Mental Fight, / Nor shall my Sword sleep in my hand: / Till we have built Jerusalem, / In England's Green & Pleasant Land.' A similar conviction is found in the Ghent Altarpiece by Jan van Eyck, which depicts the New Jerusalem in the background as a Flemish city like Ghent or Bruges.

In the Lectionary

Apocalypse 21:9-14 is an optional reading for the feast of the Dedication of a Church in the Easter Season.

Detail of Singing Angels, from the left wing of the Ghent Altarpiece, 1432 , Hubert Eyck, (c.1370-1426) & Jan van (1390-1441)

Live the Word of God

Listen again to the reading: Apocalypse 21:9-27

Suggestions for reflection and prayer

What aspects of John's description of the New Jerusalem speak to you? Are there any which remain puzzling?

Read and reflect on words from Pope Benedict XVI in the margin.

The Woman who suffers in history, the Church which is persecuted, appears in the end as the radiant Bride, the figure of the new Jerusalem where there will be no more mourning or weeping, an image of the world transformed, of the new world whose light is God himself, whose lamp is the Lamb. (General Audience, 23 August 2006)

John saw the New Jerusalem as a city, a place of human society and human culture.

❖ Give thanks for friends and family, and for the enjoyment of literature, music and art.

John saw the New Jerusalem as a garden-city, with the tree of life in its midst.

❖ Give thanks for the natural world, and its capacity to speak of God.

John saw the New Jerusalem as a temple-city, shining with the glory of God and the Lamb.

❖ Give thanks for the presence of God in the Church, and especially the gifts of the Scriptures and the Eucharist.

The Book of the Apocalypse ends with the Church's cry 'Maranatha! Come, Lord Jesus!'

Picture Credits

Cover	The Adoration of the Mystic Lamb, from the Ghent Altarpiece, lower half of central panel, 1432 (oil on panel), Eyck, Hubert (c.1370-1426) & Jan van (1390-1441) / St. Bavo Cathedral, Ghent, Belgium / © Lukas - Art in Flanders VZW / Bridgeman Images
P.9	St John the Evangelist at Patmos, from the Mystic Marriage of St Catherine Triptych, 1479 (right wing) 1479 (oil on panel), Memling, Hans (c.1433-94) / Memling Museum, Bruges, Belgium / Bridgeman Images
P.11	Cave of the Apocalypse, Patmos, Greece, www.oedipusblog.com
P.16	Patmos, Greece, © Photos.com
P.19	St John the Evangelist on the Island of Patmos, c.1618 (oil on canvas), Velazquez, Diego Rodriguez de Silva y (1599-1660) / National Gallery, London, UK / Bridgeman Images
P.20	Alpha and Omega
P.22	Seven churches of Asia in stained glass (East window of York Minster), John Thornton, © Andrewrabbott, www.commons.wikimedia.org
P.24	Map of the Seven Churches, © Alive Publishing
P.28	Philadelphia in Asia, © 2015 David Padfield, www.padfield.com
P.29	Laodicea in Asia, © www.gregorysmagee.wordpress.com
P.31	The Light of the World, c.1852 (oil on canvas), Hunt, William Holman (1827-1910) / Manchester Art Gallery, UK / Bridgeman Images
P.34	Polyptych of the Apocalypse, 1343 (panel gold ground) / Alberegno, Jacobello / Galleria dell' Accademia, Venice, Italy / Mondadori Portfolio/Electa/Osvaldo Böhm / Bridgeman Images
P.36	Papyrus Scroll, © Yulia glam/www.123rf.com
P.42	Thurible, Cathedral of Santiago de Compostela, www.rwotton.blogspot.co.uk/www.santiago-compostela.net
P.43	The Four and Twenty Elders Casting their Crowns before the Divine Throne, c.1803-5, William Blake (1757-1827), © Tate, London 2015
P.44	UK, England, London, Portrait of German-English composer George Frideric Handel (1685 - 1759), 1726 / Attributed to Balthasar Denner (1685-1749) / De Agostini Picture Library / Bridgeman Images
P.46	Germany: The Four Horsemen of the Apocalypse, Revelation 6:1-8. Illuminated miniature from the Ottheinrich Bible / Gerung, Matthias / Pictures from History / Bridgeman Images
P.48	Battle of the Somme, www.independent.co.uk
P.53	Mountains of Samos, © www.abettergreece.com
P.54	The Four Horsemen of the Apocalypse: the Rider on the White Horse, c.1878 (oil on canvas), Watts, George Frederick (1817-1904) / © Walker Art Gallery, National Museums Liverpool / Bridgeman Images

P.56   Sistine Chapel (Cappella Sistina), by Michelangelo Buonarroti, 16th Century, fresco (post restoration), Buonarroti, Michelangelo (1475-1564) / Musei e Gallerie Pontificie, Musei Vaticani, Vatican City / Mondadori Portfolio / Bridgeman Images

P.60   Workshop of Andrea del Verrocchio, Tobias and the Angel © The National Gallery, London

P.63   Nea Kameni volcanic island, Santorini, Greece, 2012, © Norbert Nagel, www.commons.wikimedia.org

P.64   Deforestation, www.deckup.com.au

P.66   John the Theologian, Monreale (mosaic in Santa Maria Nuova di Monreale, Sicilia), 12th Century, www.01varvara.wordpress.com

P.71   Cardinals at Conclave swearing on the Gospels, © photo from AFP, www.rappler.com

P.73   Sistine Chapel Ceiling: The Prophet Ezekiel, 1510 (fresco) (post restoration), Buonarroti, Michelangelo (1475-1564) / Vatican Museums and Galleries, Vatican City / Bridgeman Images

P.74   Olive Trees on Thassos, 9th July 2006, © Petr Pakandl, www.commons.wikimedia.org

P.75   N. Novgorod Elijah icon, late 15- early 16 c, www.commons.wikimedia.org

P.76   Olivier Messiaen, www.tygpianoduo.blogspot.co.uk

P.78   Spain: The Woman and the Dragon (verso). From the Beatus of Leon version of the Apocalypse (1047 CE). / Pictures from History / Bridgeman Images

P.83   The Woman Receiving Wings to Flee the Dragon, no.37 from 'The Apocalypse of Angers', 1373-87 (tapestry), Bataille, Nicolas (fl. 1363-1400) / Musee des Tapisseries, Angers, France / Bridgeman Images

P.85   The Archangel Michael defeating Satan (oil on canvas), Reni, Guido (1575-1642) / Private Collection / Bridgeman Images

P.87   Our Lady of Guadalupe, 1531, Basilica of Our Lady of Guadalupe, Tepeyac Hill, México City, www.sheepofkephas.wordpress.com

P.88   Germany: The beast with ten horns and the beast with lamb's horns. Illuminated miniature from the Ottheinrich Bible / Gerung, Matthias / Pictures from History / Bridgeman Images

P.90   Ancient ruins in Rome, © Nikolaj, www.zastavki.com

P.95   Bust of Nero, Musei Capitolini, Rome, © Cjh1452000, www.wikipedia.org

P.98   The Whore of Babylon, from the Luther Bible, c.1530 (coloured woodcut), German School, (16th century) / Bible Society, London, UK / Bridgeman Images

P.101   Caricature gillray plumpudding, 1805, James Gillray, Library of Congress, www.loc.gov

P.102   Britannia on a 50 pence piece, www.thesilverforum.com

P.103   Domus Aurea, January 1, 2005, © Boticario, www.wikipedia.org

P.104   Palatine Vergil, 5th to 6th century, www.ibiblio.org

P.106   Pope Paul VI's Coronation Tiara, January 20, 2008, Elizabeth Roy (Original uploader was Della Balda at it.wikipedia), Magnus Manske, www.commons.wikimedia.org

P.108   The Angel Standing in the Sun, exhibited 1846, Joseph Mallord William Turner (1775-1851), © Tate, London 2015, photo credit John Webb

P.114   Christ mosaic, 6th century, Archbishop's Chapel, Ravenna, Italy, www.03varvara.wordpress.com

P.116   The End of Borodino Battle, 1899-1900, Vasily Vereshchagin, www.wikiart.org

P.118   The Revelation of St John: 15. The Angel with the Key to the Bottomless Pit (woodcut), Dürer or Duerer, Albrecht (1471-1528) / Universal History Archive/UIG / Bridgeman Images

P.124   Great White Throne, Zion National Park, Utah, © Sylfred1977, www.en.wikipedia.org

P.125   The Martyrdom of St Paul Miki and Companions: The 26 Nagasaki Martyrs, www.catholiccompany.com

P.126   Depiction of Satan, c.1866, Gustave Doré, Paradise Lost, www.en.wikipedia.org

P.128   Heavenly Jerusalem, Apocalypse of Saint-Sever, 11th century, www.studiesincomparativereligion.com

P.132   Sistine Chapel Ceiling (1508-12): The Fall of Man, 1510 (fresco) (post restoration), Buonarroti, Michelangelo (1475-1564) / Vatican Museums and Galleries, Vatican City / Bridgeman Images

P.135   Germany: New Jerusalem. From the Bamberg Apocalypse, 1000-1200 / Pictures from History / Bridgeman Images

P.136   Detail of Singing Angels, from the left wing of the Ghent Altarpiece, 1432 (oil on panel), Eyck, Hubert (c.1370-1426) & Jan van (1390-1441) / St. Bavo Cathedral, Ghent, Belgium / © Lukas - Art in Flanders VZW / Photo: Hugo Maertens / Bridgeman Images

Notes

Notes

THE

BOURNE SOCIETY

Village Histories

2. CATERHAM

Editor: Gwyneth Fookes

Series Editors - Roger Packham & Gwyneth Fookes

ISBN 0 900992 42 5

Acknowledgements

As can be seen from the Contents page, a large number of people have contributed to this volume. All are members of the Bourne Society who have devoted a great deal of time and effort to research their particular subject. However, no work of this nature could be written without the co-operation of many other people. The talents of authors' partners and friends are exploited unmercifully. Local contacts are invaluable in adding the human element to what are often bare facts and bringing them to life. The staff of record offices and libraries are always founts of wisdom and their help is greatly appreciated.

Roger Packham can always be depended upon to provide old photographs from his extensive collection, and his knowledge of faces and places make his contribution especially valuable.

Modern methods of printing make the production of a book of this kind possible at reasonable cost, but also demand computer expertise in the presentation of the text and illustrations. The Society has depended on Dr Robert Warner for this work for some years now and his enthusiasm is also much appreciated.

Cover photgraph: shows the southern end of High Street, Caterham on the Hill, and includes four notable symbols associated with Caterham. In the centre is the 200 year-old cedar tree To the left is 'Wilderness House', the oldest dwelling in Caterham. On the right is the 'Old Rectory', part of which date from the 16th century. In the foreground is a Caterham Super 7 sports car. Caterham Cars have been in the town for 40 years and the cars are sold to enthusiasts worldwide.

Photograph by Roger Hammond

Thanks to Caterham Super 7 owner/driver Jason Sutherland of Caterham Cars and co-driver Neil Hammond.

CONTENTS

LIST OF ILLUSTRATIONS

Page No.

Page No.

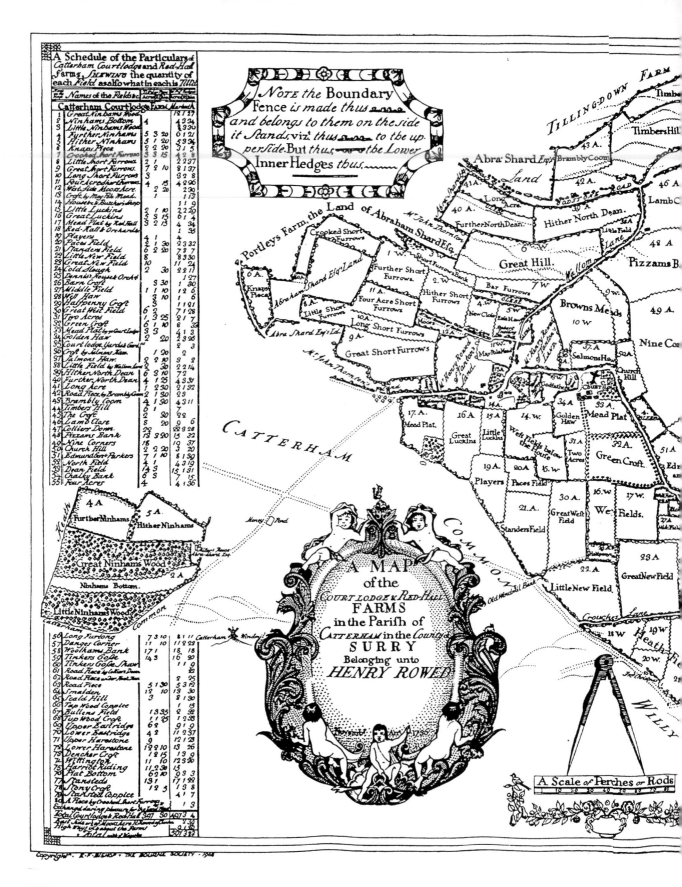

A Schedule of the Particulars of Catterham Court lodge and Red-Hall Farms, SHEWING the quantity of each Field as also what in each is Tilled

NOTE the Boundary Fence is made thus ···· and belongs to them on the side it Stands, viz. thus ···· to the upper side. But thus ···· the Lower Inner Hedges thus ····

A MAP of the COURT LODGE & RED-HILL FARMS in the Parish of CATTERHAM in the County of SURRY Belonging unto HENRY ROWED

A Scale of Perches or Rods

VIII

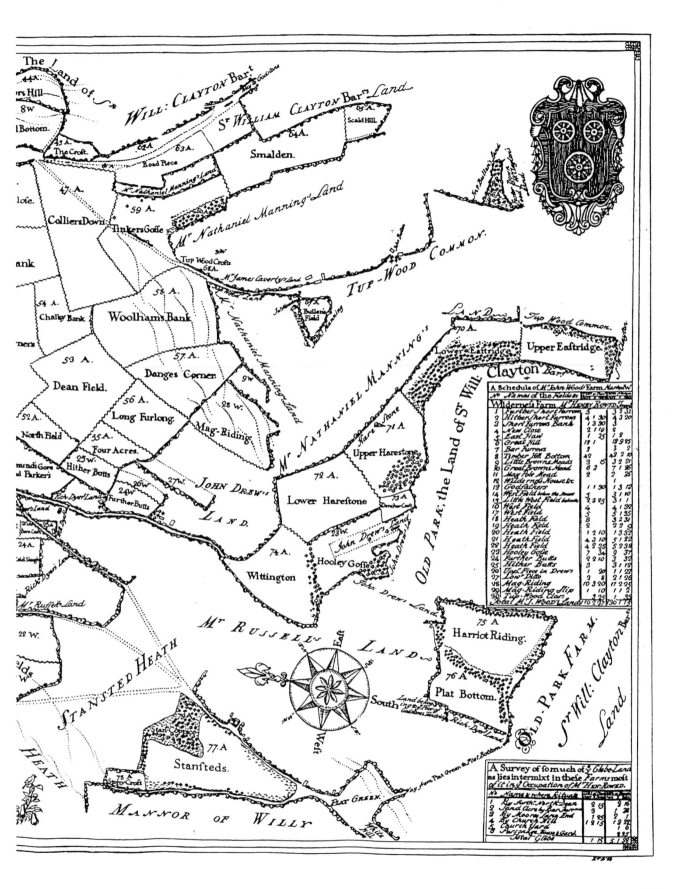

The Land of Sr
...A.
...s Hill
8w
...Bottom.

WILL: CLAYTON Bart

Sr WILLIAM CLAYTON Barts Land

85 A.
Scald Hill.

Say to Godston

45 A.
The Croft.

62 A.

63 A.

Road Piece

84 A.

Smalden.

47. A.

...ose.

Colliers Down

Tinkers Gosse

Mr Nathaniel Manning's Land

59 A.

Mr Nathaniel Manning's Land

30W
Tup Wood Crofts
58 A.

Mr James Caverly's Land

87 X
Bullens Field

TUP-WOOD COMMON.

Butter Brow

Land

70 A.

Lower Eastridge

Upper Eastridge.

Tup Wood Common.

54 A.
Chalky Bank

58 A.
Woolham's Bank

Mr Nathaniel Manning's Land

53 A.
Dean Field.

57 A.
Danges Corner.

9w

Sr Will: Clayton Bart

52 A.

56 A.
Long Furlong.

28 W.

Mag-Riding.

Old Park, the Land of Sr Will.

North Field

55 A.
Four Acres.

25 w.
Hither Butts

27 W.

JOHN DREW's

Hare Stone

71 A.
Upper Harestone

A Schedule of Mr John Wood's Farm Marked W

...mundi Gore
d Parker's

26w
Further Butts

LAND.

Lower Harestone

72 A.

73 A.
Doncher Croft

Nº	Names of the Fields &c				
	Wilderness Farm Mr Henry Rowed Tenant				
1	Further Short Furrows	5		3	2 32
2	Hither Short Furrows	4 1 30		4 3 20	
3	Short Furrows Bank	1 3 30		3	
4	New Close	2 1 19		2	2
5	East Haw	1 25		1	9
6	Great Hill	13 1		13 9 95	
7	Bar Furrows	3		3 2	
8	Timber Hill Bottom	42		4	
9	Little Browns Meads	3 6		3 21	
10	Great Browns Mead	2		7 1 25	
11	May Pole Head	2		2 25	
12	Wilderness House &c				
13	Godfathers	1 1 30		1 3 17	
14	West Field below the House			3 1 10	
15	Little West Field behind	3 2 25		3 1 1	
16	Hart Field	4		4 1 30	
17	West Field	5		5 1 35	
18	Heath Field	3		3 2 31	
19	Heath Field	2		2 2 9	
20	Heath Field	9		9 3 59	
21	Heath Field	4 2 10		1 3 59	
22	Heath Field	4 3 25		5 2 38	
23	Hooley Gosse	3		3 7	
24	Further Butts	2 2 10		3 32	
25	Hither Butts	3		3 1 13	
26	Uppr Piece in Drews	1 20		1 1 22	
27	Lowr Ditto	2		2 1 26	
28	Mag-Riding	10 3 20		11 2 25	
29	Mag-Riding Slip	1 10		1 2	
30	Tup-Wood Clos	4 25		3	
	Total Mr J. Wood's Land	110 2 37	30 T 7 S		

Rich Dyer's Land

Further Butts

24w

74 A.
Wittington

John Drew's Land

23 w.
John Drew's Land

Hooley Gosse

John Drew's Land

75 A
Harriot Riding.

Old Park Farm.

Sr Will: Clayton Bart Land

22 W.

STANSTED HEATH

Mr RUSSELL's LAND

East

South

West

Land belonging to yᵉ Vicaridge of Coddens landed on Rich Dyer

76 A
Plat Bottom.

HEATH

Han Copse

77 A.
Stansteds.

Sr T. Croft

Way from Plat Green to Plat Bottom.

PLAT GREEN.

MANNOR OF WILLY

A Survey of so much of yᵉ Glebe Land as lies intermixt in these Farms most of it in yᵉ Occupation of Mr Henr Rowed.

Nº	Name & where Situate				
1	By Furth: North Dean	2 6		9 16	
2	Land Acre by Bar Furrows	2		30	
3	By Moors Lane End	1		1	
4	By Church Hill	1 9 15		1 9 17	
5	Church Yard			1	
6	Parsonage House & Gard			1 16	
	Total Glebe	1 8	51		

IX

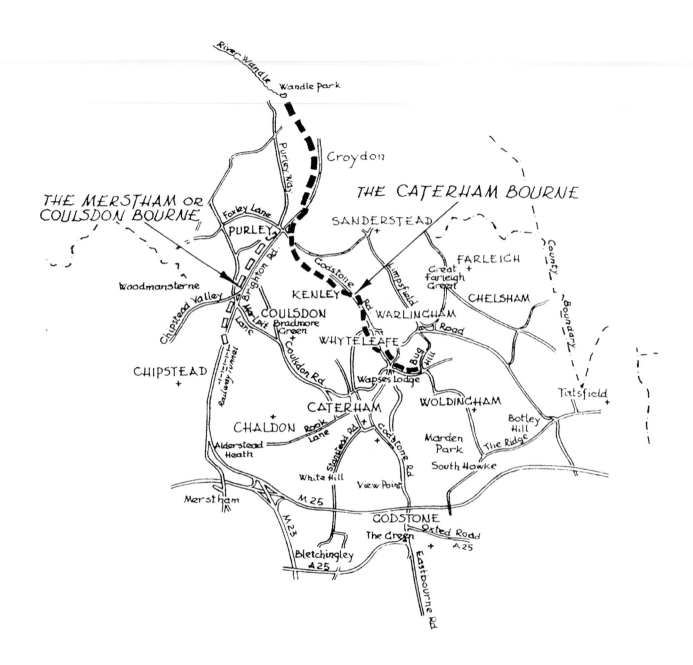

The Bourne Society Area

Introduction

THE BOURNE SOCIETY set itself the task of publishing a substantial general history of each of the several parishes within its study area - this volume is the second. The first volume on Purley was produced in autumn 1996 and was received with great enthusiasm, to such an extent that ten excerpts were published in *the Advertiser* and the first print run was sold out just after Christmas.

A research team has been formed for each of the proposed books, which include some members who have considerable experience in researching and publishing their particular subject. Others embarked on researching for the first time and have often found that their subject expanded and became more intriguing the more they explored.

It has often been said of Caterham that it was of little significance before the railway came, but the research team has been able to tell a substantial story of its history over many centuries. Caterham's past was rooted in agriculture, its residents scraping a rather meagre living from the poor soils. After the coming of the railway, so came the City gentlemen, the Asylum and the Barracks. Despite the impression of a traffic-jam prone suburb at the end of the twentieth century, there are still farms to be found, the tiny flint cottages of old are interspersed with modern housing and deer still roam in the woods. The volume of material gathered by the writers of this book about more recent times has to be seen to be believed. So much of it has had to be condensed to make the finished product a manageable size. Caterham's research team is to be congratulated on its enthusiasm and industry.

This history of Caterham does not claim to be the definitive history and it is hoped that it will serve to stimulate the interest of residents in their locality and some may be sufficiently enthused to become involved themselves in their local history.

Roger Packham
Gwyneth Fookes

May 1997

Chapter 1

Chronology

by Roger Packham and Jean Tooke

c. 250,000 BC	Evidence of early man from the discovery of a flint hand-axe.
c. 50 BC	Construction of Iron Age hill-fort at War Coppice.
AD 100	Construction of Roman Road through Caterham.
1086	Church at Tillingdown recorded in Domesday Book.
c. 1095	St. Lawrence's Church built.
c. 1200	Roger of Guist, Norfolk, granted his manor of Caterham and parish church to the canons of Waltham Abbey. His name is commemorated in Gaist Avenue.
1200	Date ascribed to font in St. John's Church. It was donated by the old parish church of St. Lawrence.
c. 1200-1300	Evidence of occupation of *King & Queen* site postulated following excavations in 1981.
1300s	17 taxpayers recorded for Caterham.
1401	Caterham's five tithingmen were Stephen Smyth, John Ropkyn, John Aleyn, Richard Godfrey and Walter Godfrey.
1447	Thomas Best of Catterham was MP for Lewes (and again 1460-1).
c. 1485	Wildernesse House, (84 High Street) built. It is now an employment agency.
1532	Survey of lands of Waltham Abbey show that the Abbey had a substantial house in Caterham
1597	Reputed date on fireplace beam in Box Cottage (demolished 1964).
c. 1650	Three (or four) taverns or ale houses recorded in Caterham. They were kept by Mary Rabbett, William Brown, Thomas Staples and (probably) Thomas Benett.
1660	Town End Farm built. It is still one of the most attractive flint buildings in the area.
1660s	Caterham's Hearth Tax Returns show over 50 households, of which half are liable for tax.

**Town End Farm
in 1994**

A HISTORY OF CATERHAM

c. 1700	The earliest part of the Old Rectory is dated to the late 16th/early 17th century. It is now occupied by Buxtons.
c. 1700	Population was 201, including John Blanch who was running a school in Caterham.
1705	Local voters were Lawrence Rowed, Robert Ockley, John Medhurst, Walter Hatcher, John Haswell, John Drew, Richard Dye, Jeffrey Hatcher and John Rowed.
1736	Rowed Map of Caterham made for Henry Rowed of Court Lodge (later Caterham Court).
1767	First recorded cricket match between Caterham and the celebrated Hambledon Club of Hampshire.
1788	Infants' School noted.
1804	School built at Caterham by Thomas Clarke, Lord of the Manor.
1820	The *Blacksmith's Arms* was opened. Demolished in 1878 it was re-built on an adjacent site.
1845	*Ye olde King & Queen* was first licensed as a beerhouse with Richard Cullingham the first beerhouse keeper.
1856	Caterham Railway was opened on the 4th August.
1862	Caterham Spring Water Co. established by Act of Parliament.
1866	Consecration of St. Mary's Church on 7th May by the Bishop of Winchester.

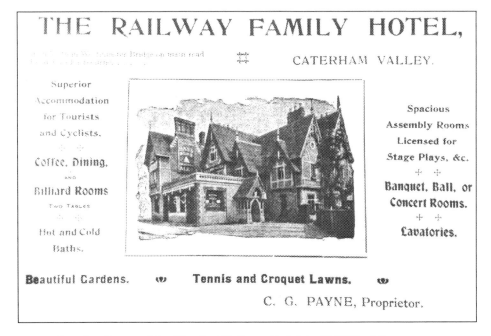

An advertisement for The first Railway Hotel, built 1856 at the same time as the station

Photo courtesy of Caterham Library

1868	'The Priory' built next to the station for William Garland Soper.
1869	Foundation stone laid on 17th April for the Metropolitan Asylum (later re-named St. Lawrence's Hospital) by Dr. Brewer MP.
1869	Caterham Gas Company established.
1872	Caterham Temporary Cottage Hospital opened in May - situated in Godstone Road, Riddlesdown.

CHRONOLOGY

1873	Caterham Hill Board School opened on 2nd July.
1875	New Cottage Hospital opened in Croydon Road on 23rd August.
1875	Congregational Church built in Harestone Valley for c.£14000 (now United Reform Church).
1876	Caterham Valley Board School opened on 10th January (now Adult Education Centre).
1877	Guards' Depot opened as the Recruiting Depot for the Grenadier, Coldstream & Scots Guards
1879	'Harestone' built for William Garland Soper (now Marie Curie Centre).
1881	Roman Catholic Church of the Sacred Heart was opened on 11th August with Cardinal Manning, Archbishop of Westminster presiding.
1882	St. John's Church, Caterham Valley, consecrated on 27th December by the Bishop of Rochester.
1884	School for the Sons of Congregational Ministers (renamed Caterham School in 1912) moved to Harestone Valley from Lewisham.
1884	St. John's School opened on 24th March by Revd. J.B.Heard (now the Miller Centre).
1890	Fire Engine house built in High Street; it remained in use until 1928.
1890	First issue of *Caterham Free Press* published. Renamed *Caterham Weekly Press* in 1901.
1895	First meeting of Caterham Parish Council on 2nd January.
1898	Pilgrims Fort built.
1898	Soldiers' Home built in High Street.
1899	Caterham Urban District Council held first meeting on 17th April.
1900	Caterham railway line 'doubled' and new station built.

The Soper Hall, opened in 1912 in memory of William Garland Soper, photgraphed in 1930

Photo courtesy of Caterham Library

A HISTORY OF CATERHAM

1900	Queen's Park opened on 23rd May as a memorial to H.M. Queen Victoria's 'long and conspicuous reign'.
1902	Demolition of first Railway Hotel.
1902	Borer Memorial Ambulance Station in Queen's Park opened on 24th June.
1903	Electricity supplied by Caterham Urban Electricity Supply Co.Ltd. in Croydon Road.
1903	Enlarged Cottage Hospital opened in Croydon Road on 3rd June by HRH Princess Christian of Schleswig-Holstein.
1907	Wesleyan Methodist Church opened opposite Guards' Depot.
1908	Death of William Garland Soper on 20th December.
1910	Present Post Office built opposite Caterham Station.
1912	Soper Memorial Hall opened on 4th January.
1912	Roman Catholic School in Essendene Road opened on 25th August by Bishop Amigo of Southwark.
1915	Recruitment Day on Wednesday, 15th April, involving over 3000 men.
1932	Dedication of St. Paul's Church, Banstead Road.
1939	Opening of Caterham Bypass.
1940	Congregational Church, Harestone Valley Road, hit by bomb.
1956	Centenary of Caterham Railway celebrated by the Bourne Society.
1964	Demolition of *the Greyhound, Capitol* Cinema, Box Cottage and Roffey Cottages.
1982	Supermarket opened by Waitrose on site next to Caterham Station.
1988	Valley Hotel (formerly Railway Hotel) demolished.
1990	Church Walk shopping precinct opened.
1996-7	Demolition of part of Caterham Hill Primary School (1872).
1997	Return of Asprey Fountain to Church Walk on 11th April.

———————————————

Chapter 2

Prehistory to Roman Times

by Mary Saaler

The pattern of settlement in the Caterham area is clearly related to the landscape. In prehistoric times the area of the North Downs attracted people who sought out the deposits of flint to shape into tools. Flint, which can be readily worked and shaped, was an important commodity in the daily lives of prehistoric people, providing them with items such as knives, axes, scrapers, blades and arrowheads. The earliest local example of worked flint is a hand-axe which was made some time between 500 000 and 40 000 years ago. It was found in a garden in Westway. The British Museum holds a collection of scrapers and flakes which were found in Caterham in about 1900 but, apart from these, Caterham has produced relatively few surface finds of flint tools and waste flakes. This is in clear contrast to neighbouring places such as Chelsham and Limpsfield, where flint tools have been found in large numbers.[1] The contrast is probably the result of different land use, since most surface finds occur on ploughed land.

WAR COPPICE

Aubrey, writing about Surrey in the 1690s, provides the earliest description of the prehistoric hill-fort at Caterham when he noted that 'at a place called the War-Copice is a Camp, or Fortification on the Top of a Hill'[2]. In the 1870s Wickham Flower gave a more detailed description and mentioned a double rampart which

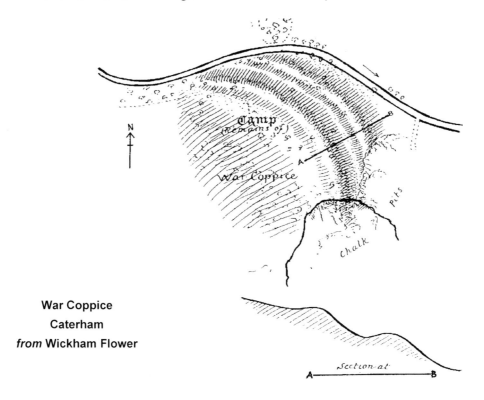

War Coppice
Caterham
from **Wickham Flower**

stretched for 150m, of which the inner rampart rose to a height of 4.5m, while the outer rampart ranged in height from 2m to 5m.   At this date the only visible remains lay on the northern side, since the south and south-eastern sides had been quarried away [3].   Hope-Taylor carried out a small excavation on the north-east side in 1950 when he recorded that he found two banks and ditches, with traces of a third bank outside them, all extending for about 60m. He also noted that the inner banks had been palisaded with the local stone which outcrops nearby [4]. If we project the existing lines of the ramparts we can estimate that the fort once covered an area of about 20-25 acres and lay in a dominating position, with extensive views over the countryside to the south, east and west.   It is one of a series of hill-forts that extends along the North Downs.

While Aubrey regarded War Coppice as a camp or fortification, studies of other Surrey sites have shown that they were usually sparsely inhabited and may also have served as trading posts or enclosures for animals at pasture. The Surrey hill-forts generally date from about 200BC until the time of Caesar's landing in 55-54BC. [5]

THE ROMAN ROAD

The Roman road which passes through Caterham is part of the route which runs from London to the Brighton area. Margary has traced the line through Streatham, Croydon, Godstone and East Grinstead to the South Downs near Brighton. To the north of Caterham most stretches of the road have been obscured by suburban development, but at Caterham there is visible evidence of the track. The modern route, known as Tillingdown

The Roman road visible as a bank at the top of Tillingdown Hill

Hill, marks the line of the Roman road which first becomes visible as a bank running through a children's playground.   To the south of the playground a hedge-line partly shows the line of the road as it runs along the side of the valley, but much of it has been obscured by earth washed down from the fields above. The road may have been built on the steep slopes of the valley to avoid low ground which would be liable to flooding. The London to Brighton road was probably constructed at about the end of the first century as part of a network which was designed to transport commodities from the south-east to supply the London market. The line of the road was used in later times to mark the parish boundary of Caterham [6,7].

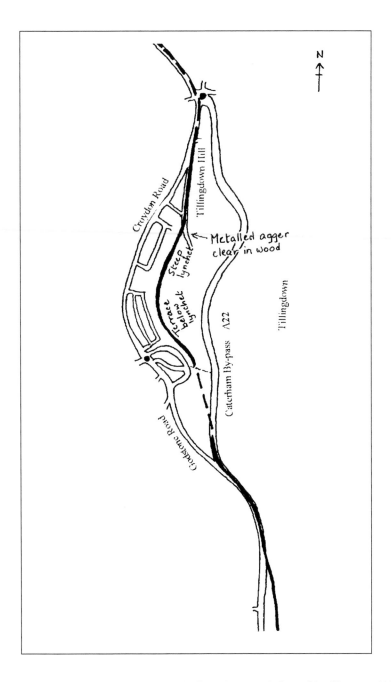

The route of the Roman road through Caterham as inferred by Margary (1937)

SOURCES

1. Bird, D., & Bird, J., (eds.) *The Archaeology of Surrey*, p. 77

2. Aubrey, J.,   *The Natural History and Antiquities of the County of Surrey.* 2 p.17

3. Wickham Flower, J. 'The War Coppice Caterham, Surrey', *Surrey Archaeological Collections.*   5, pp. 177-85

4. Report of the Council, *Surrey Archaeological Collections*, 52, p. 101

5. Bird, D., & Bird, J., (eds.) *The Archaeology of Surrey.*   pp. 157-9

6. Margary, I. *Roman Ways in the Weald*, p. 110

7. Saaler, M., 'Excavation of the Roman Road at Caterham', *Local History Records* 8, pp. 21-22

Chapter 3

Origins

by Peter Gray

Caterham as we know it today includes Caterham Valley, Caterham on the Hill, Tupwood, Portley and Tillingdown, although the latter was once part of Tandridge parish. The historic parish of Caterham included areas now thought of as being outside its boundaries – such as Whyteleafe, which did not exist until a house of that name was built in the 19th century. For the origins of these places and of modern Caterham we must look back to the formation of the modern administrative area at the end of the 19th century, and much further, over 1000 years, to late Saxon times and the subsequent development of the parish in the medieval period.

In the past 100 years there have been many changes to the extent of the place we know now as Caterham. When Caterham Urban District was formed in 1899 it replaced the historic parish in a civil sense and had identical bounds. In 1910 the bounds of the urban district were changed to include Tillingdown.[1] After that date there were other changes and amalgamations with adjoining areas until, in 1974, Caterham Urban District was joined with Godstone Rural District to form the much larger Tandridge District. For electoral purposes Caterham Urban District was divided into wards.

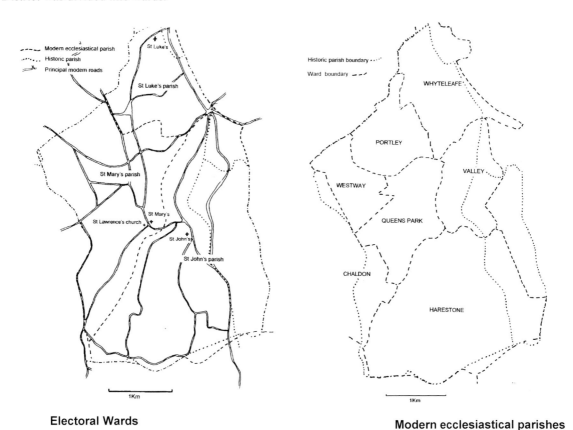

Electoral Wards

Modern ecclesiastical parishes

Caterham and Tillingdown historic parishes and their modern subdivisions. The historic boundaries are becoming lost.

The term parish can have two meanings. It can be either administrative or ecclesiastical. Originating historically in a religious sense, it evolved into an administrative unit, initially with identical boundaries. These boundaries generally did not change until modern times. By about 1200 parishes had usually achieved the form and extent which came down to us in the 19th century.[2]   Initially they formed the area served by a parson from the parish church and to whom tithes were due. Law and order and other legal matters were the concern of the manors. These manors often had very different areas to parishes. Later, particularly in the 16th and 17th centuries, various Acts of Parliament gave secular duties to the parish. Over time these duties superseded the role of the manorial courts in most things except the regulation of transfer of estates by sale or inheritance. Nevertheless the civil and religious parishes operated side by side with identical areas until the last century.

Prior to the coming of the railways the population of the historic parish of Caterham was such that only one church was needed. The increase in population brought by the railways resulted in a demand for additional churches which were built and new parishes formed out of the old. Most of historic Caterham is now divided into the ecclesiastical parishes St Mary's and St John's, the latter including most of Tillingdown. In 1866 the new parish of St Luke's in Whyteleafe was created. It includes parts of Coulsdon, Warlingham and historic Caterham.

This book is largely about the modern extent of Caterham, with Whyteleafe including Portley being the subject of a separate volume. However since inevitably early documentary evidence relates to the entire historic parish and cannot readily be separated, the early evidence for the whole of the historic parish is covered in this volume. The Saxon and medieval origins of Caterham are described later.

SOURCES

1.   *Victoria County History of Surrey*, **IV**: 264. 2

2.   Morris, Richard, (1989). *Churches in the Landscape*, 229

Chapter 4

Until the Conquest

by Peter Gray

There are no written documents relating to Caterham itself until well after the Norman Conquest. There is however much other evidence from which we can build up a picture of the area in pre-conquest times. Some landscape features such as trackways must be of pre-conquest origin because of their relationship to early archaeological features; other aspects can be deduced from later sources, and still others can be presumed with reasonable certainty from evidence related to immediately adjoining areas.

SETTLEMENT PATTERNS

The first large-scale map of the area as a whole was made in the early 19th century, when maps were produced for most parishes in connection with the commutation of tithes for money payment. These maps show details of each piece of land involved. The Caterham map when set against the topography of the area gives a good basis for considering the likely origins of the settlement pattern. (The 1736 Rowed map *(pages VIII/IX)* gives a useful earlier view for much of the parish).

The land is mainly one of high chalk downland, gently sloping towards the north but with a steep scarp slope to the south. The chalk downland (covered with clay with flints) is described as 'unenclosed rough pasture' in the Tithe Award of 1841. It is interspersed with deep north-facing valleys besides several relatively shallow ones. The deep valleys have sides which are steep enough to be very significant obstacles to communications. Places where hilltop and valley land are joined by relatively gentle slopes are limited almost entirely to the northern part of the parish – the area of Burntwood and Salmons Lanes – perhaps significantly the site of early estates and sub-manors.

The steep scarp slope on the south face of the Downs is another equally dominant feature, with only a single break in Tandridge District – the Caterham/Godstone gap. Despite the apparent attraction of such a gap as a natural route, it was not the focus of the principal north/south roads. At its southern end until the 16th century there was no village of Godstone. Most roads, except the Roman road, avoided the gap and made for the top of the Downs, sometimes, as at Whitehill, with some difficulty. Even the Roman road avoided the valley bottom as far as possible, following the side of Tillingdown Hill rather than the line of the present Croydon Road in the valley bottom. The reason must have been the liability of the valleys to flood and their general wetness. There are now no surface streams even in the deep valleys but the *Victoria County History* in 1911 stated that 'a winterbourne still broke out intermittently in the neighbourhood of Caterham.... (but) extensive waterworks have made this bourne less frequent'[1]. It seems likely that the position was worse in earlier times when the water table was higher.

From another point of view availability of water was a significant factor in the settlement of the area. Although the chalk plateau is covered extensively with clay with flints, water could not be obtained easily. Sources were either deep wells, clearly expensive and only to be associated with large houses, or from surface ponds which were unreliable, or from springs breaking out from the valley sides. In Chaldon there is a 19th century memorial stone recording the provision of a pond '... for the sole use of cottagers ... and no cattle to be watered and no sheep washed here'.[2]

The effect of this topography and the related geology can be judged from the Caterham tithe map of 1841. The deep valleys were virtually uninhabited and people generally lived on the tops, near the lips of the valleys. Most of the enclosed land was on the valley sides whilst on the tops enclosure tended to be limited to near the valley

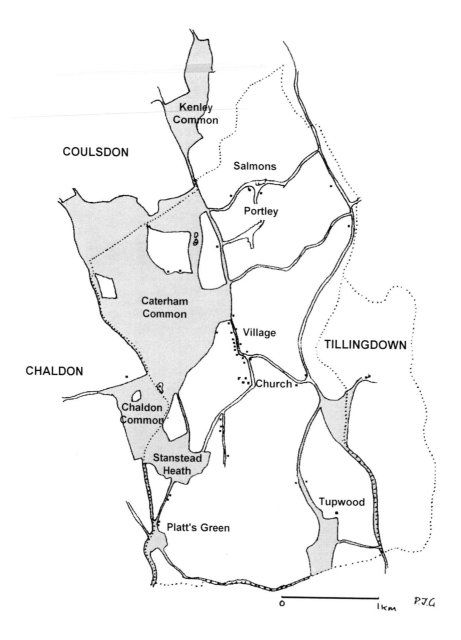

Caterham and Tillingdown in early 19th century (based on tithe maps of 1841) showing the extent of unenclosed commons and location of houses and cottages. A map of the 15th century would probably not have been very different apart from the fact that the commons would have been a little larger.

margins. All the large areas of unenclosed waste were on the tops. Most of the houses were poor. The combination of deep valleys, probably wet, and north facing, with downland tops of poor land with difficulties arising from poor water supplies meant that until recent times the area has never been one which would have attracted a large population; only the advent of modern drainage and piped water supply has changed the position.

Tillingdown seems to have been significantly different, and this may well arise from its topographical position. It is on a hill surrounded on three sides by deep valleys and connected to the North Downs ridge by a relatively narrow neck of land, surely – one might think – a naturally defensible area. Today, as it has been probably since the land was acquired by the Claytons of Bletchingley in 1672,[3] it is little more than a single farm. They replanned the fields so that there are no clues from ancient hedgerows of the earlier development of the landscape. Certainly there is no evidence of unenclosed commons such as occur elsewhere in Caterham. However there is documentary evidence of Tillingdown in Saxon times. In Domesday Book (1086) it had its own entry and as will be seen later there is other evidence suggesting its importance in pre-Norman times.

Old Forge Cottage (Stanstead Road): Originated as a tiny timber framed 1½ storey cottage with one room on each floor. Probably late 17th century. Additional bay added perhaps c.1800 followed by encasing framing with flint later in 19th century.

In the years before the Norman Conquest the only part of modern Caterham with a relatively significant population is likely to have been on Tillingdown. There may have been some habitation in the area of Old Park, where there are extensive earthworks.[4] Also the very name 'Old Park' and the odd way that the obvious boundaries show that it was incorporated into North Park, Bletchingley (the post-Conquest hunting park) suggest that there was something special about it, although what exactly is not at all clear. Any small farms were probably on the top, on dry land but within

Harestone Farm (26 Harestone Lane): Originally a timber framed 2-bay 2-storey end chimney house c.1700. A distinct step up in quality and size compared with cottages on the edge of the common but still very poor when compared with farms below the Downs. Originally thatched.

Stanstead Cottage: Originated as a tiny cottage, single storey with just two rooms. The largest room was only 9' 6" square – an indication of the relative poverty of such houses on the edge of Stanstead Common. Probably always flint. c.1700.

reach of water. Only towards the northern part of the district where the slopes become more gentle may there have been rather more agricultural activity.

EARLY ROADS AND TRACKWAYS

Interpretation of the ancient system of roads and tracks can provide a key to the early history of an area. In early times, broadly before the Romans arrived, when man-made features were few and far between, tracks could follow the most direct route between natural obstacles. As the population grew and the area was settled the early routes changed. Some sections became disused, others were diverted and generally tracks became much more devious. A major stage of this process had been completed by the time of the Black Death in the 14th century when there was a major fall in population. Changes thereafter appear to have been small until the surge in population and consequent development in the 19th century.

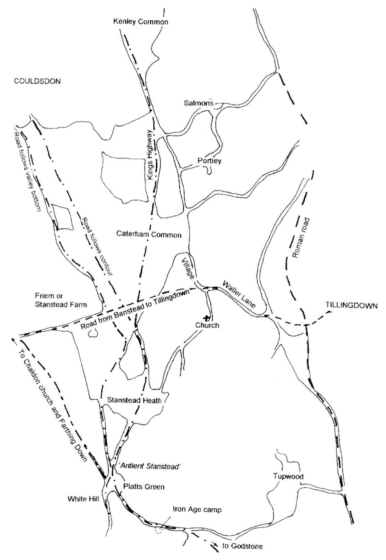

Pre-conquest roads superimposed on a map of early 19th century with the unenclosed commons

Although the local population may have been minimal in the Saxon period, people would undoubtedly have passed through the area on their way between centres of population or other activities. The routes they used would often have been basically the same routes that we use today. Such tracks would obviously relate to known earlier sites such as the Iron Age hill-fort at War Coppice, the Saxon field system on Farthing Down in Coulsdon, and the settlements at Tillingdown and Banstead. Several of the main modern routes in the area can be traced to such origins.

There is evidence of north/south tracks rather earlier than the Roman ones. The most obvious and easiest way from the south is via the col by War Coppice at the head of Harestone Valley. At this point the route is 'guarded' by the Iron Age hill-fort. South from the col relatively gentle gradients go down to the south-west to join the track, now followed by parish boundaries, from Whitehill to Outwood and the Weald. Another goes to the south-east to Godstone. Most of these routes are still rights-of-way, on foot at least. North of the col the road followed the narrow ridge to Platts Green, by the modern *Harrow* Inn, where several routes diverged. One of them, Whitehill – the road due south from Platts Green – is very steep.

North of Platts Green the road divided into three. One branch went along the modern drive to Willey Farm and originally on to Doctors Lane, Chaldon Church and Farthing Down with its Saxon barrows and roadway.[5] Another went along Roffes Lane, following the valley bottom past the eastern boundary of Friern Farm in Chaldon, then climbed out of the valley to go across Coulsdon Common past Coulsdon Church. This road seems to have been referred to as the 'Antient Stansted' or Stane Street.[6] Friern Farm in Chaldon is also referred to as Stansted Farm,[7] no doubt confirming that Stansted (or Stone Street) passed nearby. There is another early reference, for Coulsdon, to the Ancient Stansted [8] which is obviously the same road. Both the *Victoria County History* and Manning and Bray in their *History of Surrey* suggest that it could have been a minor Roman road joining the London/ Brighton road at Godstone but it does not appear to have been considered by Margary in his *Roman Ways in the Weald*.[9]

The third road north from Platts Green is the 'Via Regia' or King's Highway of a 13th century document.[10] It followed the first part of the modern Stanstead Road before cutting across what is now Willey Lane to join Hayes Lane, Kenley, on the parish boundary. Traces of it (called Crouches Lane on the 1736 Rowed map) exist as a causeway across the fields east of Roffes Lane. Further north its route is marked by Foxon Lane. This is the same King's Highway referred to in the 14th century boundary charter.[11] In that charter the road is referred to as 'to Blechingley' rather than Caterham, probably indicative of the relative unimportance of Caterham at the time.

No mention has so far been made of the most famous early road of them all, the so-called Pilgrims Way. One may suppose that the pilgrims in question were on their way to or from Canterbury in Chaucer's England. The ordnance map shows a very curious route for the trackway in this part of Surrey, sometimes at the foot of the Downs, sometimes on the top. It climbs the steepest slopes and never seems to go near any villages or places where weary pilgrims might obtain food and lodging. It is alleged to run from near *The Harrow* Inn towards Chaldon church, but turns left by Willey Farm instead of taking the obvious route along the crest of the downs. It seems most unlikely that it ever existed – in this part of the country at least – in the medieval period.[12]

One road did take an east/west route. This ran eastwards from Rook Lane, where it took a line direct to the curious kink in Caterham-on-the-Hill High Street, down Waller Lane past what is now the railway station, and on via Tillingdown Lane to the pre-Domesday settlement of Tillingdown. It would have provided pre-Conquest communication between Tillingdown and Banstead, both important local settlements under common ownership at that period.[13] The road's diversion to the modern line along Chaldon Road past the *Clifton Arms* can be explained by the formation and subsequent growth of Caterham village and by the demise of Tillingdown. The present T-junction by the *Golden Lion* is thus the result of gradual growth of the village over 600 or 700 years. In the natural order of things Nature abhors a T-junction!

There were clearly other roads in the medieval period but they were of purely local importance. The modern Stanstead Road leading from near *The Harrow* to the top of Church Hill probably did not exist until the post-Conquest foundation of the church. Church Hill, such a significant road today, was the private drive to Caterham Court until the coming of the railway in the 19th century.

DOMESDAY BOOK AND LOCAL REFERENCES

Domesday Book was compiled in 1086 for William the Conqueror as a register of taxable lands in his new realm. Caterham is not mentioned, but Tillingdown is. *Domesday Book* lists the various manors and gives some details of inhabitants and of buildings such as mills and churches with a taxable value. Parishes were not yet in existence and frequently – particularly in Surrey and Sussex – were not coterminous with the manor.

Caterham until the 19th century was an area of largely open unenclosed downland lacking readily available water, and barely inhabited steep-sided deep valleys. In view of the uninviting nature of this land it is not surprising that there is no reference to an estate here in the Saxon period. Caterham manor seems therefore to have been a post-Conquest creation.

In adjacent areas of east Surrey the pattern of manors is of long narrow estates stretching from the top of the Downs in the north to the Surrey/Sussex boundary in the south. Godstone and Tandridge manors provide typical examples. Immediately south of Caterham the boundaries of Bletchingley and Chevington manors seem to have followed clear – almost straight – lines (now tracks and roads). It is reasonable to guess that Bletchingley and Chevington – the manors to the south of Caterham – originally extended onto the Downs in the area later called Caterham. The possible extent of these Saxon estates are indicated on the map below. Chevington, still commemorated by Chevington Farm, was absorbed into Bletchingley manor in the Middle Ages.

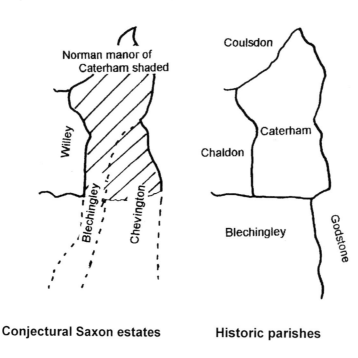

Conjectural Saxon estates   **Historic parishes**

Tillingdown is mentioned in *Domesday Book* and is clearly an important holding. It is described under the 'Land of Richard, son of Count Gilbert' and includes —

'Salie's wife holds Tillingdown herself from Richard. Alnoth held it from King Edward *(the Confessor)*. Then it answered for 10 hides now for 1½ hides. Land for 4 ploughs.... 5 villagers and 8 slaves ....A church.....'[14]

Tillingdown's population as stated may be read as families and would equate to no more than 60 or so persons, very many more than there are now or have been for many years. (For comparison the population of Caterham parish in 1801 was 301, in an area more than four times that of Tillingdown).

Because Tillingdown was later joined with Tandridge as part of a single parish it is usually stated that the Domesday Tillingdown church was really the one at modern Tandridge.[15] However the location of the church at Tillingdown is not known, and perhaps it was near the present farm.

One of the most interesting aspects of Tillingdown is the possible extent of the Domesday manor. The later parish boundary occupies only about half the natural hill top, an unexpected and odd situation at a time when the area was not densely occupied. We know from elsewhere in the area that parishes and manors are by no means necessarily the same thing. Examination of the boundaries in relation to the natural features, the deep valleys and Roman road which was one historic boundary, suggests that an earlier, more logical extent of the 'estate' would have been to use the deep valley to the east, Marden Valley, as the boundary. In spite of the English Place Name Society's derivation[16] could the name (Marden) have a 'boundary valley' origin? [17]

Why, if it had a church, did not Tillingdown become a parish in its own right, instead of as part of Tandridge? It may be that within a century or so of the Norman Conquest the importance of the area had diminished, and it had become just a minor part of the de Clare estate. The final straw was no doubt the Black Death in the mid-14th century with the consequent great reduction in population. The church may no longer have existed by the time parishes came to be formed in the 12th century.

SOURCES

1. *Victoria County History of Surrey*, **IV**: 265

2. Gray, Peter, (ed.), *Chaldon Explored*, 12

3. *Victoria County History of Surrey*, **IV**: 324

4. *See* Gray and Fookes in *Surrey Archaeological Society Bulletin*, **268** and *Surrey Archaeological Collections*, **83**: 202

5. Bird J and Bird D G (eds), (1987) *Archaeology of Surrey*, 106, and *Surrey Archaeological Collections*, **L**: 47-72

6. Manning and Bray, *History of Surrey*, **II**: 443

7. *Ibid*, **II**: 437

8. *Ibid*, **III**: 620 (printed as 720 but preceding page 621)

9. Margary, Ivan, (1948) *Roman Ways in the Weald*

10. Manning and Bray, *History of Surrey*, **II**: 443

11. Morris, Richard, *Churches in the Landscape*, 229

12. See *Surrey Archaeological Society Collections*, **XLIV**: 47-83, and **LXXII**: 1-13 where the question has been thoroughly examined. The idea seems to have originated in the 18th century and 'set in stone' by the Ordnance Survey in their early editions

13. Æthelnoth (Alnoth) an important Kentish thegn held both Tillingdown and Banstead in the mid-11th century. — Blair, John, *Early Medieval Surrey*, 116-9

14. Morris, John. *Domesday Book*

15. It may be that everyone quotes from the *Victoria County History*, **IV**: 324 without considering the evidence for a significant settlement at Tillingdown

16. *The Place Names of Surrey*, 318 but see 313

17. A hide is a fiscal term although it probably had its origins in area. The premise that at Domesday it equated to an area of 100 to 120 acres is now disputed, but nonetheless for the purposes of comparison with neighbouring Domesday entries for Woldingham and Chaldon it may provide a useful indicator of the comparative extent of the various manors when the possible boundaries of each are related to natural features, and other evidence is considered. On this basis the whole of the Tillingdown hilltop makes more sense as forming the extent of the Domesday manor

---

Chapter 5

Foundation of Historic Caterham

by Peter Gray

The years following the Norman Conquest saw the foundation of historic Caterham, the foundation of the church, the formation of the parish and the development of the village on the hill. It was the Caterham that remained until modern development commenced in the mid-19th century.

THE CHURCH

Today the old church of St Lawrence is dwarfed by St Mary's, surrounded by tall trees and houses and close to a busy road. When it was built in the 11th-century it would have been very different. The spot would have been very remote, with no road nearby (Church Hill was not constructed until the 19th century), no houses and possibly few if any trees. Its position overlooking the valley would have been quite prominent.

The original dedication of the church was to St. Leonard[1], who was a 6th century hermit[2]. The remote location might well be the sort of spot a Saxon hermit would have chosen for his cell[3].

The earliest parts of the church are believed to date from about 1100. They show a small nave only 26'0" x 14'6" with evidence of an apsidal chancel – an exceptional feature. Small churches like this – and Chaldon is another – were probably built purely for household use[4]. There is no direct evidence for a Norman manor house nearby, but Court Lodge – the known 18th century house – was doubtless the successor to a much earlier building. When the church was built, it would seem that it was related to a manor house alone without a village nearby.

Part of the church showing the evidence of the apsidal chancel – the curved wall can still be seen just below the roof of the present chancel.

PARISH BOUNDARIES

Parishes in the sense that we know them today were established in the century or so after the Norman Conquest. Their boundaries can provide important clues to aspects of the history of the area.

The boundaries of the historic parish of Caterham follow natural features, valley bottoms and/or early man-made features such as the Roman road. The straight line marking the junction of Caterham with Coulsdon is interesting because today Coulsdon is still an unenclosed common whilst Caterham Common adjoining had been enclosed. The need to define the precise line probably only occurred when Caterham Common was enclosed in 1853. (See map in previous chapter.)

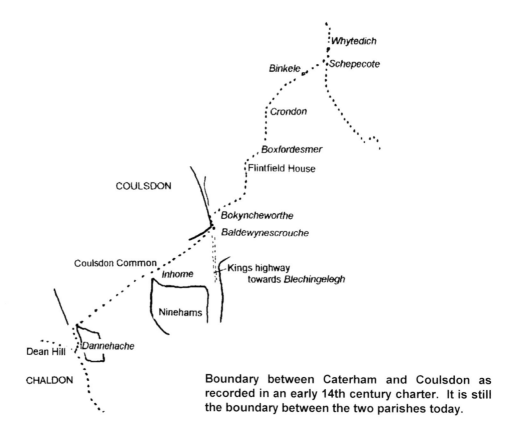

Boundary between Caterham and Coulsdon as recorded in an early 14th century charter. It is still the boundary between the two parishes today.

One section, at the boundary with Coulsdon, is recorded in an early 14th-century Chertsey Abbey charter. This charter has been studied in detail by A.R. Rumble[5]. It gives some interesting information about place names and the medieval landscape apart from the boundary itself. To quote from the translation –

> '(from) the king's highway which leads towards Godston called Walstret (at) the ditch called le Newedych or Whytedich, and so by that ditch as far as the place that is called Schepecote, and so by Binkele as far as the croft called Crondon, and so by fences and hedges as far as the pit called Boxfordesmer, and so as far as the field called Bokyncheworthe, and so by the king's highway that leads towards Blechingelegh as far as the cross called Baldewynescrouche, and so by fences and hedges as far as the field of Caterham called Inhome, and so across the heath as far as a place called Dannehache, and....'

Newedych or Whytedich may refer to a ditch carrying the Bourne stream near Whyteleafe Station, a ditch whose origin may point to the need to channel the occasional waters of the Bourne since it otherwise had no distinct channel. The boundary then climbs out of the valley to follow the top of the steep slope above the present Whyteleafe Road. Binkele may be the ancient name of the area before it came to be called Whyteleafe in modern times. The pit at Boxfordsmer is a deep hollow in Coxes wood which could once have formed a flint working. Flint Field House is nearby today. The 'King's highway' here is the southern end of Hayes Lane and is part of the same road mentioned at Stanstead in Chapter 4. Its line at Baldwynescrouche approximates to Ninehams Road, Ninehams being a corruption of Inhome, meaning intake or enclosure from the heath. The enclosure itself can still be traced in modern street lines. The boundary goes across the heath, still open to the north as Coulsdon Common, to Dannehache, which marks a hache or gate on Dean Hill on the edge of the common. This point is at the junction of three parishes, Caterham, Coulsdon and Chaldon. The charter then goes on to describe the boundary between Coulsdon and Chaldon.

The Caterham boundary from this point goes south following the valley bottom, a shallow downland valley, rising to the crest of the Downs near the *Harrow*. For the last part of its route it is identical with Roffes Lane. From the top of White Hill the line turns east following field and wood boundaries close to the crest of the Downs until it reaches the Roman road at the top of Godstone Hill. The remaining length northwards to Whyteleafe follows a line of typically early character, first the Roman road and then the bottom of the deep valley beyond Wapses Lodge roundabout to the starting point of the boundary in the valley at Whyteleafe.

ORIGIN OF CATERHAM VILLAGE

The only settlement of any size in Caterham up until the 19th century was on the hill. There are no early written documents which record the origins of the village, so we must use the evidence of maps and relatively recent records to trace its probable origins.

The first large-scale map of the village of Caterham is the 1736 map of the Rowed Estate. Comparison of this map with the first edition of the 25" ordnance map of 1869 provides a clue to the likely origins of the village.

The 1869 map shows the village as modern development was starting. New roads were laid out, and many hedgerows had been cleared but their basic lines are still indicated by trees. The map had been drawn just in time for our purposes. The one significant difference from the Rowed Map (apart from the enclosure of Caterham Common) is the enclosure of land for the school at the northern end of the village, known to have occurred in 1805.

The Rowed map shows twelve or so buildings mainly on the west side of the road north of the kink by Waller Lane. None of the buildings is close to the church. The picture seems hardly to have changed 100 years later when the tithe map was produced in 1841. Several buildings had been added, however, by the time of the 1869 OS map, but the basic picture is still the same.

Nearly half of the buildings shown in 1736 remained until recent times, and several still do. They provide important evidence of the size and quality of buildings in the village. Almost all were originally very small although they had been subsequently extended. A mid-19th century deed[6] describes eight of the buildings – they were built of a variety of materials, with tile or slate roofs, timber, brick and stone walls. One was described as a butcher's and grocer's shop with granary and slaughterhouse, doubtless as outbuildings at the rear. This building is now apparently No.84 High Street. It seems to have been the most substantial building and the only house of medieval date in the parish, probably dating from about 1500[7].

Some details are available of three or four other 1736 buildings. Box Cottage where Ainsworths homeopathic shop now stands was demolished in 1964. Judging from early sketches and photographs, it seems to have been timber-framed and similar to No. 84, and thatched, but rather smaller[8]. It is reputed to have had *1597* on the fireplace beam. Part of *Ye Olde King & Queen* is also timber-framed. Judging by the quality of the workmanship it appears slightly higher in status than Box Cottage and was built before 1736[9]. Originally weather-boarded, it

84 High Street, Caterham on the Hill in 1994

was encased in brick and extended in about 1800. The only other building standing in 1736 for which we have much evidence is the parsonage (now Buxton's offices). Hidden behind several 18th, 19th and 20th-century additions is a single bay of an earlier building which could have been a simple one-up one-down cottage. It was built of white hearthstone, and is possibly of late-17th or early-18th century date[10]. Roffey Place was a row of three small 18th-century cottages with the front doors entering the single living rooms, also demolished in 1964[11]. Where Butlers' premises now are the roof line of Roffey Place can still be seen on an adjoining wall. Both the maps and the recorded evidence suggest a village largely composed of small, poor cottages[12].

Box Cottage

DEVELOPMENT OF CATERHAM ON THE HILL VILLAGE FROM 12th TO 19th CENTURIES

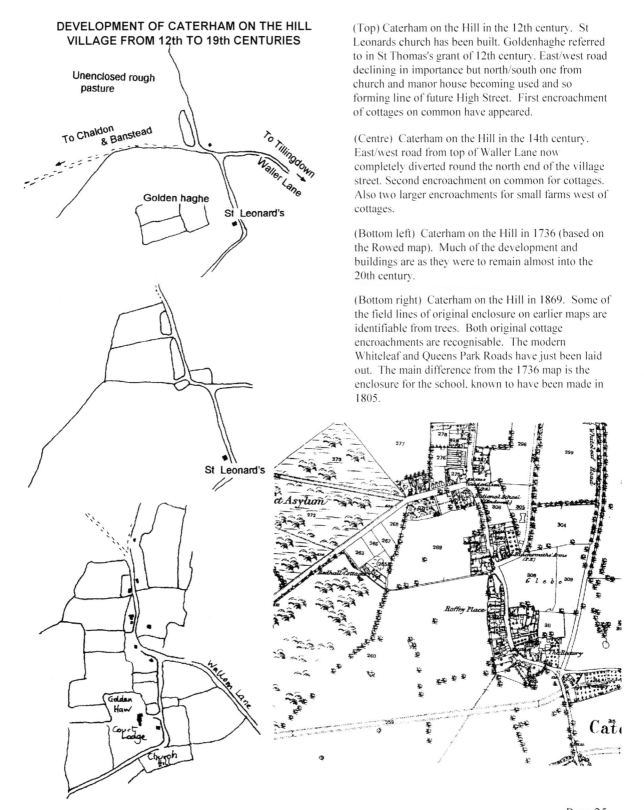

(Top) Caterham on the Hill in the 12th century. St Leonards church has been built. Goldenhaghe referred to in St Thomas's grant of 12th century. East/west road declining in importance but north/south one from church and manor house becoming used and so forming line of future High Street. First encroachment of cottages on common have appeared.

(Centre) Caterham on the Hill in the 14th century. East/west road from top of Waller Lane now completely diverted round the north end of the village street. Second encroachment on common for cottages. Also two larger encroachments for small farms west of cottages.

(Bottom left) Caterham on the Hill in 1736 (based on the Rowed map). Much of the development and buildings are as they were to remain almost into the 20th century.

(Bottom right) Caterham on the Hill in 1869. Some of the field lines of original enclosure on earlier maps are identifiable from trees. Both original cottage encroachments are recognisable. The modern Whiteleaf and Queens Park Roads have just been laid out. The main difference from the 1736 map is the enclosure for the school, known to have been made in 1805.

Apart from the Rectory almost all the old houses were on the west of the High Street. This fact and the 1805 enclosure for the school referred to above provides the key to the origins of the settlement.

The process started after the Conquest. At that date – or soon after – the main enclosures of farming land were already in existence to the east and south of the High Street.   New dwellings were being built on the edge of the common rather than the previously enclosed land, a process which can be seen in many other places in Surrey. At that time road patterns were changing. The east/west road was becoming less important whilst a new one northward from the manor house and church was being created.

The process is best illustrated in the accompanying maps. *(Page 25)*

Early documentary evidence is hard to come by, but documents of the 12th and 13th centuries belonging to the Hospital of St Thomas of Southwark show that there was building activity in the area[13]. Those documents also include reference to 'Golden Haw' shown later on the 1736 Rowed map. Archaeological evidence from the site of *Ye Olde King & Queen* has revealed evidence of occupation commencing about 1200[14].

MEDIEVAL LANDSCAPE AND PLACE NAMES

There is not much written evidence relating to Caterham before 1400. The only major collection of documents is the cartulary of St Thomas's Hospital preserved in the Stowe manuscripts in the British Library. These documents, supplemented by later evidence and the context of the physical landscape, give one or two glimpses of early medieval Caterham.

Until the 19th century the landscape of Caterham parish was roughly half-unenclosed manorial waste. This was on the tops of the downs; the rest of the parish was enclosed. Field and place names in 13th and 14th century documents show that the extent of the enclosed land and the commons in Caterham was much the same as it was when the first Ordnance Survey map was prepared 1805 *(Opposite)*.

The St Thomas's documents[15] show that much of the enclosed land was farmed – normally as arable – in strips, though not in the classic medieval two- or three-field system. The strip fields were widely scattered on the lip of the valley and flat lands in the bottom of Harestone valley. The actual strips, with their medieval names, are traceable on the 18th century maps and in one or two cases on the 1841 tithe map.   One acre of land in Withindene field lying between the land of Roger Ros and Richard Colyer next Longfurlong[16] documented in the 13th century can be found near Wittington on the 1841 tithe map. The process of aggregation of the strips into single compact holdings had already begun in the 13th century, as reference to two- and three-acre strips [17], shows but judging by the Rowed map it was not complete by the 18th century. Not all the enclosed land was in strips. The charters suggest that some virgate (32 acre) holdings were divided into four or five fields[18]. There was also the demesne – the home farm – which can be traced from the 18th century maps. Portley and Salmons may also have been compact holdings rather than common fields. Evidence of the use of the steep valley sides is provided by place names. Stone Riding and Little Rudene are forms of ryding (OE for cleared land) enclosed and used for grazing since the land was far too steep for use as anything else. In one case the name Row Tye (rough pasture) confirms this.

The influence of the topography, the steep-sided valleys and the difficulties with water – possibly too much in the valleys and too little on the tops – gives a picture of poor farming country.

EARLY PLACE NAMES

The St Thomas's documents contain a number of place names which can be traced to modern times and some which have been lost but can nevertheless be located by implication.

The main names, Stanstead, Upwood (Tupwood), Porkle (Portley) and Salmons are easily recognised. Others which were of obvious importance, such as Gatiers and Halyngbury associated with Waltham Abbey, have not been identified. It is worth noting that Halingbury[19] is a place-name near Waltham Abbey in Essex so although the reference here is doubtless to Caterham there may be a connection in some way with Essex. More obscure

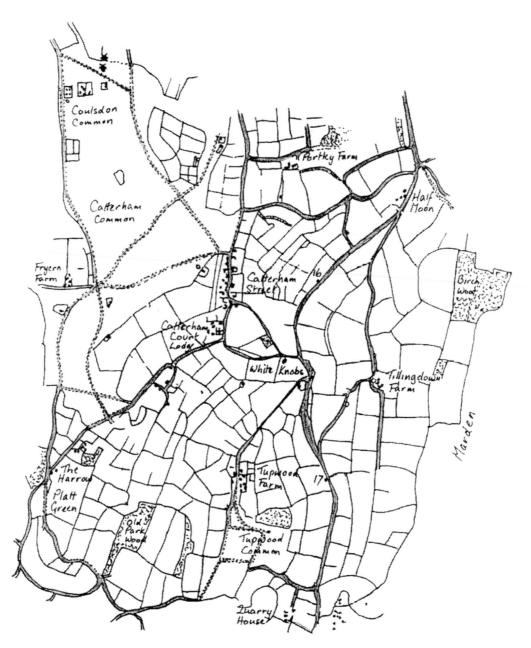

Caterham about 1805

based on Ordnance Surveyors' draft map (original 2" = 1 mile) of Caterham , Tillingdown and part of Coulsdon (available in the map library of the Britsh Library). The extent of the commons does not seem to have changed much since the end of the medieval period.

names can be located as follows: 'hoca' – meaning a hook or point of land – seems to refer to the land by the church, which fits the description well when considered against the valley below. 'Apleton' by deduction seems to refer to the land near the manor house now traversed by Manor Avenue. There is no evidence that Harestone

Valley was ever so called at that time[20]. Instead the upper part of the valley seems to have been referred to as 'cumbe' with 'utercumbe' (in modern times Aldercombe Farm), and the lower part 'lievenecumbe'. Field-names such as Goldenhaw, Bromfield, and Withindene can be traced from the tithe and Rowed maps.

The Iron Age hill-fort near Whitehill is the place called 'werc or rawlneswerc on the hill between the vill of Blecingle and Stansted"[21]. Werc is Old English for 'work' in the sense of a fort or defensive earthwork. There is a reference to a 'grove called Shuntesdon' close by, with a way called Smetheswei on one side[22]. In 'werc' not only do we have the origin of the 'war' in the modern War Coppice Lane but also we have probably the 13th century name of the coppice and the road itself.

Finally what of the name Caterham? Unfortunately place-name scholars are unsure of its meaning because of lack of early evidence. However, it is suggested that the first element may be related to the Welsh *cader*, 'fort hill-fort', which could be a reference to War Coppice[23].

SOURCES

1.   *Victoria County History* of Surrey, iv, 270

2.   *Oxford Dictionary of Saints,* Oxford, 1978

3.   From discussion with Rosalind Ransford, pers. comm

4.   See Blair, John, *Early Medieval Surrey*, 134

5.   Rumble, A.J., Medieval Boundaries of Coulsdon, Surrey, *Journal of the English Place Name Society*, **IV**. Surrey Record Office ref. 7/2/17

6.   Author's survey 1995

7.   *Bourne Society Local History Records*, **V**:19

8.   Author's survey 1976

9.   Author's survey 1974. *Bourne Society Local History Records*, **IV**: 9

11.   *Bourne Society Local History Records*, **IV**: 9

12.   Town End on the <u>east</u> side is outside the old village and it is of flint and more substantial but probably had farming rather than village origins

13.   St Thomas's 811 for example (see footnote 15)

14.   Russell, M.J., Surrey Archaeological Society Collections LXXIV, 1974. 123-133

15.   These notes are based on the translation of the Cartulary of St Thomas's Hospital privately published 1932. The references are to the deed numbers (e.g. St. Thomas's *xxx*), quoted in that translation

16.   St. Thomas's 827

17.   St Thomas's 799, 800, 822 for example

18.   St. Thomas's 813

19.   Manning and Bray, *History of Surrey*, **II**: 436

20.   EPNS, 313, gives the first reference as 1605

21.   St. Thomas's 812

22.   St. Thomas's 836

23.   EPNS, 312

Chapter 6

The Manor and its People

from Domesday - 19th Century

by Mary Saaler

We can see from the records of the middle ages that there was no single unit of land which might be called 'The Manor Caterham'. On the contrary, the land was divided up between great lords and landowners who held various parts of Caterham. The manor or estate of Tilllingdown is a good example of this subdivision – it was held as a separate estate by the Clare family at the time of Domesday and continued to be a separate holding from then on.[1] Some of the other parts of Caterham came to be associated with Tillingdown during the later middle ages; for example, the estates of Portley, Upwood, Hallingbury and Caterham were all administered from Tillingdown, or later from Bletchingley.[2]

Clare, *Or three chevrons gules*

(Three red chevrons on a gold ground).

We know very little about other areas of Caterham until about 1200, when Roger, of Guist in Norfolk, granted his manor of Caterham and the parish church, which was then known as St. Leonard's, to the canons of Waltham Abbey in Essex.[3] Waltham Abbey was originally an Anglo-Saxon foundation and was refounded by Henry II in 1177. Because of its size and royal patronage, it became one of the most important religious houses in the country. By the gift of Roger of Guist, the abbey was the major landowner in Caterham until 1540, when it surrendered all its property on the dissolution of the monasteries. Other religious houses also held land in Caterham, usually through gifts and grants. Chertsey Abbey acquired land here and the Knights Templar held property, known as 'The Manor of Caterham', until the order was disbanded in 1307. After a few years, the property of the Templars passed to the Hospitallers of the Order of St. John of Jerusalem, who retained it until the dissolution. Other great London-based houses, such as the Hospital of St. Thomas in Southwark and the Hospital of St. Thomas of Acre in Cheapside, also held land in Caterham. There are problems in identifying the lands they held, since these landlords were also renting and sub-letting land and property to one another.

THE FOURTEENTH CENTURY

The scattered nature of the holdings gives us a picture of Caterham being a fragmented place, with local people paying their rents to the bailiffs of distant landlords. However, the officials of these great lords visited Caterham to supervise their property and a few of these records have survived. We can see from the accounts for Tillingdown that landlords had to cope with the effects of the Black Death, which reduced the population by about a third in the period 1348-61. The fall in numbers left areas of land vacant and reduced the landlords' income. The solution was to convert vacant land to sheep pasture and derive income from wool, the chalk downland being ideal for this purpose. The same records also give us information about local employment in the middle ages. Most people were directly involved in farming, but there were also craftsmen such as the blacksmith who provided iron and steel to repair the ploughs and make shoes for horses and oxen. Other craftsmen, such as stone-masons, tilers, thatchers and carpenters were concerned with building work. Since most buildings were timber-framed, there was plenty of employment for carpenters and it is noticeable that they were frequently paid to dismantle redundant buildings and move them to different sites; at Portley the old kitchen was taken down and moved to Tillingdown, while barns and cattle-sheds were similarly moved to other sites.

The tax returns of the 1330s allow us to identify some of the local inhabitants at that time. Only the wealthiest people paid tax, being taxed at the rate of one fifteenth of the value of their land or possessions worth more than 10 shillings. There were 17 taxpayers in Caterham who paid amounts ranging from 1s to 7s. The following table gives their names—

William Baldwyne	William the Pleyer
Walter at Bromfeld	Geoffrey Loveday
Thomas at Roke	Geoffrey the Pleyer
Richard at Suthale	John the Strong
John Baldwyne	Elias of Blythe
Gilbert of Northeye	Henry the Foder
William the Whyte	Edmund Dakers
Charles Colgrym	John ----
Peter East	

As these men were probably householders we can guess that there were at least 17 houses in Caterham at this date. As we might expect, most of them were taxed on their crops of wheat, oats and barley and on their sheep and cattle. Two members of the Baldwyn family were tax-payers in Caterham and their name appears in the place-name of Baldwyns Cross in later documents. Even as late as 1543, the names of East, Loveday, Pleyer and Northeye were used to identify pieces of land in Caterham.[4]

FIFTEENTH CENTURY

During the 15th century parts of the manor known as Portley, Upwood, Gayters, Hallyngbury and Fosterdown, together with Tillingdown, continued to be administered from Bletchingley as part of the estate which had passed by marriage from the Clares to the Earls of Stafford. The Stafford lands in Caterham, which lay north-east of Waller Lane, were rented or leased to local farmers.

Other areas were administered by Waltham Abbey, and we have a record of the Abbey of 1401 which gives us the names of the local officials at that time. The five tithingmen of Caterham were Stephen Smyth, John Ropkyn, John Aleyn, Richard Godfrey and Walter Godfrey. This shows that Caterham was divided into five separate tithings, with the tithingmen being the equivalent of local policemen, who were responsible for maintaining law and order within their own tithings. They also had the task of collecting 'the common fine' which each tithing paid to the sheriff of Surrey to finance the administration of the king's justice within the county. In the case of Caterham, each tithingman collected three farthings, giving a total of 3¾d from Caterham.

The aletaster was the local official who was responsible for supervising the brewing and selling of ale. John Ropkyn combined the duties of ale taster and tithingman, but he failed to carry out his duties of supervising the ale and so paid a fine of 4d. However, two women – the wives of Stephen Smyth and William Ropkyn – paid for licences to brew and sell ale. (It was fairly common for women to do the brewing for their household and earn money by selling the surplus).[5]

Other information about local people comes from tax records. We can see the emergence of the Best family which held land in Caterham over several centuries. Between 1419 and 1442, Thomas Best 'of Caterham' and then Richard Best regularly acted as collectors of Surrey taxes.[6] Thomas Best 'of Catterham' was MP for Lewes in Sussex in 1447 and again in 1460-1. By the 1490s Robert Best had become tenant of the Stafford estates of Portley, Upwood, Gayters and Caterham.

SIXTEENTH CENTURY

The 16th century was marked by the effects of the dissolution of the monasteries. All the religious houses gradually gave up their interests in property, which was transferred either to local farmers or outside investors. We should not underestimate the problems faced by local people at this time of upheaval. A survey of the lands of Waltham Abbey made in 1532 shows that the Abbey then held a substantial house in Caterham, which had a hall, an upper room and a cellar, with a garden, courtyard and two acres of land. The same property also contained a barn which was 13m long and 9m wide 'in a good state of repair'. The survey shows that the Abbey held 281 acres of arable and woodland scattered throughout Caterham, together with the right to cut wood in 150 acres of common land which was held by 'the Lady Dyonise of the Hilly Feilde in Caterham'. In addition, the Abbey was entitled to take every seventh tree in the wood of Upwood and had the right to graze 200 sheep on the common pasture, while it also had income from rented properties.

Seal of Abbey of Waltham Holy Cross, showing two angels on each side of the cross.

Photo courtesy of the British Museum, ref seal XV

Because the Abbey also had the right to appoint the clergy in Caterham, local people felt that the Abbey lands comprised the true manor of Caterham. We can see this clearly when they stated in a survey of 1543 that 'The manor of Caterham, with the parsonage, has gone by the name of the manor of Caterham, otherwise called the abbot's land'. The parsonage and its garden were valued at 10s in 1535 but perhaps the house was in a bad state and was demolished after Waltham Abbey lost possession of Caterham. Another enquiry in 1544 referred to the Bishop of Winchester's officials building a new parsonage 'in the abbot's garden'. This new parsonage is probably the one depicted on the Rowed map of 1736 and is now known as the Old Rectory.

The Best family was well represented on the juries of local people who made these surveys, while various members of the family held the lease of the manor during the first half of the 16th century. An effect of the dissolution was to put large amounts of land on the open market. In Caterham the abbot's manor was acquired by William Sackville, who was a member of the household of Henry VIII. Sackville sub-let his manor to John Best. Sackville also took over the lands in Caterham and Chaldon previously held by the Hospital of St. Thomas in Southwark, which had been sub-let to Thomas and Joan Best. His holding included the site of War Coppice – being described as 'four acres of wood and coppice wood, called Warke Copices'.

Caterham continued to be divided into at least two manors and the estates formerly held by the Staffords were then held by Richard Best. The evidence of place-names such as Smalden, Northdene, Shortfurrow, Longacre and Timberhill suggests that part of the former Stafford estates lay to the north and east of the present Waller Lane. The common at Caterham Heath was also part of this holding.[7]

Like many other manors throughout the country, Caterham was bought and sold as an investment by wealthy lawyers and businessmen. In 1553 Sackville sold his part of Caterham to Robert Hartopp, who was a citizen of London and a goldsmith. Hartopp paid £400 for the manor of Caterham and it remained with this family until

1625, when his great granddaughter Elizabeth Hartopp married Robert Coppin of Kensington. Similarly by 1616 the former Stafford lands were in the hands of Jasper Ockley and afterwards Sir Isaac Shard.[8]

As in many other places in Surrey, there is evidence of land shortages as the population increased. Families needed more land to provide food and they began to enclose parts of the waste or common for their own use. This caused more problems in Caterham by reducing the amount of land available to the poor to graze their animals.

Various documents tell us about the lives of local people during the 16th century. For example, the muster rolls listed the able-bodied men, with or without armour, who were fit enough to defend their country. In Caterham these included Richard Best and John Kempsale, who also served as jurors at meetings of the manor court. We know the names of other jurors, such as Simon Burningham, William Eton, Richard Ropkyn and John Wenewryght, who were tenants of the manor.[9]

The assize records for the reign of Elizabeth I give the names of those who committed crimes and of their victims. There were two cases of highway robbery in Caterham; the first occurred in 1569 when three labourers, Stephen Anstie, John Canfield and Thomas Massie, assaulted Richard Pecton and stole his money and his dagger. In 1589 another local resident, Abraham Giles, also a labourer, was hanged at Croydon assizes for a similar offence. Elizabeth Nicholas was found guilty of theft of clothes from Richard Geale, but she was remanded because she was pregnant. While many crimes were committed by the poor, some better-off people went poaching for fun. In 1580 a crowd of local people, including John Basset of Caterham, took 14 ferrets and six dogs on a poaching expedition to Beddington Park and caught 40 rabbits.[10]

Members of the Basset family were among the more wealthy local residents, and the will of Anthony Basset in 1596 shows that he had a dwelling house in Caterham, with a barn and orchard, and scattered holdings of land throughout the manor. He left his house and some property to his wife Margaret, and made bequests to his brothers, James, Thomas and William, while his son William was his executor.[11]

The tax lists of the Elizabethan period show that 12 local people had enough income to be paying tax. The roll for 1593-4 shows the continued importance of the Best family, with Richard Best paying the largest amount of 13s.4d and William Best paying 8s.0d.[12]

SEVENTEENTH CENTURY

For the first time in the history of Caterham, official records begin to give us clues about the size of the community. Church records show that there were 82 members of the church in 1603, which number had increased to 119 by 1676. The lists of those who supported the protestant reforms in the Church of England in 1641-2 named 59 men in Caterham who were over the age of 18. The Hearth Tax returns of the 1660s show us that there were just over 50 households in Caterham, and about half of these were too poor to pay the tax of 2s a year payable on 'every hearth or stove'. Only three households had six or seven hearths, the majority of families having just one fireplace. This was a very unpopular tax with all levels of society, and was soon abandoned. Samuel Pepys wrote in his diary: 'The people clamour against the chimney money and say they will not pay without force'.

We can find additional information for the 17th century in the records of the quarter sessions. These show us that most people still earned their living by farming. However, there are references to a few other workers, such as a blacksmith, a quarryman, bricklayers, ale-house keepers, a food supplier, a weaver and a shoemaker. Further information about the people of Caterham in the early years of the 17th century comes from the notebook of Bostock Fuller, a JP of Tandridge Court. He kept notes about his daily work and recorded the activities of Caterham people. He noted the names of the local officials who served as tithingmen and constables, as well as those who committed minor crimes. We can see that men like Thomas Bassett, John Bearde, William Best, William Comyns and George Heath were tithingmen and constables, while others were charged with disturbing the peace. Various members of the Rowed family were charged with hunting and killing rabbits, and Elizabeth

Lye was sent to gaol for setting fire to the bedding and other goods of William Best, her master. There was also a confrontation between George Heath, the constable and William Comyns, the tithingman, for which Comyns was bound over to keep the peace.[13]

By the middle of the 17th century we begin to have information about leisure activities. The quarter sessions were dealing with ale-house licences and show that there were three or four taverns or ale-houses in Caterham. Three ale-house keepers, named as Mary Rabbett, widow, William Brown, shoemaker, and Thomas Staples, a food-seller, were charged with failing to have licences to trade. However Mrs. Rabbett clearly kept a popular house since the local people petitioned the JPs to allow her to trade and the JPs supported the recommendation. Thomas Benett, the constable, may also have been an innkeeper, since he was charged with allowing people to play unlawful games in his house. These were described as 'Cards, Dice, Tables and Shovell groat (shove-halfpenny) for his monetary advantage and to the great disturbance of the neighbours'. Since these were typical pub games he was probably running a tavern.[14]

Two 17th century inventories of goods made on the death of a tenant show contrasting pictures. When Richard Ladd – a quarryman – died in 1609 his house consisted of three rooms and his furniture was a table, a form and a bench; he also had eight sheep and five lambs. In contrast to this the inventory made in 1614 for Richard Woodroffe (alias Sharpe) – a local blacksmith – shows a more comfortable scene. His house consisted of a hall, a kitchen, a bedchamber and a workshop. The kitchen contained a number of brass and pewter plates and dishes, while the bedroom held two beds and other furniture. His anvil, bellows and hammers were in the workshop. Men who were local officials such as John Beard and William Best carried out the probate valuations.[15]

While the official records give us a certain amount of information, private transactions help to fill out the picture. A property dispute in 1638 gives us a clue about the location of a windmill and refers to a house called *le White Harte*, which may have been one of the ale-houses or taverns mentioned at the quarter sessions. In this dispute Thomas Ponnsett – 'a gentleman' – brought a charge against Edmund Jordan 'lately of Chaldon' concerning property in Caterham consisting of 200 acres of pasture at Stansted Heath with a windmill lately built on it, a house known as le White Harte, and two acres of land called Green Close. The Rowed map of 1736 shows a windmill on Caterham Common, but it also marks the site of Old Windmill Bank, which may give a clue to the existence of an earlier windmill at Stansted. Ponnsett claimed that the Lord of the Manor, George Evelyn, had granted him the property in 1628 but that Jordan had taken it over illegally. Ponnsett won his case and Jordan was fined £65.

The lordship of the Evelyns passed to James Linch of White Parish in Wiltshire, and although his main home was far from Caterham he remembered the poor people of Caterham in his will and left them £1 'to be distributed by the overseers of the poor'. Linch left his manor of Caterham to his granddaughter, Susan Gauntlett. She married Robert Hussey of Corfe in Dorset, who transferred the manor to George Roffey, a gentleman of Southwark, in May 1699. The agreements which accompany this transfer show that the land was part of the manor held by William Sackville in 1544, and before that by Waltham Abbey. It included Stansted and other land in Caterham defined as:

>   3 acres of arable, meadow and shaw in Caterham, adjoining Stansted
>   16 acres at Webhaw with the shaws
>   3 acres at Webhaw Coppice
>   16 acres at Aldercombe
>   4 acres at Aldercombe Coppice
>   6 acres at North Stoneridden
>   7 acres at South Stoneridden
>   2 acres at Stoneridden Coppice
>   12 acres divided into plats
>   14 acres at Fryarn Hill
>   4 acres at War Coppice 'now arable'

10 acres at Stubbs alias Crouches
2 acres at Stubbs Coppice
2 acres at Collerslow
22 acres at Broadwood 'two acres now arable'
20 acres at Denhill Wood 'four acres now arable'
9 acres at Bromehill Wood
3 acres in two little coppices on the west of Broomswood
10 acres at Homewood
5 acres at Broadfield Wood, alias the Little Wood

This total of 156 acres was leased to William Field. However, George Roffey also took over a large area of common grazing land and an agreement made in June 1699 recorded the use of this land. It referred to the rights of tenants to feed their animals on Caterham Heath, which adjoined Stansted. By this agreement, the local tenants paid George Roffey for the right to graze their animals on the common as they had paid the previous landowners. The Roffey family continued to hold lands in Caterham until 1770.[16]

EIGHTEENTH CENTURY

Church records reveal that the population of Caterham had increased to 201 at the beginning of the 18th century. This figure included two nonconformists and one of these, John Blanch, was running a school in Caterham. By 1788 the population had risen to 230 and there was one school for infants. While these figures relate to the whole population, poll-books of the 18th century show that few of these people had the right to vote. Voting was restricted to people who held freehold land worth more than £2 a year, and there are seven lists of voters in Caterham spanning the period from 1705 until 1780. We can see that about 16 people had freehold land in Caterham but only about half of these lived in Caterham. The list for 1705 names the local voters as:

Lawrence Rowed   John Drew
Robert Ockley   Richard Dye
John Medhurst   Jeffrey Hatcher
Walter Hatcher   John Rowed
John Haswell

Since they had the right to vote, these men were the more wealthy tenants who employed others as labourers. The list shows the predominance of the Rowed family who held the estate shown on the Rowed map of 1736. By 1775 the poll-books reveal a fall in the number of local voters, and list them as:

John Smith   Thomas Drew
Thomas Brooks   Henry Rowed
Thomas Snellinge

In addition, other people such as Napkin Brooker and John Thornton, lived in Caterham, but held their freehold land in Coulsdon.[17]

The Rowed map of 1736 shows the estates of Caterham Court Lodge Farm, Red Hall Farm and John Wood's property of Wilderness Farm. All of these were farmed by Henry Rowed. When he died in 1764 the inventory of his land – which then included Tupwood – shows the basis of mixed farming, divided between arable, pasture and woodland.

The parish registers give a few clues about local occupations. There was an innkeeper at the *Half Moon Inn* in Caterham Valley at the junction with Burntwood Lane, formerly Stonham Lane. Other occupations included a butcher, a chandler, a wheelwright, a gardener, farmers, labourers and servants, while there were many without occupations who were described as paupers and travellers. The registers also mention the baptism of Richard Rowed, son of Henry and Mary Rowed 'of the Court House at Caterham', and the marriage of Napkin Brooker, a farmer and widower, aged 49, to Mary Wicking of Godstone, aged 48.

An inventory of Brooker's goods on his death in 1780 shows that he held a substantial amount of property in Caterham. His comfortably furnished house contained 12 rooms, including a parlour with a dining table and writing desk. There were four bedrooms and the bedroom over the parlour held two beds, a dressing-table, a mirror and three chairs. His house contained fashionable items such as a chocolate pot, a coffee pot and a tea kettle, as well as plenty of strong drink. He farmed land in Caterham, Coulsdon and Warlingham and held the lease of the *Half Moon* 'in Stonham Lane in Caterham'. Much of his Caterham land lay in the valley and extended from the present-day Colliers to the south to Burntwood Lane to the north.[18]

During the 18th century the separate manors or estates of Caterham passed into the hands of a single lord of the manor. The land that once belonged to Waltham Abbey and the former Stafford lands were both held by Thomas Clark, as Lord of the Manor of Caterham.

NINETEENTH CENTURY

By the early years of the 19th century the population of Caterham had increased to 301. There were 71 families living in 63 houses, with seven houses being left empty. By 1826 the number of local residents who qualified to vote had dropped to two; these were John Fairall and John Richardson. As in previous centuries, most of the people were employed in agriculture. The Crop Returns of 1801 show that almost one third of the parish was used for crops, mainly wheat, oats and barley. The remainder consisted of woodland and pasture.[19]

We have information about Caterham Court Farm in the early years of the 19th century. In 1827 the architect Charles Waisthall published a book to promote the design and improvement of farmsteads. He used Caterham Court Farm as his model, since this was a place where scattered and inconvenient farm buildings had accumulated with no regard for efficiency. He showed plans of realigned buildings to make a better layout and added a piped water-supply served by a pump to replace the 'water as black as treacle' in the farm pond.[20]

Thomas Clark of London, who was Lord of the Manor at the beginning of the 19th century, provided Caterham with a school. In 1804 he enclosed just over an acre of land on the common – 'at the North end of the Village' – and built a house for a school, with an orchard and garden adjoining. This was to be rent-free for the schoolmaster, who had the right to take the produce from the orchard and garden. During the later 19th century the lordship of the manor was held by Charles Day; on his death it passed to his trustees and then to George Drew.

Lashmar Cottages

Manor court meetings were being held at the *Half Moon Inn*. The records of the court show how Charles Day, who later became Lord of the Manor, gradually bought up small pieces of land as they fell vacant. The court also gave tenants permission to enclose parts of the common and waste for their own use if they could afford it. For example in 1846 John Marchant Lashmar, a brewer from Oxted, was allowed to enclose land at Platts Green adjoining his house on payment of a shilling a year. He also took over the public house at Platts Green, known as *The Old Harrow*, at a rent of 3d a year. In 1846 Jesse Brooker of Caterham – a carpenter – was bailiff of the manor, while James Balch was elected keeper of the pound for stray animals, and William Reading was the parish constable.[21]

SOURCES

1.   Morris   *Domesday Surrey*, 19.5

2.   Saaler, M., 'The Manor of Tillingdown',   *Surrey Archaeological Collections* 81, pp. 19-39

3.   Ransford, *The Early Charters of Waltham Abbey*, pp. 429-431

4.   SRO.   2575/box 3F; 7/1.14

5.   PRO.   SC2 173/31

6.   PRO.   E 179/184

7.   BL.   Add Ch. 54009-11.   PRO.   LR2/254

8.   BL.   Add Ch.   54014-18

9.   SRO.   7/1/14

10.   Cockburn, *Surrey Indictments, Elizabeth I*

11.   Surrey Wills, *Herringman Register*, Surrey Record Soc. No. 3, pt. 1, p. 43

12.   PRO.   E179 186/352

13.   Whiteman & Clapinson, *The Compton Census of 1676*
    Carter, 'Surrey Protestation Returns', *Surrey Archaeological Collections 59.* p.64
    PRO. E179 188/481
    Leveson-Gower, 'Notebook of a Surrey Justice', *Surrey Archaeological Collections, 9.* pp. 190-223

14.   Jenkinson & Powell *Surrey Quarter Sessions Records 1658-68.* Surrey Record Society

15.   HRO.   1609B50/1-2; 1614B64/1-2

16.   BL.   Add. Ch. 54033-62

17.   Ward, *Parson & Parish in Eighteenth-Century Surrey.* Surrey Record Society
    Surrey Poll Books. Bannerman, Parish Register of Caterham

18.   PRO. PROB. 31/728/422

19.   Parton, 'The 1801 Crop Returns', *Surrey Archaeological Collections, 64,* pp. 113-23

20.   SRO.   7/1/9-7/2/6

21.   Harvey, *Modernising the Farmstead: The First 'Before and After' Case Study*

Chapter 7

Victorian Caterham

by Jean Tooke

The Victorian era saw the dramatic growth of Caterham from a small insignificant downland village to an expanding town. This remarkable transformation is vividly illustrated by comparing the 1841 and 1891 census returns.

CATERHAM IN 1841

In June 1841, the rector, the Revd. James Legrew wrote in the margin of the baptism register:

> 'On Monday June 7th of this year, the Relieving Officer went round the Parish to take an Account of the number of persons who abode therein on the preceding night, when he found there were 477 persons, 245 males, 232 females - 86 inhabited houses or tenements - 2 uninhabited.'

After collecting the census schedules, Luke Teather, the 28 year-old enumerator from Limpsfield, copied details into the enumeration book. He noted the 86 houses, some occupied by several families. For each inhabitant he carefully listed the place of abode, age and occupation, adding 'yes' if born in Surrey or 'no' if born elsewhere.

Unlike nearby villages, there was no resident lord of the manor. Manorial lands were administered from Court Lodge Farm by the bailiff, John Everet, responsible to 'the executors of Charles Day Esq.' The tenant of Court Lodge, an attractive but unpretentious house, was farmer Edward Stanford. The only other properties of note were the Parsonage, Grove House, belonging to churchwarden William Dyer, and Manor Cottage where the occupants could be described as gentry. James & Mary Sadd, Dr. John Williams, barrister Henry Aglionby, and four ladies of independent means were looked after by five servants.

By contrast, the majority of men worked on the land, although the official classification 'ag lab' (agricultural labourer) covered dairymen, shepherds, carters and other specialist farming trades. Of the 245 males listed, 85 were boys under 15 years. Two thirds of the remaining 160 men – 107 in total – gave their occupations as agricultural labourers.

Seven men over 70 years of age were still in employment, including five 'ag labs', the Revd. James Legrew, rector since 1797, and George Pratt appointed schoolmaster in 1821. The oldest inhabitant, however, was 90 year-old pauper, Mary Boorer. Sarah Rowed – one of four female octogenarians – was of independent means, cared for by two servants, Edith Waghorn and James Dabner. It is known that Mary Boorer and Sarah Rowed lived at each end of the village street, for the enumerator conveniently copied schedules in the order in which they were collected. Each group of houses was entered under the local place name.

The round began at Little Marden, Up Wood (Tupwood Lane), occupied by six families including lime burners Thomas and Joseph Atkins. At Up Wood Farm, further down the hill, five farm workers lodged with William Brooks, looked after by his wife Mary and servant Sarah Dalton. The small hamlet of Platt Green was next stop, situated a mile from the tiny parish church across desolate Stanstead Heath. Standing at crossroads, both *The Harrow* public house and blacksmith William Wright's smithy were essential for travellers.

The village street stretched from Court Lodge to the School House in Town End. The *Blacksmith's Arms* was the only public house. *Ye Olde King & Queen* was not opened until 1845, when Richard Cullingham, listed as an 'ag lab' in 1841, applied for a licence to sell beer from his cottage. Traditional trades were represented by blacksmith Solomon Biles and wheelwright William Reading, but new businesses were in evidence. A tailor's shop had been established by James Balch, son-in-law of Henry Bryant, butcher and cheesemonger.

Ye Olde King & Queen, **Caterham on the Hill (1994)**

Thirty two properties were dotted around Caterham Common, including the Old Workhouse and 'Birdcage', home to four farm labourers' families. The last person visited was Ann Buckstone, a lady of independent means, whose surname is remembered in present-day Buxton Lane.

Salmons Farm adjoining the Common was occupied by farmer and parish overseer Thomas Ellis, his family and four young farm-workers. Married labourers lived nearby in Portley Green and Salmons Lane. At the bottom of this lane by Wapses Lodge stood the busy *Half Moon Inn,* where Jane Balch – the village tailor's sister – and two other guests were staying on census night.

The only property in the valley between the *Half Moon Inn* and White Nobs was Stanford's Gate Lodge, named after the Court Lodge tenant. Now used as offices, it stood at the entrance to the steep Court Lodge drive, (Church Hill). Final schedules were collected from White Nobs, where Ann Fairall farmed with the help of son Jonathan and grandson Esau Bellchambers.

CATERHAM IN 1891

Fifty years later William Brough, vestry clerk, and Henry Harland, the Croydon Road jeweller, recorded in their census enumeration books that 4350 persons spent the night of Sunday 5th April 1891 in Caterham – 2268 in St. Mary's and 2082 in St. John's parishes. These figures represent a nine-fold increase when compared with the 1841 census returns.

The initial expansion started in 1853. George Drew, an astute speculator, became Lord of the Manor. He realised that there was a demand for substantial, spacious houses in the Surrey hills, provided transport could be arranged to the City of London. Prosperous businessmen wishing to escape frequent epidemics – and wealthy expatriates planning retirement – were searching for such properties. As Lord of the Manor, George Drew could provide the land. As director of the Caterham Railway Company, he could provide transport for these early commuters.

It was no coincidence that on 21st November 1856, three months after the Caterham Railway opened on 4th August, George Drew put manorial lands up for sale at the Auction Mart in the City of London. All the plots were large, with stringent covenants governing the type of house. An early example was the Woodlands estate, Stanstead Road, in a prime position overlooking the valley. John Harrison bought this land for £170 at the auction, selling it in 1859 for £300 to Henry Hall, who built the elegant mansion, now converted to a nursing home.

High Street, *c.*1890 opposite the Rectory.

The building on the right survives as 84 High Street but the other two have been demolished. They were Rectory Cottages (left) and Clematis Cottage. The photograph shows the character of Caterham before the arrival of the institutions and large houses. Clematis Cottage was replaced by a Victorian house, which was itself demolished for a recent development.

These transactions could be slowly assimilated, but later massive developments completely changed Caterham's character. Not only was the Metropolitan Asylum opened in 1870, but in 1877 the Guards' Depot for young recruits was built on an adjoining site.

The effect of these developments can be seen in the 1891 census returns. These show a remarkable increase in the number of houses and inhabitants, while a study of residents' birthplaces reveal that they were born in neary every county of England except five northern counties. An immediate effect of the rapid population increase was to divide the town into two parishes. St. John's Church, built in 1882, became the centre of a second parish created two years later in 1884. This new situation led not only to two enumeration districts but two distinct communities, with some residents seldom venturing up or down Church Hill or Waller Lane.

CATERHAM ON THE HILL

Between 1841 and 1870 the traditional community on the Hill developed slowly. Imposing houses were built in Whyteleafe Road and Stanstead Road, including Portley, Essendene and Woodside, adjoining 'Woodlands', owned by Lloyds underwriter Joseph Street. Properties standing in 1841 were enlarged. Miss Buckstone's property, renamed 'The Buxtons', was occupied in 1891 by Harry Mitchell, a vulcanised-fibre merchant.

'Woodlands', Harestone Lane, now (1997) a nursing home.

After 1870 open fields and common lands west of the village street were covered not only by two sprawling institutions but by rows of small terraced houses built to accommodate workers and tradespeople. Gladden Cottages, named after the builder, Woodville Place, Alma Terrace and the appropriately-named Asylum View appeared on local maps. In Coulsdon Road were found asylum attendants, soldiers, brickmakers, stationary engine drivers, fitters and stokers together with innumerable general labourers. It is not surprising that five new public houses were opened.

With so many opportunities for employment, trade prospered. In 1884 Robert Vigar, fire brigade captain and master blacksmith, built his new forge and ironmonger's shop in Town End. His former workshop was soon rented by Devon-born fishmonger John Greenslade, who had previously worked in Croydon. Linford Balch inherited his father's tailoring business, but transferred to a larger double-fronted house in the High Street at the corner of Park Road, letting two rooms to the Revd. Frederick Bright, St. Mary's Church curate. Nearer the Asylum, front rooms were converted to tobacconists' and general dealers'. James Bunce, an Asylum tailor, also sold newspapers from 9 Hope Cottages with son George, age 14, as newsboy.

Families living in outlying hamlets seemed hardly affected by these momentous changes. George Skinner of Stanstead Cottage by *The Harrow*, his brother Albert, and father-in-law Isaac Dodd, from nearby Hollidays Bottom, were all born in the parish. They were three of only six heads of household in the town whose wives and children were also born in Caterham.

THE METROPOLITAN ASYLUM

The Metropolitan District Asylum for the Reception of Imbeciles and Chronic Harmless Lunatics listed 126 officers, 927 male and 1065 female patients resident on 5th April 1891.

Each patient is listed individually. The first entry shows 70 year-old George Bolton, an imbecile, single, general labourer, his birthplace not known. In the column relating to infirmity, inmates were classified imbecile or lunatic, stating whether or not from childhood. Where appropriate an annotation blind, deaf or dumb was added.

The patients were under the supervision of superintendent Dr. George Ellis, assisted by two other registered medical practitioners. Elizabeth Moseley, 60 year-old head matron, had two granddaughters living with her, both deaf and dumb. Her assistant matron, four head attendants, 23 male and 45 female attendants were noted. Resident staff worked in the kitchens, laundries or carried out domestic duties organised by housekeeper Martha Coates.

The Metropolitan District Asylum, later renamed St. Lawrence's Hospital

The Asylum was planned to be self-sufficient. This was reflected in two important appointments. William Jones, the farm bailiff, was in charge of the 100-acre farm and John Barker from Crockham Hill, head gasman, was responsible for the complicated gas and hot water system shared with the Barracks.

THE BARRACKS

Captain T.W. Gunton, chief resident officer, sent in the census statistics for the Guards' Depot for Recruits, but curiously he was not resident on census night. There were no officers present, only 629 men. The only army officer from any regiment staying in Caterham was Lieut. Baden-Powell, brother of the founder of the Boy Scout movement, recorded at 5 Providence Villas.

As fourteen soldiers, ranging from 27 to 43 years of age, were in married quarters, it must be assumed that they were sergeants or corporals instructing the recruits. An example is George Nightingale – living with his wife, sister and three daughters including eight year old Florence. Ireland may have been his previous posting, as two year old May was born in Dublin.

Any clues to the identity of the regiments can only be gleaned from soldiers living outside the Depot. George Bone served in the 1st Battalion and Thomas Ison in the 2nd Battalion Coldstream Guards, while the Scots Guards were represented by William Davids of 3 Prospect Cottages.

CATERHAM VALLEY

By 1891 the Valley had been developed beyond recognition. White Nobs Farm, in existence in 1841, was farmed by John Kendell, a 63 year-old Cornishman, but virtually every other property had been built in the intervening 50 years.

According to Kelly's 1891 Directory—

> 'Caterham valley is delightfully situated, many of the houses being built on the hilly ground
> surrounding the valley, which is wooded to the hill tops'.

The census returns show 'Eaton Tower', 'Riddings Court' and 'Kilmarnock Lodge', occupied by a wholesale druggist, an East India merchant and a solicitor, Edmund Chalk, and listed in Tupwood New Road (Harestone Hill). 'Tupwood Lodge', Tupwood Lane, had been built three years earlier in 1888 by James Greville Clarke, replacing Up Wood farmhouse listed in the 1841 census. The farm was originally purchased by his father, James Clarke, the nonconformist publisher, who later bought Beech Hanger, from where he promoted the transfer in 1884 of the Congregational College (Caterham School) from Lewisham to Caterham.

This move had been supported by William Garland Soper, described in the census returns as an Australian merchant with a BA degree. 'Harestone', his splendid residence, dominated the Valley. Designed by architect John Sulman, it required a large staff to maintain it. Two cooks, a kitchenmaid, parlourmaid, housemaid and nurse comprised the female resident staff. It was also the only establishment to boast a footman, 17 year-old George Simmons born in Caterham. Coachman William Ashdown lived in one gate lodge, assisted by two grooms living above the stables. The second lodge was assigned to farm bailiff Albert Wood.

These servants would have been augmented by local labour, perhaps from Orchard Cottages, for the work undertaken by the occupants of these seventeen Godstone Road cottages reflects very clearly part of the town's character. Bricklayers, carpenters, painters, plumbers and the eight gardeners would have been employed building and maintaining the new houses and gardens. James Kilby, fly driver, lived at No 11. Three doors away was postman William Barber from Beccles, Suffolk, with sons William and James. The baker, grocer's assistant and 13 year-old butcher's boy, Horace Humphrey, would have worked in the local shops which relied on the more affluent households for their livelihood.

William Edmunds, parish overseer, whose store in The Square adjoined the *Old Surrey Hounds* advertised in the 1891 Directory:

> 'Wholesale & family grocer, wine, spirit & provision merchant, patent & homeopathic medicines,
> perfumery & general household sundries, with a branch in Westerham, Kent.'

The Square had become the focal point for the growing community. This was recognised by Charles Asprey of 'Beechlands', described as a retired dressing-case maker. In November 1890 as befitted the chairman of Caterham & District Gas Co. he had donated a drinking-water fountain surmounted by the town's first gas lamp. The first buildings in The Square were the railway station and hotel, erected in 1856 and designed 'in the old English style of domestic architecture'. To these had been added Kilby's stables and Lloyds Bank. Elliff & Martin's estate office, still standing opposite the station, had been transferred from Richard Martin's home (now the East Surrey Museum). The new police station in Timber Hill Road was manned by Sergeant James Brice and Constable Joseph Wedge on census night, guarding one prisoner, Mary Gibbs, a female agricultural labourer from Jersey.

Traditional country trades were still essential. George Tremain, conveniently positioned near Kilby's stables, described himself as blacksmith, ironmonger, wheelwright and coachmaker. By 1891 he had shrewdly opened a second business on the Hill.

Tradespeople and gentry from both Hill and Valley were united in their efforts to promote the town. Their names, faithfully recorded in the *Caterham Free Press*, were on subscription lists for churches, chapels, the hospital and public hall, where in 1893 – two years after the census – the splendid Industrial, Fine Art & Loan Exhibition was held.

Richard Martin's house, now the East Surrey Museum, at
N° 1 Stafford Road. It was formerly a dentist's surgery.

SOURCES

Census Returns – 1841: HO-107-1077/10 – 1891: RG-12-582 & 584

Parish Registers – St. Mary's Church, Caterham

Kelly's Post Office Directories for Surrey

Caterham Free Press and *Caterham Weekly Press*

For further information see:

Census Returns – 1851, 1861, 1871 & 1881

Tooke, J. (1982) Who was Who in 1851. Bourne Society *Local History Records* **21**:5-14

Tooke, J. (1985) Caterham – 100 Years Ago. Bourne Society *Local History Records* **24**:4-15

Tooke, J. (1986) Caterham's Great Exhibition of 1893. Bourne Society *Local History Records* **25**:16-23

Tooke, J. (1988) *Bygone Caterham*. Phillimore.

Tooke, J. & Packham R. (1986) *Caterham in Old Picture Postcards*. European Library.

Building the New Huts Guards Depot 1914

The New Buildings. Guards Depot.

Chapter 8

The Great War 1914 - 1918

by Basil Hebben

1914

On Bank Holiday Monday, 3rd August 1914, it was clear that the annual influx of trippers from London was down in numbers. After rumours spreading over several weeks people seemed to sense that war was coming; there was a feeling of expectation in the air.

DECLARATION OF WAR

On 4th August, as a result of Treaty obligations arising from the German invasion of Belgium, Britain declared war on Germany. Within a week the Royal Proclamation, calling up Army Reservists, had been posted at Caterham Railway Station. This brought a spontaneous outburst of patriotism; crowds gathered in the Square, sang the National Anthem and cheered enthusiastically.

VOLUNTARY WAR EFFORT

Appeals were made for volunteers to serve in the St. John Ambulance Brigade, as Special Constables, to join the National Reserve and to become members of working parties which would knit, sew and make bandages. Women residents of both Hill and Valley formed a Voluntary Aid Detachment under the British Red Cross Society. By the end of September a significant proportion of the population had become involved in some branch or other of voluntary war effort.

The plight of the Belgian people was not forgotten and refugees were welcomed to Caterham. A Committee was formed and found accommodation for these homeless foreigners, some in Sylva House off Waller Lane. Harrowing accounts were told of their experiences and escapes when their country was overrun by the invading German Army.

MILITARY CASUALTIES

On 14th September Lt. E. C. DAUN, serving with the 2nd Btn Royal Sussex Regiment, was killed in action. He was the first man from Caterham to be killed in the war. He died at the Battle of the Aisne as the British Expeditionary Force, having held up the German Army's advance at the River Marne, counter-attacked and put the Germans on the defensive. [For a detailed study of Caterham's casualties in the Great War see *The Soldiers of Caterham 1914-1918* by Peter Saaler.]

Casualty lists were now appearing with depressing regularity in local newspapers. On 24th October it was reported that a Caterham man, 1st Class Stoker W. D. WHITE, was missing when HMS *Hawke* was torpedoed in the North Sea. A month later two more Caterham sailors were lost when HMS *Bulwark* blew up at Sheerness.

POPULATION EXPANSION

The war brought a rapid increase in personnel at Caterham Barracks both from the call-up of reservists and volunteers for Lord Kitchener's New Army. Kitchener, the Minister of War, appealed to the public to assist soldiers under training by encouraging hard work and sobriety and begged everyone to avoid treating soldiers to alcoholic drinks and to help them to resist 'temptations'.

FIRST CIVILIAN CASUALTY

In November it was reported that, following a reduction in the amount of lighting allowed, the death had occurred one night of a pedestrian, Mrs HANNAH DUNN, who had been hit by a motor-cycle. The accident had taken place near a point where one of the street lamps had been extinguished. Mrs DUNN might be regarded as the first Caterham civilian casualty of the war.

INVASION THREAT

A meeting was held in December at the Drill Hall in the Valley to establish a local unit of the Volunteer Training Corps. The VTC was raised to meet what was considered at the time to be the real threat of invasion.

ALL OVER BY CHRISTMAS

As the end of the year approached, initial optimistic hopes faded. Kitchener's gloomy forecast of a long war was coming true.

1915

The first winter on the Western Front brought an end to the war of movement as both sides dug themselves in. From now on it would be trench warfare, success depending more on massed artillery and machine-guns rather than infantry skill-at-arms.

RISING PRICES

In January the Retail Food Price showed an increase of 18% over July 1914; the *Weekly Press* commented on increased costs of fuel and food and on profiteering arising from shortages. Inevitably there had been the few, with the money to do so, who from the outset of the war had bought up stocks of food, some even making special visits to London for the purpose.

ZEPPELIN RAIDS

Following the first Zeppelin raid on towns in Norfolk in January, the rather sketchy defences were hastily reviewed and, to protect London, a mobile defence force was improvised with a headquarters at Newmarket. Soon afterwards a section was detached to operate from White Hill at Caterham. This local mobile unit consisted of one searchlight and four vehicles each with two high-angle machine-guns.

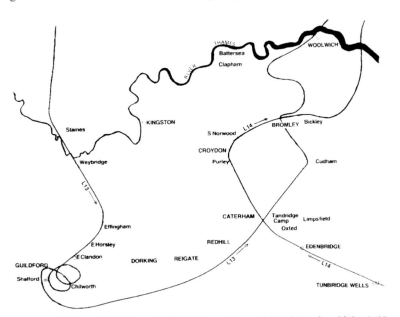

Courses of Zeppelins L13 and L14 during raid on night of October 13/14, 1915.

Whilst several airship raids occurred during the summer it was not until 13th October that two Zeppelins were reported over Caterham – an eyewitness recounted how they passed over at a low altitude, easily seen with the naked eye. One had flown over the Guards' Depot and he thought Caterham being in practically complete darkness had saved the depot from attack. One of the two Zeppelins which flew over Caterham that night dropped several bombs on Croydon, killing nine persons and causing much damage to residential property.

CATERHAM MAN DECORATED FOR BRAVERY

On 4th September it was reported that Caterham Hill man Sgt HARRY YOUNG of the Kings Royal Rifle Corps had been awarded the Distinguished Conduct Medal and the Russian Order of the Cross of St. George.

RECRUITMENT

The *Weekly Press* continued to publish a Weekly Roll of Honour naming those who had joined the Armed Services and voluntary units such as the VTC, St. John Ambulance and British Red Cross Society.

The local newspaper played a significant part in all patriotic activities. It listed contributions to funds designed to alleviate hardship among servicemen's dependants, carried optimistic accounts from serving soldiers, and supported the 'Grand Combined Recruiting March of Three Thousand Officers and Men' held on 14th April.

This campaign, which continued for several weeks, was judged to be successful and by the end of May it was reported that, since the previous August, 800 men from St Mary's and St John's parishes had enlisted out of a total population of 8000. Twelve families in the area had five or more sons in the armed services.

THE SOLDIERS' HOME

The Caterham Soldiers' Home, established in 1898, was situated near the junction of High Street and Chaldon Road. Run on strictly nondenominational and temperance lines, it was supported by the local clergy and provided an alternative for young recruits who might otherwise have been attracted to the numerous public houses. At the Home's Annual Meeting, held in October, the need for the Home to be extended was made clear when it was pointed out that at the Guards' Depot the peacetime strength of 1200 had increased to 15,000. To relieve the pressure on the Soldiers' Home, branches were established at the Drill Hall and at Harestone Hall.

HOSPITAL FOR WOUNDED SOLDIERS

In December the *Weekly Press* announced the opening of a War Hospital, under the British Red Cross, at 'Burntwood' at the top of Burntwood Lane. The property had been offered to the War Office by Mr E. H. COLES and was intended to accommodate 25 beds.

MEETINGS AND ENTERTAINMENTS

WEDNESDAY NEXT.

GRAND COMBINED
RECRUITING MARCH
OF
THREE THOUSAND OFFICERS AND MEN
(By courtesy of the G.O.C. and C.O.'s) from
THE BRIGADE OF GUARDS;
THE "EMPIRE" BATT. ROYAL FUSILIERS;
THE 11th BATT. MIDDLESEX REGT.

ON WEDNESDAY NEXT
(14th APRIL).

THE REGIMENTAL BANDS will accompany the March.
The Column will leave the Guards' Depot at 4 p.m.

BRIG.-GEN. R. H. TWIGG, C.B.
will take the Salute in the Square at 4.15 p.m.

ANY YOUNG MEN in the District who are still hesitating now have another chance, and can give in their names at the Fountain on Wednesday. Fall in behind the Column, and attend afterwards at the Recruiting Office, Drill Hall, Caterham Valley.

THIS IS "THE DAY"!
and
THIS IS THE HOUR!!

DON'T WAIT till you are "MADE TO GO," but do your Duty as a FREE CITIZEN, and help the Old Country through in its hour of trial.

"GOD SAVE THE KING."
cb6

Recruiting advertisement from the *Caterham Weekly Press*, Saturday, 10th April 1915.

Guards Depot - Crystal Palace Naval Depot - April, 1915

'St. Patricks Day.' Caterham. 1915. W.F.W. No. 5.

1916

To relieve the French Army defending Verdun, the BEF attacked on 1st July, the opening of the Battle of the Somme which continued until November. British casualties for the year were over 600,000, nearly 60,000 of these on the first day. At least four of those killed on 1st July were Caterham men.

CONSCRIPTION

With the introduction of compulsory service in the Armed Forces came military-style tribunals to consider exemptions. On 26th June, when 20 cases were heard at Caterham, all were granted exemption subject to joining the Volunteer Training Corps. As the war went on, however, it became progressively more difficult to gain exemption.

'In the public interest' casualty lists stopped showing the identity of a soldier's battalion.

A Guards platoon at Caterham   *ca. 1915*

ST LAWRENCE'S CHURCH TOWER SAVED FROM FIRE

Sparks blown by a high wind were blamed for the fire which occurred on 16th April. Fortunately the Fire Brigade under Captain VIGAR was quickly alerted, rapidly on the scene and the 11th-century church was saved.

FIRE AT THE *OLD SURREY HOUNDS*

Fire broke out in the basement in the early hours of 2nd May when the landlord, Mr. ARTHUR BEARD, was awakened by what sounded like an explosion. His prompt action enabled the occupants to leave safely by knotting sheets together to make their escape from an upstairs window. However, the building was almost totally destroyed.

FOOD PRODUCTION

Seeing that shortages would continue, many householders and organisations took up growing vegetables for their own use. Caterham School joined the 'Grow Your Own' movement and even enjoyed success when they won awards for their exhibits at the Godstone Show. The keeping of poultry and rabbits also became popular.

CATERHAM VALLEY CINEMA

The cinema continued to be popular with its usual offering of an evening film show. Occasionally a wartime documentary would be included.

Unusually, for three evenings in July, the cinema presented a film and slide lecture by Mr. Kennedy Ellis entitled 'My experiences with the German Army in the Field'. This was not quite what it seemed – Mr. Ellis had been the proprietor of an hotel in Namur, Belgium, which was overrun by the Germans.

The *Weekly Press* reported in September that the authorities had visited the cinema to check the audience for deserters or call-up dodgers – but none was found.

AIR RAIDS

On 3rd September watchers at Caterham saw the destruction of the Zeppelin brought down in flames over Cuffley by Lt. W. Leefe-Robinson, Royal Flying Corps, who was awarded the Victoria Cross for his exploit.

Later in the month – on 24th – two Zeppelins were brought down over Essex. One of these airships had been reported by Caterham Police, and four bombs were dropped in the Purley area.

A further success against the Zeppelins followed on 1st October. Encouraged by the earlier events, many people gathered on the hills and were watching the searchlights when a ball of light was seen in the sky over north London. As if by magic the light burst into great brilliance, and a cheer went up as the blazing mass fell to earth. This Zeppelin fell at Potters Bar.

1917

The Germans intensified the war at sea; the number of Allied ships sunk increased from 468 (1915), 1157 (1916) to 2673 ships lost in 1917. Food and other imports were drastically affected and inevitably shortages led to rationing.

PRIVATE MOTORING

From February, when petrol licences were suspended, virtually all private motoring ceased. Petrol was now available only for official purposes and on a reduced scale of allowance.

BLINDED EX-SERVICEMEN

On 6th March a concert was held at the Drill Hall in aid of the St. Dunstan's Appeal. The concert was presented by blinded artistes of the National Institute for the Blind and was very well attended. The evening was concluded by a presentation of the work of St Dunstan's Hostel and a total of £333 was raised.

FOOD ECONOMY EXHIBITION

For some months the *Caterham Weekly Press* had devoted considerable space to the need for everyone to grow their own vegetables and local authorities had also taken increasing interest. The Food Economy Exhibition held in Whitsun week at the Drill Hall provided a focal point, and all aspects of food economy were illustrated with contributions from foodstuff traders and a cookery presentation by the Caterham Urban Electric Supply Company. As an alternative method of cooking, the Hay Box was demonstrated.

The Caterham area was assuming the appearance of a garrison town with the Guards' Barracks on the Hill, 17th (Empire Battalion) Royal Fusiliers at Warlingham, and the 11th (Public Schools' Battalion) Middlesex Regiment at Woldingham.

In the *Caterham Weekly Press* of 21st November appeared an advertisement for the new Dining, Tea and Supper Rooms to be opened in Croydon Road, Caterham Valley – to be called 'The Mons' (after the first major battle of the BEF near the Belgian town of this name).

A determined lady (possibly Ms Florence Lloyd) alongside the Soldiers
Rooms and school chapel in William Road, opened in 1901

FUEL AND FOOD RATIONING

From September onwards rationing was introduced on a national basis. By the year end coal, sugar and bacon were included, with butter, margarine and tea supplies subject to local rationing (within six months these commodities were also under the national rationing scheme). With the start of rationing came the fixing of meat and milk prices.

TANKS

These new armoured and tracked war machines had been used for the first time in September 1916 and had immediately caught the imagination of the public. Local people who so wished could have seen the film *Advance of the Tanks* at the Picture Pavilion at Redhill, in January.

In July, Caterham had its chance of seeing at close quarters what a tank looked like. An exact replica of a tank had been made, and this was drawn through the town. The replica was complete in all details including its own guns.

ROYAL VISIT

King George V inspected the Irish Guards at Caterham Barracks in November and showed particular interest in the cookhouse where a number of female cooks were now employed.

BUNCE BROTHERS – CATERHAM'S PHOTOGRAPHERS

When George and Herbert Bunce established themselves at Westway they soon found that much of their activity was centred on the Guards' Depot. Good relations were established, and with the wartime influx of recruits business boomed. In 1917 when George Bunce joined the Royal Naval Air Service the business was carried on by Herbert, now assisted by George's wife. The photographers' work was particularly appreciated by the soldiers' mothers and sweethearts. A photograph was a long-lasting souvenir and keepsake of war service, of especial importance where the soldier became a casualty of the war.

1918

After initial success the German spring offensive was halted. Gradually the Allies – now joined by the Americans – turned the tide of battle, leading to the signing of the Armistice on 11th November and the cessation of hostilities.

PAPER SHORTAGE

In February the *Caterham Weekly Press* was forced to follow its earlier reduction from six pages to four with a reduction of the number of copies printed each week. In July, by acquiring a supply of pink newsprint, the paper was restored to its original six pages.

COMMUNAL RESTAURANTS

To lessen the impact of food rationing, especially on poorer people, two 'National Kitchens' were opened – at Chaldon Road and in the Valley. A three-course meal cost around 10d depending on choice of vegetables. 265 portions were served at the Chaldon Road kitchen on its opening day, rising to 365 on the second day.

YOUNGEST CATERHAM SERVICEMAN

Private BENJAMIN PAYNE, of Park Road, was killed in action in France on 26th April. He was probably the youngest Caterham lad to join up. He was only 15¼ when he enlisted in the Army Service Corps in 1914. After 15 months' service on the Western Front he was returned to England and subsequently transferred to the Durham Light Infantry. Going back to France, he was killed before his 19th birthday.

WAR WEAPONS WEEK

During the second week of July much effort was devoted to selling National War Bonds. Caterham optimistically aimed for £40,000 to be subscribed as the Air Ministry would name an aeroplane after the town for this achievement. 'Aeroplane Banks' were opened on the Hill and in the Valley to sell the Bonds. Whilst the actual amount collected was just £30,000 the authorities nevertheless said a plane would be identified with Caterham. *Caterham Weekly Press* clearly liked the idea of 'the Caterham machine flying over enemy lines and giving the Huns a fright by treating them in the same way as they have so cruelly treated the civilian population in our country'.

FUND-RAISING APPEALS

Hardly a month went by without at least one appeal on behalf of a voluntary organisation, for example the Cottage Hospital, Roehampton Appeal, Primrose League, Smokes for the Wounded and many others.

FRENCH AWARD TO A CATERHAM WOMAN

It was reported in November that Mrs. ASSHETON-BENNETT of Whitehill Gardens had been awarded the *Croix de Guerre* for her service with the French Red Cross as a motor ambulance driver, in connection with the great retreat in March.

CATERHAM SOLDIER DIED AT SEA

Cpl. ARTHUR HEWITT of Park Road was serving with the Military Foot Police on duty on the Irish Mail Packet *Leinster* when she was torpedoed in the Irish Sea on 10th October. At 6'5", Corporal HEWITT was regarded as one of the giants of the British Army. He had already survived being wounded twice in France.

ARMISTICE SIGNED

In reporting the celebrations following the Armistice on 11th November, the *Weekly Press* respected the subdued reactions of most of the general population; no one could forget the large numbers of young men who had laid down their lives serving their country. However, a large party of mainly American airmen marched down to the Valley from Kenley Aerodrome with their jazz band playing all sorts of popular ragtime tunes.

WAR DISABLED

On 30th November an appeal was made for walking sticks for wounded servicemen.

CHRISTMAS CELEBRATIONS

By common consent nearly all the traders on the Hill and in the Valley made strenuous efforts to decorate and stock-up their shops for the Christmas period.

At last, too, the churches were able to celebrate with the ringing of bells, not allowed during wartime.

Childhood in the Thirties

The author with his big brother during the construction
of Newstead Rise

Chapter 9

Childhood in the Thirties

by John Bailey-Smith

My father, Albert, was a partner with his father and brother, Ralph, in the family firm of J.A.Smith & Sons (builders and decorators) at 11 Godstone Road, Caterham. Granddad was a master signwriter by trade and had moved south, first to Catford in 1900 and then to Caterham in 1907. I was born on Monday, 11th August 1930. I had an elder brother, Albert, who was six years older than I was and who attended St. Francis' RC School in Essendene Road.

**My father and uncle Ralph in the doorway of the family
business at 11 Godstone Road, Caterham.**

I don't remember much of my pre-school days other than being taken to watch the building of the houses in Newstead Rise which were being built by father now trading as A. Smith & Sons (Builders) Ltd, his father having retired. My grandfather's retirement had been made possible by my grandmother's foresight. During the depression in the late 1920s she had purchased 'every roll of wallpaper in the south of England' and in the 1930s, when the economy improved, she 'sold for 6d and a shilling a roll what she had bought for a farthing and a halfpenny'. This enormous stock of paper was stored in a warehouse at the back of 11 Godstone Road. Although not wealthy, we had a comfortable lifestyle and my father could afford to run a Lagonda open tourer; this meant my brother and I had no shortage of friends who were only too pleased to accompany us on trips to the newly opened Whipsnade Zoo or the seaside.

I attended The Winnats Prep School run by my Aunt Margery before going on to St. Francis' School in September 1935. Our lives, alas, were to be turned upside down when my father went bankrupt in 1936. My only memories of this are that it was an unhappy time, that we did not go on outings any more, and that food was not always so plentiful. Perhaps the most abiding memory is of asking for a pot of jam at the little shop in Beechwood Road run by Mrs. West. I can still see her leaning over the counter and saying 'I'm sorry but can you tell your mother that she can't have anything more until she has paid her bill'. My father supported us for some time by working as a carpenter and undertaking odd jobs and as he was both conscientious and skilful we survived.

My first two years at St. Francis' were in the infants' section, which was a room attached to the church, and the teacher was a Miss Walsh. Miss Walsh was a very fierce lady who seemed to take delight in frightening her small charges by constantly threatening to cut our tongues out if we were slow or were guilty of the slightest misbehaviour. She would take out a clean duster, lay a pair of shiny scissors on top and then put the kettle to boil on the cast iron stove that provided the heating. We were terrified of her and although we used to reassure each other that she wouldn't dare to carry out her threat we were never quite certain. While I was in the infants' I was accompanied to school by my brother Albert, who first got me into the habit of walking to school. Our mother gave us the money to pay our bus fares from the stop at the Cottage Hospital which used to be at the corner of Beechwood Gardens and Croydon Road, and the single-decker bus would take us to the *Golden Lion* leaving us just a short walk to school. My brother, however, got me to walk the whole way – going via the bridge over the railway line, into Stafford Road, up the incline into Milner Road, then up Milner Close to 'The Slopes'. The steep path followed by the even steeper flight of steps was a challenge for a five year old, but I am sure that it helped develop the strong legs that have stood me in good stead for some 60 years since.

Having walked to school, after school we would walk home via the High Street, Waller Lane and Croydon Road, although this often entailed having to fight our way past the boys from the Dene School. The Dene was a private school in the building now part of the hospital and standing adjacent to Waller Lane; the boys considered themselves superior to us, and also we were 'Valley boys'. The walk down Waller Lane could be quite magical in summer as there were many red squirrels in the giant beech trees whose boughs interlaced overhead, and at the junction with Church Hill there was a huge rookery which would be a scene of activity and noise. Alas, the building of the block of flats and the increase in traffic drove the rooks away, and when the great storm of 1987 felled many of the giant beeches the red squirrels had long since departed.

The Square in summer would be filled with swallows and martins which nested under the eaves of the surrounding buildings; now there are just a few pairs. Having reached the Valley we would head for Bromley Hall's which stood at the corner of Timber Hill Road and the Square, and supplied animal feed of all kinds. The owner, Mr. Prescott, would deliver the larger items in his pony and trap, which was stabled at the rear of the premises next to the police station. The attraction here was the large parrot which lived in the front of the shop and fascinated us small boys with its raucous greeting of 'hello'. The shop had a glorious smell of the various foodstuffs, dog biscuits, maize, corn etc, all stored in large sacks. Having tired of saying 'hello' to the parrot, we would walk on to Dorothy's Café, which was just past Woolworth's, in order to spend our bus fares on home-made Turkish Delight, something I still enjoy to this day. Most of my friends attended the Beechwood Road Primary School, and treated my long walk to school with a mixture of amazement and envy. The envy was caused by the thought that I could escape parental supervision for several hours, whereas living but an hundred yards from the school they could never have any excuse for being late home.

Our free time was often spent either playing in one another's houses or gardens, usually combining our Hornby Dublo train sets or vying to build the best structures with our Meccano sets. Our next door neighbours, the Skinners, had a garden shed and this was our 'den', the place we could escape to in wet weather. Many happy hours were spent playing with steam engines, although I can't think what we actually did with them other than feed them methylated spirits and watch the flywheel whiz round. As we grew older this innocent enjoyment changed to fiercely competitive games of pontoon and brag, initially using matchsticks as stakes but with increasing affluence, money. If the games became too heated, parental attention might be drawn and hasty explanations invented to allay any suspicion that we 'were up to no good'.

CHILDHOOD IN THE THIRTIES

Our playground was the Marden Park Estate which stretched eastwards from the top of Beechwood Gardens to Oxted and from Wapses Lodge southward to Flower Lane in Godstone. The Estate was renowned for its breeding of shire horses and these magnificent animals did much of the work, tractors being used mainly for ploughing. These vast acres provided a wonderful playground, trees to be climbed, camps to be built and games of 'tracking' to be enjoyed. At Paddock Barn there was a large Dutch barn, usually well stocked with bales of straw, which made a snug place to shelter, hide or play; there was an old 'stage coach' which provided a wonderful basis for numerous games.

We also liked helping the farm staff and we became quite expert at 'stooking' – this was the piling of the sheaves of cut corn into lines with three a side and one at each end. I discovered years later that the pattern of stooking varied from county to county. When the corn had dried it would be loaded onto large carts (wains) and towed by a pair of shires to the place where it would be built into a rick. Riding on the horses was one of the great thrills, our little legs poking out sideways on their broad backs. Occasionally someone fell, but I don't remember any serious accident and there was no Health and Safety Executive to spoil our fun. Grinding up turnips in the winter for cattle feed may seem rather tame to today's generation but it was healthy exercise with a purpose and we would undertake it with a will, as we did any of the jobs. Threshing the corn was another high point, because we could help toss the sheaves up to the 'feeder' on the threshing machine or, being horrid little boys, wield clubs to kill the many mice that emerged from the rick as it was gradually demolished.

One abiding memory is of helping at Hill Boxes Farm where my friend Jim Cowie lived, his father being the Farm Manager to the Estate. It was a warm day and we were building a rick. After lunch I fell asleep on top of the rick and Mr. Cowie took four pitchforks and quietly pinned my ankles and wrists down. When I woke I couldn't move and this gave much amusement to the others, and the opportunity for the other boys to take unwarranted liberties while I was unable to defend myself.

Christmas 1936 was the time of the abdication crisis and there was much singing of 'Hark the herald angels sing, Mrs. Simpson's pinched our King'. Just before this the Crystal Palace had burnt down and although we were some distance off, the glow in the sky was quite vivid and, of course, very exciting to a small boy.

In May 1937 came the coronation of George VI which was the cause of great excitement; after all, there hadn't been a coronation for some 25 years so it was a novelty to much of the population. There was much exhibiting of flags and we had a large one on a blue pole fixed under our bedroom window at the front of the house. Shops were similarly decorated and did special displays and I seem to remember a grand firework display on Timber Hill.

In September 1937 I moved to the main school in Essendene Road and my brother went to John Fisher School in Purley, leaving me to make the long walk to and from school on my own. In those days a wooden stockade stood beside the school; this was the village pound where stray cattle and horses were put, except there weren't any in 1937! My new teacher was Miss Enright, a young Irish girl who was totally different from Miss Walsh as she was kind, made classes interesting and seemed to have no problem in keeping control – probably because we all adored her. She had a great love of nature which she communicated to us children, no doubt making us rather more civilised than many of our age group. I don't remember who took the next class up, that is the 10 and 11 year olds, but the headmistress, Miss Beesley, took the top class, the 12 and 13 year olds. Miss Beesley was known as 'Beeswax' and I remember her as a tall, thin woman with glasses and hair in a bun. Our contact with her was very limited, but she seemed to be respected by the older boys.

On my walk home down the High Street I would sometimes pause, with nose pressed against the window, at Mason's Toy Shop which was at No. 61. I probably bought my first Dinky toys there as well as the latest additions to the Meccano range, and as Mr. Mason knew my father I was always on my best behaviour.

I had two years of my lonely walk to and from school. It was during this period that the Caterham bypass was being built, and from the lofty viewpoint at the top of 'The Slopes' I could survey the northern progress. The bypass also provided a weekend playground, as tip-up trucks were used to transport the excavated chalk from the southern end to build the embankments necessary from the bridge along to Wapses Lodge. The trucks were left at the southern end on Friday night ready for filling on Monday. However, naughty boys soon discovered that there was a downhill slope and that a truck once moving would trundle at an increasing speed at least to the curve beyond where there is now an underpass. Why nobody was seriously injured I feel must be sheer luck. We collected many cuts and grazes in leaping from trucks before they derailed on the bend. There was a watchman, but he was too old and slow to be effective.

Saturday mornings were frequently spent at the *Capitol* cinema where the usual diet of cowboy films was eagerly digested along with quantities of sweets and apples. A favourite was Palm Banana Split toffee, which was purchased from Wood's bakery in Croydon Road at the junction with Beechwood Road, where Mrs. Wood – a large lady with a mop of white hair – would break the large slabs of toffee with a small hammer. This toffee was very hard and needed to be sucked for some time before one could chew it, sticking one's teeth together and being generally delicious! From time to time trouble broke out in the cinema and the manager and staff would frantically try and restore order, although most of it was just noise and high spirits caused by the hurling of apple cores and other minor missiles.

Occasionally we would be taken up to London by our parents, not on the train but by bus to Purley and then a 'shilling all day' on the tram. This gave us great freedom as arriving at the Embankment we could travel by tram right across London whether to the Science Museum, Madame Tussaud's or the Zoo, all for a shilling! Another favourite outing was to Croydon Airport to see the big passenger biplanes, Hannibal, Horsa, Hercules, etc. with the smaller de Havilland Rapides and many other aircraft. Alas this idyll was about to come to a close from 3rd September 1939 with the war, blackout, blitz and rationing.

Croydon Airport and a Handley Page Hannibal passenger biplane

Also in September 1939 my life took another turn; my father now being in regular employment, he was able to send me to John Fisher School to start in the Prep. school and, of course, a few days earlier war had been declared. To us small boys the thought of war was very exciting; to our fathers who had survived World War I it was a rather more grim prospect. Despite John Fisher being close to Croydon Aerodrome I started there in the second week of September, travelling by bus to Purley. I was once more with my brother walking to school,

CHILDHOOD IN THE THIRTIES

Trying on our gas masks at St. Francis School in June 1939
The author is second from left, the one who wouldn't take his pullover off

from Purley Fountain up Foxley Lane to Peaks Hill Rise and school in order to save the bus fare on the 234 single-decker. The change from a small single-storey school to a rambling two-storey building was quite daunting.

Something the war ended was the Empire Day celebrations and the regular Sports Days. On Empire Day the children would gather round the school flagpole which would be flying the Union Jack and sing patriotic songs. The songs would be Rudyard Kipling's 'Land of our birth we pledge to thee' and 'I vow to thee my country', all sung with immense pride bearing in mind that much of the map of the world was coloured pink showing the extent of the British Empire. There were also celebrations on Timber Hill recreation ground, consisting of displays and fireworks. Sports Days were held at White Knobs recreation ground, and continued after the war for a time but ceased some time in the 1950s. They attracted quite large crowds and many entries to the various events – running, cycling, children's competitions and tug-o-war between local teams. There would usually be displays by the Fire Brigade, St. John Ambulance, Scouts and, of course, the Brigade of Guards whose training depot was on the Hill. The various sporting events provided the opportunity for the local lads to display their prowess (or just show off) in front of the girls, leading to much rivalry and boasting and too often ending with feeble excuses. Strangely I seem to remember that it was the slow bicycle race that created some of the keenest interest.

Caterham's War — 1939-1945

World War II Wardens' Posts

Above – this one was demolished in 1992 to make way for landscaping the new development on the corner of Whyteleafe Hill and Hornchurch Hill.

Below – this one, preserved in good order, is in a garden in Caterham on the Hill.

Chapter 10

Caterham's War — 1939-1945

by Patrick Jones

By the spring of 1939 there was a growing realisation in the country that all was not well in Europe, and that war could find us unprepared and vulnerable. The Government and the District Council put into motion plans for such an eventuality; Pelham House in Harestone Valley Road was selected for use as the Chief ARP (Air Raid Precautions) centre. Structural alterations were made, doors and windows were sandbagged and another entrance from the road made to allow easy access for ambulances and other vehicles. The siting of over 50 public air raid shelters was decided, together with wardens' posts and other vital communication and rescue centres.

**This surface shelter, still standing in Queen's Park, was typical of the
emergency shelters provided to accommodate about 50 persons each.**

Caterham was originally designated as a Category II area; this meant that no evacuation of local people would be arranged under the official scheme and it would not be a receiving area for evacuees. No account seemed to have been taken of the proximity of Kenley, Croydon and Biggin Hill aerodromes, nor the strategic implications of Redhill and West Malling airfields.

Air raid sirens were first tested on 3rd April 1939. They had to be collected from Pelham House by divisional wardens and fitted to cars with 12-volt batteries, which then toured predetermined areas. If no cars with 12-volt batteries were available they were told to obtain batteries – or even cars – from the Caterham Motor Company! Eventually the sirens were installed on buildings such as the Council Offices, and the Post Office provided a system by telephone wires, whereby they could all be activated simultaneously from Pelham House.

Gas masks were issued, though for some months there was a serious shortage of the bellows-type respirators for babies and the colloquially-named 'Mickey Mouse' masks for very young children. Identity cards were issued and ration books were printed. The Government called for volunteers for the new ARP units, firewatchers, heavy rescue, first aid and decontamination units. The District Council transferred workers from their Parks & Gardens and Refuse Departments.

On Friday 1st September 1939 evacuees started to arrive at Caterham Station; four special trains arrived, another four on Saturday, and four again on Sunday. 4300 children and their teachers were shepherded along from the station to the Harestone Hall reception area by ARP workers, Boy Scouts and Girl Guides, where refreshments were organised and served by the members of the WVS and the Harestone Young People's Clubs.

This was followed by a medical examination, then each child was given a bag of biscuits, a ¼lb packet of chocolate, a tin of corned beef and two tins of milk (all supplied by the Ministry but packaged by local volunteers), before being guided to the buses and coaches that would disperse them to the various reception areas. A few days later, Major Stather, the Organising Secretary, received a grateful letter from the Headmaster of Brockley Central Boys' School, countersigned by 22 members of his staff, thanking everyone involved for their 'splendid work on our behalf'.

The blackout was now strictly enforced, pedestrians were advised to wear something white or reflective, the accident rate went up, white lines were painted on the kerbstones, and white bands painted around trees and other obstructions on the pavements.

By the middle of March the District Surveyor reported that 2530 garden shelters (the 'Anderson') had been delivered, out of a total of 3350 requested, but that only about 1200 had actually been erected. There was, he said, 'a marked reluctance by members of the public to erect their own shelters'. However, many people had dug the necessary pits in their gardens only to find that they flooded easily due to bad siting or lack of drainage.

During this period, labelled the 'Phoney War', many of the evacuees returned home. They were missing their families, the fish and chips shop around the corner, and the pub along with the conviviality of lifelong friends and neighbours. The expected air raids had not materialised, and by January 1940 it was estimated that 88% of the mothers who had been evacuated had returned to their homes, taking with them 86% of the children below school age.

An item in the local newspaper related the case of a young soldier from Caterham Barracks, answering a summons in the Magistrates' Court. He had been reported for speeding in the blackout, travelling at 30 to 38 mph when the legal maximum was 20 mph. He was fined £2 and his licence endorsed; the magistrates accepted his explanation that he was hurrying to get back to his barracks before his pass expired at midnight. He had taken advantage of a rare opportunity to play for his club at Arsenal Football Ground – his name was Gunner Denis Compton.

The first reported bomb in the district fell in Whyteleafe Road on 3rd July 1940. There were no casualties. By the end of September bombs had fallen in many parts of Caterham. One – in some reports described as an 'aerial torpedo' – left a huge crater in the grounds of St. Lawrence's Hospital. It uprooted two large trees, throwing one of them over 60 feet to land on the hospital roof. Fortunately there were no casualties and the hospital was not severely damaged, nor did it receive a direct hit at any time afterwards.

In October the King announced the creation of the George Medal, to be given for gallant or meritorious service by civilians. One of the first three to be awarded to women was to **Sonia Straw**, and the warrant read:

> 'In the afternoon of the 1st of September, enemy aircraft dropped bombs on the area of the Guards' Depot in Caterham, Surrey, on the southern outskirts of Croydon, some of them destroying houses in Coulsdon Road and causing casualties.

'Miss Sonia Vera Carlyle Straw, the nineteen years' old daughter of a former Guards' sergeant, is an Air Raid Warden living in a nearby side road. With a number of unexploded bombs in the area, and while bombs were still dropping, she attended a number of badly injured women and children, as well as treating several people suffering from shock. She continued these ministrations entirely on her own, for a considerable period until help arrived.'

On 5th and 6th September 1940 there were heavy raids on London, and on the afternoon of Saturday, 7th September the biggest raid of the war so far took place. Hundreds of bombers and their escorting fighters filled the air, and people on high ground in Caterham watched in dismay as great palls of smoke rose into the blue sky. The watchers in Caterham could also see flames in the sky as the Docks, Woolwich Arsenal and hundreds of factories and houses along the Thames were engulfed. This was the start of the London Blitz which was to continue in all its ferocity for 56 consecutive nights.

In Caterham Salvage Drives were organised – surplus pots and pans made of aluminium were given up to make Spitfires. Other metals, rags and rubber were collected by Boy Scouts and others. The *Capitol* Cinema was a receiving depot for waste paper, and the WVS appealed for wooden cotton reels and medicine bottles.

On 28th November Caterham parishioners learned of the loss of a man who had played a very significant part in the community. Canon John Morris, Rural Dean of Caterham and Vicar of St John's, had passed away in his sleep following a tour of duty at the wardens' post the previous evening. There was hardly an organisation in Caterham that had not benefited from his influence in addition to his considerable pastoral commitments.

National Savings Weeks were launched – people were asked to put money into War Bonds, Defence Bonds and National Savings to help finance the war effort. In February, the Caterham & Warlingham Urban District Council set a target of £100,000 for the planned 'War Weapons Week'. The response exceeded all expectations and the final total saved was £426,421.

There were many Canadian soldiers stationed in Caterham and in the early hours of 6th May one of them walking along Godstone Road noticed a glow in one of the basement windows of the Surrey Hills Hotel, known locally as 'The Hydro'. On investigation he could smell smoke, and realised that flames were beginning to penetrate the heavy blackout curtains. He alerted some of his compatriots nearby, who called the fire brigade and assisted him in raising the alarm and evacuating the occupants. Four men and three women perished in the blaze, including Mrs Doris Ponting, the proprietress.

A month before this fire, a Mrs Page had persuaded the Council to let her have the use of an empty shop at 25 Station Avenue, and she appealed to the public to donate goods, old or new, for sale to raise money for the 'Spitfire Fund'. It operated in much the same way as charity shops do today, and Mrs Page, aided by an energetic band of helpers from the WVS etc, set herself a target of £1000.

On 19th September, the Scouting Association announced the award of its Certificate of Gallantry to Cub Scout **John Messer**, aged 12 years. The following account was given in a local newspaper:

'While an air raid was in progress he was sheltering under a table with some younger members of his family when the house was badly damaged by a bomb falling close by. He first moved theother children into a cupboard under the stairs, then went for assistance. The Civil Defence workers who returned to the house with him reported that they found the children safe and unharmed and "as snug and as warm as a brood in a nest".

Having given the adults an address to which the children could be moved for safety, John accompanied them there and then returned to his house to obtain bedding for them. The wardens said throughout he had showed no sign of panic or fear, which they said was "... no doubt, due to his training to remain cool and courageous in such an emergency".'

Late in 1941 the Government was encouraging the establishment of community restaurants, to ensure that people away from home during the day, especially war workers and school children, would be able to have a nourishing meal at a reasonable price. In Caterham –, after weeks of preparation – a British Restaurant opened at 59 Croydon Road, and the following display advertisement appeared in the local press:

British Restaurant

59 Croydon Road   Caterham

(Over Caterham Motor Company's new Premises)

CAFETERIA SERVICE, 12 noon - 2.30 p.m. EXCEPT SUNDAY

TARIFF

Soup	2d
Main Course	7d
Main Course (small)	4d
Sweet	2d
Bread	1d
Tea	1d

NOW OPEN

The overall costs of the establishment, such as lighting, heating and wages, were subsidised by the Council, but this was not necessary for a meal totalling about a shilling, which cost under 5d to produce.

To foster public interest, the District Council decided to 'adopt' a ship already in commission, HMS *Carnation*. The news had just been announced that the British Empire Medal had been awarded to three of her crew-members for service in the action in which HMS *Cossack* had been sunk. A commemorative plaque, made of oak, was presented to the vessel for mounting on display on the bridge. Bearing the coat of arms of the District Council, the inscription below read 'To commemorate the adoption of HMS *Carnation* by the citizens of Caterham & Warlingham Urban District Council, Warship Week, February, 1942'. (This is probably the plaque that is now in store in the East Surrey Museum).

At this time Mrs Page was in danger of losing her 'Spitfire Shop'; the Council wanted to repossess the premises for use as a Civil Defence depot and offices. Although in poor health, she had no intention of giving up until her target had been reached, and vowed to set up stalls on the pavement to sell her goods. Fortunately, she was able to move in to 8 Croydon Road, formerly Knight's the butcher's. The rear of the shop and the upper floors were already in use by the WVS and Mrs Page was able to continue there until the £1000 target was reached, when on the insistence of her doctor she had to stand down and the 'Spitfire Shop' closed on 14th August.

One of the most memorable slogans of the war was 'Dig for Victory' – it was attributed to a remark made by Michael Foot MP, according to a writer in the London *Evening Standard*. In November 1942 the District Council launched its 'Dig for Victory' Campaign. Council gardeners and other experienced growers gave demonstrations on how to break new ground, how to plant and sow, and to convince people that there were considerable financial gains in growing their own vegetables. Anyone could do it; even the schoolchildren had allotments where their playing fields used to be.

The plaque presented to Corvette HMS *Carnation*, the vessel adopted by the District Council in 1942

January 1943 saw the formation of the Caterham Sea Cadet Corps and they adopted the name 'TS *Carnation*' for their unit. Miss Letch who, with her sister, owned a drapery store in Westway, volunteered to make a set of signal flags for the Unit for training purposes. Before the end of the month she had completed the 30 constituent flags of the International Code and had started on the 90 flags required for the Naval Code.

After a lull of nearly eighteen months raids were again taking place on London and the south-east of England, twice or even three times a night. On the morning of 18th January many people about in Caterham saw one of the bombers, a Junkers 88, coming down after being attacked over Croydon. It crashed in Town End recreation ground, scattering wreckage over a wide area, but fortunately doing little damage to the houses around. The crew had baled out, but too late for most of them. Two of them crashed through the trees and were found near the wreckage and a third body was found in a nearby nursery garden. These were the pilot – a lieutenant aged 21, a sergeant aged 23 and a corporal aged 18. The fourth member of the crew did bale out successfully and landed three miles away in Whyteleafe; a 16 years old ATC cadet, Fred Ovenden, approached him and indicated that he was under arrest and that he should accompany him to Kenley Police Station. The German made no protest, but before they had gone far, they were met by police and Home Guard personnel and the cadet handed over his prisoner to them. All four crew members were wearing the ribbon of the Iron Cross. The three dead airmen were later buried in Caterham Cemetery with full military honours.

'Save your bones' was an unlikely slogan, but in June there was a drive to save bones for making glue (for aircraft). They were also used extensively in the manufacture of lubricating grease, explosives, fertilisers, and food for cattle, pigs and poultry. Collection bins were fixed to lampposts and a large one was placed in the window of the Fuel Office at 11 Croydon Road.

Presentation of an ambulance outside the Council Offices (Soper Hall) about 1941.
Photo courtesy of Caterham Library

In July, the local Savings Committee declared the 'Wings for Victory' Week as successful as before. A total of £358,881 was invested; enough to pay for eight Halifax bombers. An impressive plaque was awarded to the Savings Committee by the Air Ministry to mark the achievement.

On 5th November 1943 a raid was in progress over Croydon and Mr Arthur Taylor and his wife Catherine were standing at the front door of their house, 107 Croydon Road. While they watched the spectacle in the sky, an 'Ack-ack' shell which had failed to detonate fell in the road outside and exploded – killing them both. Mrs Taylor was a founder member of the Mothers' Union at St. John's Church, and had been very active in the parish.

On 24th March 1944 one of the heaviest raids in this area took place. It was estimated that 175 bombers heading for London were frustrated by the anti-aircraft defences and jettisoned their bomb-loads on Croydon, Bromley and Caterham. High explosive and incendiary bombs caused widespread damage; the roof of the Congregational Church (now the United Reformed Church) in Harestone Hill was hit by at least three incendiary bombs and destroyed by fire. An incendiary bomb fell through the roof of a nearby school, but was extinguished in a bedroom before serious damage occurred.

No one living in the south of England during the spring of 1944 could have failed to realise that 'something was going on', with the movements of heavy vehicles and increased activity in the skies. Caterham bypass was filled from one end to the other with every type of armoured vehicle hidden under camouflage netting. On 6th June people going about their normal daily business felt a sense of calm but with a mixture of expectancy and anxiety. When the radio announced that allied forces had commenced landing on the Normandy coast, there was little cheering or rejoicing.

CATERHAM'S WAR – 1939-1945

Barely a week after 'D-Day', the Germans launched the first of their *Vergeltungswaffen* – or 'Vengeance Weapons'. The first 'Doodlebug' (the colloquial name most popularly used for the V1 flying bomb) to land in Caterham fell on the Acme Photographic Works on the corner of Chaldon Road and Heath Road. The blast caused damage over a wide area and affected as many as 300 houses. Fortunately, over the next four weeks, more than half of the flying bombs that landed in the district fell on open ground.

Of the seven bombs that fell near Tillingdown Farm, the first was too close for comfort for one man who can remember it vividly. Peter Skinner, then only a lad of 13, was in the habit of visiting the RAF personnel manning the barrage balloon site adjacent to the farm. Seeing the Doodlebug descending on what appeared to be a course directly to where they were standing, they all dived into a slit trench under a tree. Seconds later they felt the heat of the exhaust flames as it passed through the top of the tree and exploded on the farm building at the northern corner of the farm, a short distance away. This bomb, although its motor had not cut out, was apparently losing height and had it continued on its way instead of crashing on this high ground, would most likely have fallen on heavily populated parts of Whyteleafe, Kenley or Purley.

When the Allies reached Berlin, the Germans capitulated and 8th May 1945 was declared a national holiday for 'Victory in Europe'. The Japanese Government agreed to an unconditional surrender on 2nd September.

The plaques presented to the District Council following the success of the War Savings Weeks in 1943 and 1944

Post War and into the Future

**A victim of its own success – the busy M25 motorway
at juntion 6 near Caterham**

Chapter 11

Post War and into the Future

by Roger Hammond

If a World War II pilot, returning to Kenley aerodrome in 1945, had flown into a huge white cloud to the south-east of Caterham and suddenly, but unknowingly, been time-transported forward some 50 years – in the manner of H.G. Wells' *Time Machine* – he could be forgiven if, on emerging from the cloud and checking the landscape, he did not realise that the time-shift had taken place.

Generally, residents of Caterham have been largely unaffected by major development or serious landscape changes. Only the broad scar of the M25 motorway would begin to make our pilot start to question his sanity. Only when he dropped down lower would he begin to see that the adjacent conurbations of Caterham Hill and Caterham Valley have undertaken that relentlessly creeping expansion that will eventually weld them into one amorphous conglomerate. Wherever possible landowners and developers have used – many would say abused – back gardens, orchards, woodland plots and empty ground for new houses and group developments. A new inlet here, a new cluster there, with names as creative as their architects' use of the space they occupy. Many of the large and elegant dwellings erected in and around the Caterham area in the Victorian and Edwardian eras still stand impressively, but are now too large for single-family dwellings and are being remodelled into apartment buildings or, in many more cases, into homes for the elderly.

The 'Green Belt' – that precious lifeline of protection from development for animals, birds and the enjoyment and recreation of people – is safe, or so the authorities say, but wherever it exists there are constant attempts to undermine its sanctity. Here and there around the south-east of England a little is lost, the belt is tightened and squeezed, a handshake exchanged and a boundary re-drawn. Local councils are under pressure with ever-tightening budgets and all that lovely open land waiting to be exploited in return for development fees, business rates and council taxes.

ACCESS TO AND FROM CATERHAM

Looking at old photographs taken in and around Caterham in the late 1940s, it is hard to believe that the roads shown are basically the same ones we use in the mid 1990s, subject only to the occasional widening and improvement schemes that have been carried out on them. What is so staggering is the sheer volume of traffic. 50 years on there are cars everywhere, moving or simply parked, along every road. What was once a morning and evening 'rush hour' on city-bound routes has now become the day-long norm on most A- and B-class roads in the area.

The nearby M25 motorway has been a victim of its own success, carrying an almost continuous stream of cars and lorries both day and night, with a concomitant fog of polluting fumes. A relatively small incident can cause major blockages, with jams of stationary cars often exceeding 10 to 15 miles in length. Widening schemes for the M25, from three lanes to four in each direction, commenced early in 1994. Traffic trying to join the M25 motorway from Caterham can often be backed-up onto the Caterham By-pass. Traffic trying to get to Croydon and London from Caterham regularly becomes blocked by 'bottlenecks' along the A22 at Whyteleafe, Kenley and the approach to Purley.

Frustration abounds. To avoid the queues drivers explore every possible short-cut whilst their cohorts hover like hawks waiting to swoop on a newly-discovered route. Thus are born the 'rat-runs' which can turn a quiet residential backwater into a mini-racetrack twice each working day. To compensate residents and reduce traffic speed, more and more residential roads are being fitted with traffic calming measures, such as 'sleeping policemen' (speed-reducing humps) and width restrictions. Traffic-watching cameras are also being introduced at crucial junctions.

'Let the train take the strain', was a slogan coined by British Rail for their 'Awayday' fares in 1970, and a large number of commuters do just that, travelling daily to work in Croydon and London by train from Caterham Station which moved to its present site in 1900, at the end of a double track laid from Purley. The prospect of a return to railway privatisation in the late 1990s caused many passengers to fear the emergence of inter-operator wrangling, and potential increases in the already considerable fares they have to pay, obliging many to turn back to their cars for commuting.

For nearly half a century after World War II, there was a certain logic to the buses that operated in Caterham. Green 'country' buses ruled on the Hill, one or two venturing down to the Valley, pausing at the station before slinking off south to Godstone and East Grinstead or Redhill and Reigate. Red buses ruled in the Valley, looking strident and slightly out-of-place in their brash 'town' livery, waiting to trundle back along Godstone Road to Purley. Bus routes were firmly established and familiar. Their route numbers rarely changed; for instance, when the 447 became the 440, passengers had a good decade to grow used to the new number.

Since the decision to deregulate buses in the early 1990s, a veritable 'liquorice all-sorts' of buses began to ply the existing routes; an agglomeration of vehicles in liveries of off-white, blue and cream, and orange would pull up at stops, snuffling for business. In 1997 the quantity of buses seems to have diminished, leaving orange as the apparently-approved colour alternative to the long-standing green and red. Presumably their regular passengers know which bus goes where!

A 'liquorice all-sorts' of buses now stop in the Valley

Experts say that our massively jammed roads, crowded commuter trains and buses will all become a thing of the past when office workers cease travelling to their inner city offices and begin working from home, linked by their computer terminals and fax machines. There is very little evidence of this revolution in 1997 ... but what will the 21st century bring?

SIGNIFICANT CHANGES TO FAMOUS LANDMARKS

Though at the beginning of this chapter it was said that in general there have been few changes of any major consequence in the Caterham area, there are five important sites where transmutations have been taking place throughout the 1990s.

St. Lawrence's Hospital – One of the major landmarks of Caterham Hill, the famous hospital built in 1869 for the care of the mentally ill and people with learning disabilities is now in decline, following changes which now require that wherever possible patients previously resident in mental hospitals should be released to live in the community. Nationwide many large houses have been purchased by authorities and specially-formed trusts for conversion into suitable accommodation. A number of large houses in Caterham Hill and surrounding areas have thus been appropriated by the Lifecare Trust, an organisation concerned with the purpose of carrying out the requirements of the new Mental Health Act and its consequences, and based in the grounds of the hospital.

St Lawrence's Hospital

Demolition of a large part of the hospital's buildings began early in 1995, leaving part of the main building to be redeveloped as Lifecare Trust's Headquarters. Plans for the rest of the site first proposed 360 residential buildings. A revised application for 250 dwellings was later submitted. Work began on the first phase in the winter of 1995. Perhaps it would not be too surprising to see an allocation of space for a new updated hospital building, for occupation by those ex-patients who, having tried life 'in the community', prefer to return to the sanctuary of comfortably-circumscribed perimeters.

The Guards' Barracks – Another firmly-established landmark of Caterham Hill, is one that can bring a misty-eyed memory of fear, trembling and fun to old soldiers and ex-National Servicemen all over the world who once served there. The Guards' Barracks was established in 1877, saw the making of many a military man, and was the gathering point for many young ladies from the town at the Saturday evening dances.

The Guards' Barracks

Many different regiments resided there in its long and colourful history, and the sounds of their bugle calls of reveille and taps, and parade-ground drilling, band parades and the rifle practice were familiar reminders of their presence.

Sadly the grounds will soon only hold the distant echoes of memory, as the barracks were officially declared closed in autumn 1994 as part of the programme of reduction of the British Armed Forces. Plans for the re-use of the site have not yet been finalised, though rumours abound locally.

Hillcroft School – Another major central site destined for redevelopment lies in Chaldon Road, Caterham Hill, at its junction with the High Street and opposite the *Golden Lion* pub. The site is the eastern section of Hillcroft School grounds, which also includes the old Fire Engine building in the High Street, and is commercially attractive with great intrinsic value.

A public meeting was held in early 1994 where Tandridge Council offered the public the opportunity to make suggestions for the site's future use. Some creative ideas emerged, including a pedestrian precinct, a permanent museum and a covered marketplace. Everyone who spoke was concerned for the future of the old Fire Engine building, pleading that it should be retained in good order and made some good use of. The majority opinion was that the site should be used for public recreation; a leisure centre with swimming pool and plenteous car parking was the general appeal. Time will reveal the final decision of the authorities concerned.

Hillcroft School in the snow

Eothen School – This acclaimed day school for girls, began life in 1892, at 2 Westview, Harestone Hill, with eight pupils. The present site was then an adjacent field, on which building commenced five years later.

The school closed in 1995 and the remaining girl pupils were absorbed into nearby Caterham School. The school buildings will be demolished and the prime central site devoured by developers. At the time of writing a planning application for 70 flats – 27 standard three-bedroom units and 43 sheltered units – plus a medical centre, converted from the existing science block, is under consideration and subject to a traffic impact study. Like all such developments, this is sure to disgorge at least one car per standard dwelling unit onto already overburdened existing roads which were once expected to carry little more than tradesmen's vans, the odd brewer's dray, sporadic buses and the occasional family saloon or touring car.

SHOPPING IN CATERHAM

The pattern of the shops in Caterham has remained the same for many years. Croydon Road in central Caterham Valley is lined with shop premises, while further along the road isolated parades exist. In Caterham Hill a small cluster of shops survives near *The Clifton Arms* in Chaldon Road; parades of shops persist adjacent to *the Tally Ho* and opposite the Guards' Barracks in Coulsdon Road; Westway is still shop-lined. Some of the shops in Westway exemplify the growing trend for small businesses to operate from behind the facade of a shop front, simply displaying a photo-poster, or a couple of their products – as though for sale – among the spiders that inhabit their now-redundant shop windows.

Even before the recession of the early 1990s the mix of shops in British high streets had begun to change. Building societies and bank branches, estate agencies and fast food outlets had begun to outnumber general retailers. Since the recession, shopkeepers are finding it difficult to survive in business. Decreased sales, increased business rates and unrelenting landlords demanding large annual rent increases are forcing many shop closures. In the mid-1990s shopping streets like Croydon Road, Caterham Valley, bristle with a forest of 'shop to let' estate agents' boards. 'Charity' shops – selling second-hand merchandise for the benefit of their good causes – abound, in premises left vacant by closed-down businesses.

Caterham boasts two collective shopping centres. The Raglan Precinct on Caterham Hill was erected on the site left vacant by the demolition of a half-dozen individual shops in 1971, and Church Walk shopping Centre in Caterham Valley was erected on land where once stood the Valley Hotel, its car park and market gardens to the rear. Both sites have the advantage of adjacent car parking. Car parking adjacent to or <u>very</u> near to, shops has become increasingly crucial to their success. If the parking is also free that success will be multiplied.

In the 1990s family shopping often consists of a weekly or bi-weekly trip to the free car park of the supermarket which stocks everything and therefore avoids the need to visit a series of individual shops. Though Caterham Valley has two fine supermarkets – Waitrose with integral car park, free for shoppers, adjacent to Caterham Station, and Safeway's, also with integral car park, off Harestone Valley Road – ever more mobile shoppers are tempted by alternative out-of-town superstores, all of which seem to offer 'bigger choice' and 'lower prices' than their rivals. A huge Tesco's store at Purley, a new Sainsbury store at Chelsham and a newer Safeway's at nearby Oxted beckon.

**The Valley's Church Walk Shopping Centre entrance
(left) with Waitrose supermarket on the right.   1997**

Seeing the rise of the mobile shopper, Caterham Hill's High Street petrol stations, like all others, are offering motorists an ever-expanding range of goods alongside their petrol pumps. These include flowers, confectionery, greetings cards, coal, fancy goods, chemists' sundries, groceries, newspapers and magazines – some are even offering alcohol – thus reducing yet further the sales once enjoyed exclusively by a whole variety of individual high street retailers.

A saddening consequence of the decline of the good old-fashioned walk around the high street shops is the diminishing chance to stop and chat, to pass on a little gossip, and to smile. It is now possible to withdraw money from your bank account, collect all your shopping, fill your car with petrol and wash it, and return home without saying a word to, or without smiling at, anyone. What an achievement for mankind!

Sunday shopping became legal in 1994 with the caveat that no store should open for longer than six hours. Defenders of keeping Sundays special denied that the British public wanted Sunday shopping, but a glimpse inside Alldays in the Raglan Precinct or Safeway's, Caterham Valley, at around midday on any Sunday instantly disproves their case.

Looked at half a century after the end of World War II, Caterham appears to be in good shape.

It is surrounded by rolling downlands and splendid woods which though thinned and seriously damaged by the fierce 'hurricane' wind of October 1987 have been tended and well managed, and are filling out with new growth. Some new golf courses have been constructed in outlying areas and others have been planned following a trend begun in the mid- to late-1980s when more leisure time was promised. However, as a result of the 1990s recession many people do have more time but not the income to afford golfing fees, so many of the planned courses have been put 'on hold' or abandoned entirely.

**Duke's Dene, one of the new golf courses
that now surround Caterham. 1997**

Surrounding farms, though depleted in manpower by increasing mechanisation, manage to maintain their lands immaculately, even those areas that they were paid to 'set aside' from growing crops because of over-production of food. Clay pigeon shooting is a popular pastime on the farms surrounding Caterham.

For the energetic there is a wealth of fine walking on the well-maintained commons and open spaces around Caterham. Horse riding flourishes. From the open hilltop vantage of View Point, the majestic panorama south to Sussex is intriguingly displayed. Thankfully the traditional green spaces survive, with children's play areas in Town End, Caterham Hill, and in the valley at Timber Hill Road and nearby White Knobs recreation ground. The well-maintained Queens Park on the hill offers tennis, bowls, croquet, a putting green and summer cricket matches amidst its acres of grass and beautiful gardens. The large grassy triangle of Westway Common provides a temporary home to the travelling fairs that visit, the occasional circus, and the ever-popular Caterham carnival.

Original pubs survive; clubs, associations and societies thrive and a strong sense of community shows no sign of diminishing, remains within the district. In the meantime and for the foreseeable future – assuming there are as few changes in the next 50 years as there have been in the last – there can be few nicer places in the world to live in than Caterham.

The treetops and rooftops of Caterham valley with St. John's Church to left and the Congregational Church to the right

Chapter 12

Churches and Chapels

by Joan Cadle and Sue Beach

There are many churches and chapels in the area – some have served the people of Caterham for many years, others have come and gone. We take a tour of Caterham starting with the churches on the Hill and ending in the Valley in date order of their establishment.

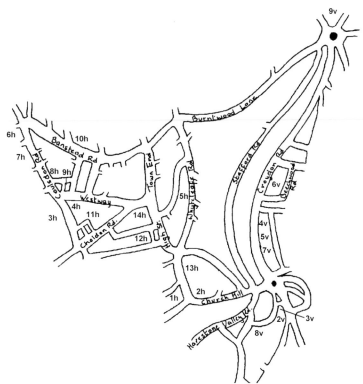

On the Hill

1h.	St. Lawrence's Church
2h.	St. Mary's Church
3h.	St. Lawrence's Hospital Chapel
4h.	Congregational Church
5h.	Church of the Sacred Heart
6h.	Mission Room
7h.	St. Michael the Archangel
8h.	Wesleyan Chapel & Methodist Church
9h.	Oak Hall
10h.	St. Paul's Church
11h.	Elim Pentecostal Church
12h.	Jehovah's Witnesses
13h.	Reformed Baptist
14h.	Revival Fellowship

In the Valley

1v.	United Reformed Church
2v.	Temporary Church
3v.	St. John's Church
4v.	Methodist Church
5v.	Bethany or Gospel Hall
6v.	Baptist Chapel
7v.	Salvation Army
8v.	Society of Friends
9v.	The Brethren

Location of churches

CATERHAM ON THE HILL

1h.   **St. Lawrence's Church, Church Road.**

The old parish church of St. Lawrence was built in 1095. A remnant of a Norman window in the south wall of the nave dates from that time. The original dedication was to St. Leonard. It is still used for occasional services and there is a comprehensive church guide available, which was published to celebrate its novocentenary in 1995.

**St. Lawrence's Church - from a sketch by Ernest
Christie (1900)**

CHURCHES AND CHAPELS

2h.   **St. Mary's Church, Church Road.**

The new parish church of St. Mary's, consecrated in May 1866 by Bishop Sumner, was designed by W. & C.H. Basset Smith with seating for 350 people. A new south aisle was added in 1883, and a 126 ft. high spire was constructed in timber and covered with cedar shingles. In 1893 the church was re-seated for 500 people and eight tubular bells were installed. In 1994 a peal of eight bells was hung in the belfry.

Building of the north aisle commenced in 1912, following a donation of £500 from Mr. Harry Lloyd of 'Woodlands' on condition that there would be no coloured glass windows as these would make the church seem too dark, and that the pews be rent free-for the use of local people.

In 1966, the centenary year of St. Mary's, improvements were necessary and it was estimated that at least £5000 would be needed. Part of the money was used to erect a new church hall adjacent to the church; other improvements included better lighting and renewal of parts of the organ. A second hall was built in 1990 following the closure of St. Paul's, Banstead Road.

3h.   **St. Lawrence's Hospital Chapel, Coulsdon Road.**

The non-denominational chapel at St. Lawrence's Hospital was closed on 20th May 1993 after many years of service to the patients and staff. One of the early resident chaplains was Revd. C.A. Greenland and the last was Revd. George Parsons, who had been involved with St. Paul's, Banstead Road until it closed in 1982. The Chapel's electric organ was donated to the Methodist Church in Coulsdon Road.

St. Lawrence's Hospital Chapel

4h.   **Congregational Church, Coulsdon Road**

On 14th November 1875 Mr. Redgate bought, on behalf of the Trustees, land known as Fowlers, Town End, on which they planned to build a Mission Hall. With the increase in population after the opening of St. Lawrence's Hospital and the Barracks, the church exchanged the land on Town End for a plot on the corner of Westway and

Coulsdon Road. The old wooden Mission Hall was re-erected on this land, was used as a church until 1892 when a new one was built, and then as a Sunday school until World War II, when it was destroyed during a raid. In 1956 Croydon Congregational Church donated a small building to the Caterham church, which was used until 1983-84 when a new brick hall was built.

5h.   **Church of the Sacred Heart, Essendene Road**

The Roman Catholic Church was opened on 11th August 1881. The family of Father Roe had donated £5000 to build the church and the presbytery. Father Roe came to Caterham during 1879 after it became known that a priest was having to come from Croydon to take mass for the many Irish catholic soldiers stationed at the Barracks. During his time as parish priest, Father Roe witnessed the building of the church, the school and a large increase in the catholic population. He died on Armistice Day in November 1918.

Father Cooksey came to Caterham as permanent priest in 1923. By 1929 plans to extend the church were drawn up. These included a north aisle, baptistry and porch, and by 1932 the work was completed, except for new lighting. During the war years, with many soldiers coming to mass, the church had to adapt and change the times of services. From 1969-75 various repairs had to be done. The chapel was refurbished after a fire.

6h.   **Mission Room, Coulsdon Road.**

The Mission Room in 1995

The Mission Room of St. Mary's was built in about 1882 to serve the needs of the people at the north end of the parish. When St. Michael's, the Guards' Depot Chapel was built in 1886, it was thought that the Mission Room would no longer be required, as the general public would be able to attend services at the Chapel. However, Caterham's population was gradually increasing and 23 years later – in 1909 – the decision was made to enlarge the room. The newly-formed branch of the CEMS undertook the extension. Over three-quarters of the £400 required was secured before the dedication service, conducted by the Bishop of Woolwich, took place in

October 1909. The extension consisted of a hall seating 300 people, and the original room remained as a chancel.

Curates to the Mission were Revd.Toplis, followed by Revd.Goundry who was there until it closed in 1932. He then became the first minister of the new St.Paul's Church.

The building itself still remains, and is used by a carpentry and joinery business, not looking very different from when it was first built, despite suffering considerable fire damage in December 1987.

7h. St. Michael the Archangel, Caterham Barracks, Coulsdon Road.

Lieut. General Smith CB provided most of the money, with a subscription from the War Office, for the construction of the Chapel at the Caterham Barracks during 1886. The dedication took place on 16th February 1887, at a ceremony attended by many distinguished military personnel. Designed by William Butterfield for 650 people, it was built mainly for the soldiers but also with the view that local residents would be able to use it. It is now one of the very few listed buildings in Caterham.

8h. Wesleyan Chapel & Methodist Church, Coulsdon Road.

When Revd. Charles E. Mees was appointed chaplain to the Barracks in 1898, he saw a need for a church for the people of Caterham as well as a meeting place for the soldiers. Land was bought in 1899 and the foundation stone was laid on 19th September 1900. Known as 'Caterham Wesleyan Soldiers' Rooms', it was opened by Revd. Thomas Allen on 21st February 1901. A year later 31 members were attending Sunday services.

It was soon evident that larger premises were required, and a new church adjoining the Soldiers' Rooms was built and opened on 1st October 1908. It was used regularly by the soldiers and in 1950 it was handed over to the Methodists. In the last few years it has undergone work to create a multi-purpose building, both for worship and other activities.

9h. Oak Hall, Francis Road

The Mission Hall in Francis Road, now Oak Hall Church, was opened to the public on 13th September 1894. Mr. Robert Best of the Beresford Chapels at Walworth and Brixton bought the land in May 1894 and Thompson Builders erected the hall, which had seating for 250.

One of the most regular preachers was Mr. Pickard of Caterham, who with Mr. Lance of Town End and Flexton Lewis rented the hall from Mr. Best in 1912 at a yearly rent of £16. When Mr. Best died in 1914 he left the premises and land to his trustees to ensure that the Mission Room continued as a place for family worship. During the war years the hall was opened in the week to enable the soldiers to have a quiet place in which to read and write their letters home. It was rebuilt in 1970.

10h. **St. Paul's Church, Banstead Road.**

On 19th October 1932, the new Bishop of Southwark paid his first visit to Caterham for the dedication of the new church of St. Paul. It replaced the old Mission Room in Coulsdon Road.

St. Paul's Church, Banstead Road

In 1930 Revd. Goundry approached the rector with regard to building a new church. As a fund of £2000 already existed – a legacy from the late Revd. Norman Campbell – there was no need to appeal for funds. Mr. L.A.G. Le Personne of 'The Oaks' was asked if he would donate a piece of land in memory of his wife, who had been well known in the area for her public work. Work commenced in June 1932. The church had seating for 250 people, hot air heating and electric lighting. Revd. Goundry, had with the help of Mr. Kensett, made most of the interior furnishings.

A fund was gradually accumulated to build a church hall. This was finally accomplished on 9th June 1954, when in spite of the pouring rain about 100 people assembled for the official opening by the Rural Dean, Revd. C.E. Fisher. The church was closed and demolished in 1982.

11h. Elim Pentecostal Church, Homesdale Road

The first meeting of the Elim Pentecostal Church was held in a tent pitched in Rignall's Field, Park Road, in 1933. The pastor at this first meeting was Felix Lloyd Smith, who stayed until 1936.

From these early days the the church then hired rooms above the Co-op in the High Street. On 9th December 1939 a new church was opened in Homesdale Road. During the following years many children attended the Sunshine Club run by Mrs. Weatherley. Sadly membership declined during the 1960s and 1970s and it was decided to close the church and transfer the membership to the Elim Church, Chipstead Valley Road, Coulsdon.

12h. Jehovah's Witnesses, Kingdom Hall, High Street

The Witnesses were in Caterham from about 1940, meeting at first at 115 Croydon Road and then for at least 20 years at the Co-op Hall, High Street, Caterham Hill. They left the hall in 1990-91 and joined the Coulsdon congregation.

13h. Reformed Baptists, Red Cross Hall, Church Road.

The Reformed Baptists, which is a new group separated from the Strict Baptists during 1982 and re-formed during 1983, hold their Sunday church meetings at the Red Cross Hall in Church Road, with two regular elders, Pat Hogley and John Pascoe.

14h. The Revival Fellowship, Hillcroft Infants School.

The Revival Fellowship Church of God used a former school building on the corner of High Street and Chaldon Road for Sunday and weekday services. Formerly it was used by a group known as the County Fellowship, which was there from the early part of 1992. Now closed and the school demolished (1997).

CATERHAM VALLEY

1v. United Reformed Church, Harestone Hill.

When William Garland Soper came to Caterham in 1863, there was nowhere for the nonconformists of the area to worship. A room in Mr. Barnham's carpenter's shop was used for a while and then services were conducted in the home of Mr. F.B. Winter of 'Bloomfield', Stanstead Road. On 9th August 1868 the church was formed with the enrolment of the first 29 members. The memorial stone of a new church was laid in 1874 and it was opened in the following year. The gallery in the main church was used only by the pupils of Caterham School, which was originally for sons of Congregational Ministers.

In March 1944 the church was destroyed, except for the clock tower, by incendiaries dropped on the last bomber raid on the district. The church was rebuilt, and opened on 13th January 1951.

2v. The Temporary Church, Clareville Road.

Land in Clareville Road was given by Mr. G.H. Cook for the erection of a temporary church. It was built by Mr. Carruthers and was opened on 3rd December 1871 with Revd. Kenrick, Rector of Caterham, taking the service. Once a full-time curate was appointed by February 1872, it was licensed for both morning and evening services. In 1882 St. John's was opened.

The Temporary Church, Clareville Road,
constructed of wood on a brick foundation

3v.   **St. John's Church, Caterham Valley**

This ancient font belonged to the
parish church of St. Lawrence,
Caterham, built in King John's reign.
It was presented by the Rector,
Revd. Jarvis Kenrick, to St. John the
Evangelist's Church, Caterham
Valley in 1871, and restored in his
memory by his widow in 1881.

CHURCHES AND CHAPELS

St. John's became a separate parish when the church was consecrated on 27th December 1882 by Dr. A.W. Thorold, Bishop of Rochester. Revd. J.B. Heard became the first vicar. The church was built by Mr. Carruthers on land which had belonged to Charles Asprey. Inside the church are many memorials to the people of Caterham Valley, who provided funds and gifts for the benefit of the church. The Revd. Kenrick gave the font from St. Lawrence's as a gift to the new church. The bells installed in 1975 came from St. Mary, Lambeth.

4v. The Methodist Church, Croydon Road

About 1882 Mr. C. Pook, a local photographer, started Sunday services in a basement room at Fairlight Villas near to the local board school in Beechwood Road. Until then local methodists attended services in Warlingham. On 15th August 1884 the foundation stone for a new chapel was laid on land given by Mr. E. Harris. It cost £600 to build and seated 150 people. From 1905 until 1951 various attempts were made to purchase land for a new chapel, but eventually it was decided that the present site could be used to better advantage. A new hall was built and opened in May 1954.

By 1969, with its membership in decline, it was decided to combine the Valley Methodist Church with the Hill church. The last service was held at Caterham Valley on 31st August 1969.

5v. Bethany or Gospel Hall, Caterham Christian Centre, 84 Croydon Road.

James Fegan first preached at Caterham during 1888 and the following year, with a membership of 20, he rented a small hall where the Salvation Army Citadel now stands. Three years later the membership had increased, and he bought land and erected a small iron chapel. The interior had tiered seating for the choir.

After a flying bomb had fallen in Croydon Road during 1944, the chapel was found to be in need of considerable repair, not from the bomb but through structural decay. It was decided to commence a building fund and eventually the church was rebuilt, having changed its name and appointed new trustees.

**James Fegan, founder
of Bethany Hall**

6v.   Baptist Chapel, Beechwood Road

Frank Marshall Pool held the first baptist meeting in his home in Croydon Road on 25th February 1894. As the membership grew a room was rented from Cutlers of 75 Croydon Road. Later land was purchased and the Ebenezer Strict Baptist Chapel was opened on 9th September 1895. Membership grew and fell over the following years and by 1927 there was no regular minister. With the election of new trustees and help from the Croydon Baptist Church, things slowly began to improve. By 1945 a rebuilding fund was opened, but it was not until 1967 that a hall was erected. On 22nd July 1978 a Thanksgiving Service was held on completion of a new chapel.

7v.   The Salvation Army, 74 Croydon Road.

The Army was 44 years old when on a cold foggy November morning in 1909 two women, Captain Beer and Lieutenant Stocker arrived in Caterham to commence their work, and the majority of the people of Caterham soon accepted them. Meetings were held in a small hall in Croydon Road, where the Citadel now stands. At first the hall was rented, but the Army was able to purchase it at auction at the Greyhound Hotel, Croydon on 16th May 1921. By November 1927 a new hall was opened. One of the first members to be enrolled was Mr. Guy Hewett, who later became a prominent member of the brass band, originally formed by Bandmaster Laker with three members.

Caterham Valley Salvation Army Band, 1935

8v.   The Society of Friends

The Society of Friends, or Quakers, have also been holding meetings in the area for many years, firstly at Eothen School, Harestone Hill and now at St. Lawrence's Church.

9v.   **The Brethren, Wapses Lodge**

In 1994 Wapses Lodge became the meeting place for the local Brethren of the community.

SOURCES

Local libraries

Surrey Record Office

Somerset House Wills

British Library, Colindale

Members of the local churches

Local reminiscences

Bourne Society *Local History Records*

St. Lawrence's Church Guide 1995

_____

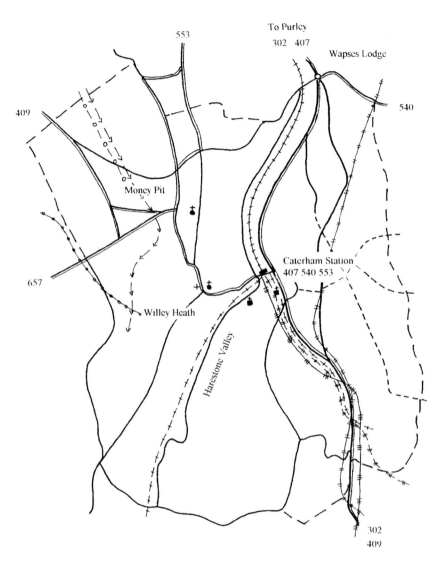

To Purley
302 407

Wapses Lodge

553

409

540

Money Pit

657

Willey Heath

Caterham Station
407 540 553

Harestone Valley

302
409

PUBLIC TRANSPORT   -   RAILWAYS AND BUS ROUTES

Caterham Railway (South Eastern Railway)
Caterham Railway proposed extensions 1855
Proposed South Caterham Railway (1873)
Proposed Caterham & Godstone Railway (1873)
Proposed Metropolitan & Brighton Railway (1875)
Proposed Caterham & Godstone Valley Railway (1876)
Proposed Coulsdon & Upper Caterham Railway (1882)
Proposed Upper Caterham Railway (1882)
Bus routes

Chapter 13

Public Transport and Roads

by Bill Gilbert

The earliest evidence of travel in the Caterham area is the ancient trackway along the crest of the North Downs. This track was used by prehistoric man travelling from settlements in the west towards the Straits of Dover. Another old road ran over Whitehill from Bletchingley past *The Harrow*. Following the Roman conquest roads were built between London and a number of places on the south coast. The road to Portslade coincides with the A22 both to the north and south of Caterham, but through Caterham Valley it ran along the side of the hill. The road in the Valley eventually became a turnpike. In 1843 at least six coaches a day passed along it between London and East Grinstead; Brighton; Lewes and Eastbourne.

RAILWAYS

In 1854 an Act of Parliament authorised the building of a railway from Caterham to the main line at Purley, then known as Godstone Road. This was the result of a scheme drawn up by a number of local businessmen (Charles Dingwall, Alexander Beattie, Alfred Smith, Francis Fuller and George Drew) to build a railway connecting the firestone mines to the south of Caterham to the existing London to Brighton railway. Firestone was a very valuable mineral used for lining chimneys and furnaces, and that found beneath the chalk of the North Downs was of high quality and sent all over the country. There were other minerals nearby so the prospects for the new line were encouraging. Unfortunately the Caterham Railway Act specified that the line should terminate in a field known as Hither North Dean, some one and a half miles from the quarries. The country along the valley where the railway would run was almost uninhabited, and Caterham itself had few inhabitants. It was therefore necessary to try to generate traffic by encouraging speculative building. Several landowners set aside land "to provide their clerks with good country residences at a moderate cost" and one, George Parbury, provided 150 acres in return for his own station, Warlingham, since renamed Whyteleafe South. The new residents, if they were shareholders of the company, would receive 21 years' free rail travel.

Building began on 5th March 1855 accompanied by celebrations which included two sumptuous feasts, one for the poor (third class) and one for the directors and friends (first class). During 1855 there were further proposals to extend the line to the firestone quarries at Tupwood and along Harestone Valley to the War Coppice quarry. It was estimated that the annual revenue from the quarries would amount to £3000. Neither scheme was implemented.

The line was built as single track, which it was to remain until the end of the century. Stations were built at Kenley (named Coulsdon until December 1856), and Warlingham, subsequently renamed Whyteleafe South. The building of the railway was completed by 21st September 1855 but the line was not opened until 4th August 1856. This long delay was caused by disputes between the two main line railway companies, the London, Brighton & South Coast and the South Eastern. One of the difficulties was that Godstone Road station (re-named Caterham Junction in 1856 and Purley in 1888) had been closed in 1847 by the LBSCR which owned that part of the main line. The LBSCR refused to reopen the station until an injunction was obtained by the Caterham Railway Co.

When the line was opened the fares between Caterham and London Bridge were 3/4d first class; 2/10d second class; and 2/1d third class. Season tickets to London at £7 per annum first class and £5 per annum second class, were available only to those building houses on the Company's property. The service began with four trains daily in each direction, and three on Sundays, passengers having to change to one of the main line railway companies at Caterham Junction. The weekday service connected with two trains of the LBSCR and two of the SER although some of the connections were rather haphazard.

Entrance to original Caterham Valley Station *c.* 1886
Mr. Foweraker, Stationmaster

The Caterham Railway Co. had experienced financial difficulties at a very early stage in the construction of the line. It was undercapitalised because of the shortage of potential passengers (the population of Caterham on the Hill in 1851 was 487) and the lack of any regular freight traffic as it was too far from the Godstone quarries. At first the LBSCR, which had supplied the engines and rolling stock, was approached to take over the line but terms could not be agreed and it withdrew its plant and sued the Caterham Railway for the cost of hire. The South Eastern Railway then stepped in and offered to buy the line for £12,000. It eventually sold for £14,000 (It had cost nearly £40,000 to build two years earlier). The takeover was authorised by Parliament in July 1859. There was great rivalry between the LBSCR and the SER since they shared the line between London and Redhill, competing for the few passengers living in the district at that time. The LBSCR would not sell tickets for the Caterham line nor allow many SER main line trains to stop at Caterham Junction station. Conditions continued to deteriorate until the mid-1860s when some passengers protested at the poor service and correspondence in *The Times* drew attention to the disgraceful state of affairs.

During the 1860s Caterham Valley rapidly developed with high-class residences, and increased traffic on the railway. In 1862 Caterham Station was enlarged. The first through train service from Caterham to London began in 1866. During the late 1890s the line to Caterham was doubled, Caterham station was re-sited and a new station opened at Whyteleafe.

PUBLIC TRANSPORT

The new Caterham Station soon after opening in 1900

During the second half of the 19th century a number of other schemes were proposed for extending the railways in the area, none of which got beyond the planning stage. Among them were:

1873   Caterham and Godstone Railway, an extension from Caterham to Godstone under Tupwood and Godstone hills.

1873   South Caterham Railway. This was to run from near Purley along the line of Old Lodge Lane and Caterham Drive, Coulsdon to terminate at Money Pit.

1875   Metropolitan & Brighton Railway from Penge and Beckenham through Farleigh, Warlingham, Caterham, Godstone and East Grinstead to Brighton with a viaduct over the valley at Woldingham and tunnels under Tillingdown and Godstone hills.

1876   Caterham & Godstone Valley Railway. This was proposed to run from the existing station towards Godstone then turn eastwards towards Westerham.

1882   Coulsdon & Upper Caterham Railway was to follow the same line as the South Caterham line but extend another mile or so and terminate at Willey Heath.

1882   Upper Caterham Railway. A branch from the main line at Coulsdon along Happy Valley to Caterham. This also was to end near Willey Heath.

After World War I, in 1923, came the "grouping " of the railways, and the LBSCR and SER both became part of the Southern Railway. The next change came in 1928 when the Caterham and Tattenham Corner lines were electrified.

Since 1945 there have been two major incidents on the line. In 1945 both drivers were killed in a head-on collision outside Caterham Station and in 1960 the Caterham train collided with the Tattenhem Corner train at Purley, causing eight injuries. A further incident of note occurred on 29th March 1974, when an unmanned train ran away from Caterham and travelled as far as Norwood Junction before being switched onto a siding; only prompt action by signalmen along the route prevented the runaway from causing a major accident.

The line was privatised in 1996 and the trains are run by Connex South Central.

The 08.56 London train ready to leave Caterham   c.1904

ROAD TRANSPORT

It was not until 1914 that a bus service reached Caterham. On 29th March the London General Omnibus Company began a service, route 152, from Stockwell to Caterham along the Godstone Road, running on Sundays only. This was mainly for the use of Londoners wishing to visit the Surrey countryside. From 11th May it became a daily service. The vehicles used were the well-known "B" type open-topped double-deckers which later gained fame as the "Old Bill" buses used by the Army in France. On 4th June the East Surrey Traction Company applied to the Caterham magistrates for licences to operate buses in the area, and by August had extended its Reigate to Godstone bus route to Caterham. There is evidence that for a short time a few years earlier an unlicensed service had run between Godstone and Caterham. In November the LGOC bus was curtailed to terminate at the *Old Surrey Hounds* at Caterham. The following year the East Surrey company had to withdraw its service as a war economy, and so there was no public transport south of the town.

1917 saw the replacement of the LGOC by Thomas Tilling as the operator of service 152 and its renumbering as 159A. Tilling took over many of the bus routes in south London owing to the number of buses sent to the Western Front.

After the war ended the LGOC reinstated its service to Caterham and in the summer extended it to Godstone.

1922 saw the reappearance of the East Surrey Traction Company buses, with two services from Hartfield and Chelwood Gate to West Croydon running every two hours. These buses, numbered S9, were the first to go up Church Hill and then via Old Coulsdon to Purley and Croydon. At first these buses were garaged at the *Tally Ho* in Coulsdon Road and then at the *Caterham Arms*. In 1925 this route was numbered 409 and the East Surrey Traction Company opened its garage at Godstone.

The next development came in 1928 when the East Surrey Traction Company started a service, route 33, from Caterham on the Hill down Church Hill and along the valley to Wapses Lodge. It then went via Woldingham and Botley Hill to Westerham Hill, running every two hours. The following year it was replaced by route 30 which came from East Grinstead, picked up the 33 route at Westerham Hill, and terminated at Caterham Station. This service did not last long and the route soon became Caterham Station to Woldingham hourly, worked by a one man operated 18-seater bus. The next year this service was extended westwards to Earlswood via Chaldon, thus providing the first public transport between Caterham and the main Brighton Road at the *Jolliffe Arms* using larger 30-seat single-deck buses; in 1931 London General Country Services took over the route as service 449.

Route 75 - Woolwich to Caterham - in Croydon Road, Caterham in the 1920s

Express coaches began operating to London on 29th September 1930 when Green Line coaches started a service from Godstone through Caterham Valley every half hour. Two days later another service was started by the Blue Belle Company from London via Purley Way to East Grinstead and Westerham passing through Caterham. It also introduced a service to Caterham Barracks from London up Whyteleafe Hill, then along Salmons Lane, Buxton Lane, Town End, Chaldon Road and Westway. In November that year the Green Line started another hourly service to East Grinstead following the same route as the 409 through Caterham.

By the end of 1931 some of these services, including that of the Blue Belle Coaches, had been withdrawn and the Green Line coaches given letters, A B C etc., to identify the routes. The East Surrey Traction Company's routes were taken over by London General Country Services Ltd on 28th January 1932, and on 1st July 1933 the London Passenger Transport Board took over the operation of all bus and coach routes in the district. The services then operating in Caterham were as follows:

A type ST bus of London Transport in Caterham in the late 1930s

A bus in Church Hill, probably in the 1950s. In early days passengers had
to alight to relieve the load when buses climbed the hill, and the conductor
stand ready with a chock in case the bus slipped backward.

PUBLIC TRANSPORT

Bus 30 Earlswood – Woldingham daily.
Bus 75 Woolwich – Caterham via Godstone Road daily.
Bus 144 Friern Barnet – Caterham via Godstone Road. Sundays only.
Bus 409 West Croydon – Forest Row via Old Coulsdon daily.
Coach K Hemel Hempstead – Caterham Station via Old Coulsdon. Daily.
Coach T Tring – Godstone Green via Godstone Road daily.
Coach U London – East Grinstead via Godstone Road daily.

Shortly after this, in October, the Board reorganised the Green Line coaches, replacing the existing services with routes H from Harpenden to East Grinstead and AH from Dunstable to East Grinstead. Both these followed Godstone Road through Caterham Valley. Coach K became G but started at Horse Guards. Prior to this the Sunday service of route 144 was withdrawn on 7th August.

In 1934 a new service, the 453, was introduced from Chaldon Road via Westway, Town End, Buxton Lane, Salmons Lane and Whyteleafe Hill to Warlingham. Initially this was run by small one-man operated single-deckers but in 1949 the double-deck "RT" bus was introduced.

In 1935 the route 30 was renumbered 449 and terminated at Redstone Estate, Redhill and a new service, route 411, between West Croydon and Reigate introduced. This followed the same route as 409 through the area.

In 1939 the Caterham by-pass was opened. The roundabout at Wapses Lodge, being raised to provide pedestrian walkways beneath, was unique in this country, having been copied from the German Autobahn system.

Just prior to the outbreak of war in 1939, all Green Line coach services were suspended and the 75 bus was curtailed to West Croydon but replaced by the 197 from Norwood Junction. In December 1940 a green double-decker bus was introduced between Victoria and East Grinstead, route 8, to replace the coach service with a 30 minute service interval. Between 1943 and 1945 Sunday morning bus services were withdrawn in order to save fuel.

Conditions began to return to normal in 1946 with the reintroduction of the Green Line, but as services 708 and 709, following the same routes as pre-war, the 449 renumbered 447 and the 197, the only red Central bus in Caterham being given the new RT type. The 709 was extended to Godstone in 1947.

The next change did not occur until 1953 when a new service, route 482 began from Caterham Station on Sundays to Smallfield Hospital. Later it also ran on Thursdays for hospital visitors. In 1959 the 447 was replaced by 440 and 440A running to Redhill and Salfords.

With the deregulation of bus services in the 1980s, London Transport lost its monopoly and quite soon the East Surrey Traction Company's buses reappeared. Sadly the Green Line coaches were withdrawn. With the growth in private motoring it could no longer maintain express services between central London and the Home Counties. London Transport was also split into a number of operating companies. The 197 route was taken over by South London Buses, extended to Wallington, and renumbered 407. The 411 service was shortened to terminate at Godstone, leaving the faithful old 409 as the only route from Caterham on the Hill to Croydon. Other routes taken over by East Surrey Buses included 302, Oxted to Whyteleafe; 540, Woldingham to Caterham Station; 553 Oxted or Westerham to Caterham Station via Whyteleafe Hill. In addition to these there are some routes limited to school days, the 303 between Redhill and Warlingham via Chaldon; 657 Warlingham to Reigate via Chaldon; 696 Bletchingley to Caterham (de Stafford College); and 810 Reigate to Chipstead via Godstone and Coulsdon. It can thus be seen that it is still possible, with some careful planning, to get around the district by bus, and with the railway continuing to offer a half-hourly service to Purley and London, Caterham continues to enjoy good communications with the rest of the South East.

SOURCES

Spence, Jeoffry *The Caterham Railway.*

King J.T. & Newman A.G. *Southbound from Croydon*

Route 409 to West Croydon at the bottom of Church Hill, Caterham in the 1950s.

Chapter 14

The Great Institutions

I. THE GUARDS' DEPOT – 1877 - 1967

(Condensed from W.D. Gaskin's Short History, a copy of which is in Caterham Valley Library.)

The site for the Guards' Depot was purchased by the War Department on 3rd August 1875 for a total sum of £6312.l0s.0d and the buildings were completed in 1877 at a cost of £46,273. Woodville House provided the Commanding Officer's quarters and stables and was situated outside the Barracks enclosure.

Guardsmen out of uniform tend to be large, friendly men. In uniform they form part of an elite personal bodyguard to the reigning monarch and as such were trained at Caterham from 1877 to 1960. Here, for some 82 years, recruits arrived from every part of the United Kingdom to carry out their basic training.

Croydon Chronicle – 23rd October 1877.

> 'ARRIVAL OF THE REDCOATS – Good news for Servantdom. On Tuesday the first portion of the 800 troops to be quartered in the new barracks at Caterham arrived at Caterham station to the number of about 300, and thence marched to their new home. On the previous day a party of some 30 or 40 men of more mature age than the new arrivals were sent down to prepare all things for the reception of their comrades. They left again on Tuesday afternoon'.

Mounting Guard, Guard's Depot, Caterham.

Croydon Advertiser – 27th October 1877.

'The owners of property in the neighbourhood seem by no means pleased with the advent of the military, considering that their property is likely to be depreciated in consequence, but the domestic servants are almost beside themselves with joy'.

Croydon Advertiser – 16th March 1878 (at the time of the Russo-Turkish conflict).

'The recruits are at drill and very well they go through their duties. They look a remarkably healthy and sturdy body of young men, and this part, at any rate, of Her Majesty's warriors in embryo do not merit the sweeping denunciations of our army reformer, Mr. Holmes. Boys they are not! Young they are, and right so, but apparently good hardy fellows....The men consist of recruits for the Coldstream Guards, the Grenadier Guards and the Scots Guards, with a sprinkling of old soldiers and non-commissioned officers from various battalions. The recruits remain here generally about four or five months, and by that time, having become efficient, they are drafted into the various battalions.

'After witnessing the drill, we turn to our left and passing the drill sheds, where a number of young men are going through their exercises, we arrive at the canteen, one of the most important parts of the establishment. Here it is that the soldiers, beside being able to obtain eatables and drinkables of all kinds, are otherwise provided for. On the ground floor is the non-commissioned officers' mess room, with a supply of papers and with facilities for bagatelle, etc. Cards are not allowed in the reading rooms, the men showing too great a fondness for them when they were. Upstairs is the reading room of the recruits, with bagatelle board, etc, and exactly opposite the door is that of the recreation room. The latter answers an excellent purpose. Here, among the men, entertainments are frequently arranged. On the left of the canteen bar is the old soldiers' room and well the latter seem to be enjoying themselves.'

'Passing on and bearing to the right, we pass the skittle alley, which now has many occupants, and halt at the four blocks of buildings which comprise the recruits' quarters. The blocks are known as 'the Wellington', 'the York', 'the Albemarle' and 'the Cambridge' with the cookhouse in the centre. The recruits' rooms are lofty, light, well warmed and ventilated on the best principles. To the right is the hospital, unfortunately rather full at the present time.

'The recruits have three drills in the course of the day, the first from 8.30 to 9.45 a.m., the second from 11.15 to 12.15 and the third from 1.45 to 3 o'clock. They go to school for an hour in the morning and an hour in the afternoon.

'Passing the drill ground we approach the gate, and on our right find the school rooms. Mr. Kidd, the schoolmaster is here engaged in his duties. In the same block, too, are various stores, and adjoining these is the armourer's shed, the shoemakers' and carpenters' sheds or shops. All that can possibly be done on the premises by the soldiers themselves is done and thus a great saving in expense is effected. The magazine is situate near the school. Turning to the right the married men's quarters appear and here we conclude our inspection.'

Having become established in their new home, it was not long before we hear of entertainments being given before an invited audience and the local tradespeople returned the compliment by inviting the sergeants from the depot to a dinner at the *Asylum Hotel* (now the *Caterham Arms*) on 21st January 1879. The Guards' Choral Society gave concerts to raise funds. Local gentry paid a Barracks' Scripture Reader's salary. Cricket and football matches were arranged. Officers hunted with the Surrey Foxhounds and the Tillingdown range was used for shooting competitions with local rifle clubs.

Firing at Miniature Range, Guard's Depot, Caterham.

Prior to the First World War a squad of men patrolled the district every evening to maintain order amongst the soldiers out on passes. The Military Police also regularly visited Croydon to keep an eye on Guardsmen who held passes to go that far from the Barracks and they always met the last train into Caterham Station.

A HISTORY OF CATERHAM

During the First World War recruits for 'Kitchener's Army' trained in their thousands at Caterham, as elsewhere throughout the United Kingdom: the first of the modern citizen armies. Their encampment in fields adjoining the Barracks was popularly known as 'Tin Town'. Extensive use was also made of Coulsdon Common to house under canvas the many thousands of soldiers who had their basic training at the Barracks prior to serving on the battlefields of France and elsewhere.

With the return of peace, social and family connections with the Depot flourished. The annual round of socials, dances, and displays of one kind and another ensured the broadest basis for friendship, love and marriage. Today there can be very few streets in Caterham that do not number some ex-Guardsman or his descendants among their inhabitants.

The first of a regular series of 'Open Days', during which members of the public were invited into the Barracks to be entertained by a varied programme of sporting and other events, was held at the Depot on 10th August 1935. From 1937 Mr. Delia exhibited his collection of model soldiers every year, except for the war years and 1950, until the final Open Day in 1959. These models were made from cartridge paper, using only scissors and razor blades. Each soldier was constructed from 98 separate pieces; even the swords could be withdrawn from their scabbards. These replicas of Guardsmen, marines, sailors and airmen inspired a number of magazine articles and were the subject of a Pathé News Film made at his home. Over the years they raised many thousands of pounds for Service charities.

The Second World War again saw a great influx of infantry into the Guards' Depot, and a rash of temporary huts overflowed onto Coulsdon Common to accommodate them. 'The Dene', previously a private school for boys, became a suitably sandbagged military hospital. Canadian and other Commonwealth troops abounded. In the bombing raids on the Guards' Depot, 25 Guardsmen lost their lives.

During the summer of 1949 a film depicting the Guards' Armoured Division was produced by Two Cities Films, called *They were not Divided*, written and directed by Terence Young. Part of the film was shot on location at the Guards' Depot, using a detachment of 22 Guardsmen.

The Household Division is made up of the Household Cavalry (the Life Guards and the Royal Horse Guards) and the five regiments of Foot Guards. These regiments traditionally form the Sovereign's personal troops. They stand guard over the royal palaces and form the Sovereign's escort on State occasions. This special relationship is reflected in the number of visits made to the Guards Depot by members of the Royal Family – 25 visits up to 1967, including five by reigning monarchs. King George V – 1917, 1926; King George VI – 1940, 1942; Her Majesty Queen Elizabeth II & Prince Philip – 1967.

II.   ST. LAWRENCE'S HOSPITAL

An extract from an article written by Marjorie Harris before the demolition of the buildings in 1996.

The hospital, when it was first opened, was known as the Metropolitan Asylum, and Westway was Asylum Road. It was not until 1930 that the name was changed to St. Lawrence's, taken from the ancient church at the top of Church Hill. Local people still talk of the 'mental hospital' or 'asylum' or of having worked 'inside'. An article about life at the hospital, written only two years after its opening, is entitled *The Idiot Colony at Caterham*! It was written by William Gilbert, father of W.S. Gilbert of Savoy Opera fame, and he was obviously impressed by what he found – the general standard of care, food, hygiene, and the whole design of the buildings, including kitchens and laundry. At that time the hospital was in effect a workhouse for the relief of overcrowded institutions in London, hence the title 'Metropolitan Asylum'. There were 1600 or so residents, all mentally ill or mentally handicapped, poor, and, for whatever reason, needing to be shut away from the rest of the community. In 1930 the London County Council took over the running of St. Lawrence's and it was not until 1948, with the advent of the National Health Service, that it became a hospital for mentally handicapped residents only.

THE GREAT INSTITUTIONS

St. Lawrence's Hospital Main Building - boarded up before demolition. *c.*1995

The original plan of St. Lawrence's was of two wings of wards, off a central administration block that housed the offices, the kitchens, the laundry, the chapel, the swimming and hydrotherapy pools, the recreation hall and the 'works' department – all that kept the life of such a big establishment going. Coping with supplies and meals for over 2000 residents as well as staff was in itself a tremendous task, apart from all the other work that had to be organised for the smooth running of the hospital, but there has always been a sense of 'belonging' among the staff, from the highest to the lowest, and this family feeling made St. Lawrence's so special and so happy.

One wing of the hospital was for men, the other for women, and in the early days 'never the twain did meet' – except for the weekly dance when they sat on different sides of the recreation hall and only touched each other when actually dancing – under the eagle eyes of the staff on duty! The segregation of the sexes was very strictly enforced and it has only been in the last 30 years or so that this has been relaxed and friendship between men and women been possible and encouraged. No longer did they have to sit on only one side of the chapel. Indeed several marriages were happily arranged with a service in the hospital church after a registry office ceremony and the couples went to live in flats, either locally or in the London area from which they originally came.

Over the years, with the wider understanding of a mentally handicapped person's potential and under the progressive influence of medical staff, opportunities for personal development and training were greatly enhanced with the setting up of various workshops. The residents became skilled at painting and assembling and then packing articles for sale supplied by the makers – such as toys and dolls. There is a film of toy soldiers being painted quite intricately. The Concrete Unit was set up and paving stones, bird baths and garden planters and ornaments became a very popular line of business. For those with less manual skill, there were plenty of opportunities for work in the gardens, the kitchens, the laundry or on the wards. All these activities earned the residents some pocket money which they enjoyed spending at the hospital shop, the shops along Westway, or at the local market, where they would be taken by members of staff or by voluntary helpers.

Staff had different ways of running wards and would arrange treats or outings for special occasions such as birthdays and holidays. At Christmas there was great rivalry to see who could produce the best-decorated ward or give the best parties. Senior staff would be invited to them all, and on Christmas Day many would be involved in carving the turkeys on the wards – in fact trying to fit in everything meant that Christmas celebrations lasted well into January.

There were often concerts, dances, plays, entertainment of various sorts held in the recreation hall, with its stage and theatrical equipment. St. Lawrence's had many clubs and activity groups meeting regularly, some run by staff, others by volunteers from outside. The largest was the Gateway Club, one of many such clubs for mentally handicapped people all over the country run under the auspices of Mencap. Once every year there is a variety show in all the regions culminating in a grand final, sometimes at the Royal Festival Hall, when Gateway members are given the chance to perform on stage. The talent of the performers has to be seen to be believed; singing, dancing, acting, all beautifully devised and presented with the help of their leaders. For several years St. Lawrence's Gateway Club went on from the south-east region to perform at the Royal Festival Hall in the national final.

St. Lawrence's received tremendous support from volunteers and the League of Friends. So many people gave their time and expertise in so many ways, and especially their friendship to the residents, helping with everything that went on there. The support of parents and relatives was invaluable. Those who ran Horizon Radio and all the many clubs, those who sang in the church choir – coming to worship with the residents week after week and at special festival services – and those who willingly befriended individuals in a deeper way as Advocates on a regular, committed basis were all greatly appreciated. It is impossible to speak too highly of the debt owed to the local shops and their staff who were always helpful to and patient with St. Lawrence's residents while they were doing their shopping, dithering over what they wanted, or fumbling with money and their other parcels. No shopkeeper was ever heard to speak unkindly to them – most knew their regular customers by name.

The League's most strenuous spell of fundraising came after the disastrous fire which destroyed part of the school – the very night before that part was due to open after being refurbished and equipped with modern TV, video aids to learning, and computers. Almost £30,000 was raised in one year. This was used to buy replacements for the aptly named Phoenix Centre. The centre has now been extended to become the Caterham therapy centre for the future. All the therapies will be available and clients will be brought in daily from their homes. More recently the League provided most of the money for the SNOOZELIN, a special sensory room which with its music and coloured lights making patterns on the walls can quieten hyperactive people or stimulate the lethargic. It also has chains of fibre optics with delicate winking lights which can be touched and held – a fairy-tale experience.

One of St. Lawrence's most famous residents was Joseph Deacon. Joey was completely spastic and unable to do anything except manoeuvre his wheelchair with his wrist, smile and make noises. In some miraculous way his friend, Ernie Roberts, also spastic but able to speak, could understand Joey's noises. When people did not believe that this was possible, various tests were set – keeping them both in separate rooms and asking Joey to pass on a message or the time – they never failed. With the help of Michael Sangster, who wrote it down in longhand, and Tom Blackburn, who typed it out with one finger, Joey's life-story was written. Tom not being able to read recognised the letters from association with a list of their friends' names. A day's work would result in five or six lines of typescript and with the help and encouragement of hospital staff the story was eventually completed and published by Mencap under the title *Tongue-tied*. Then came the BBC interest and its prize-winning film *Joey* for the *Horizon* programme, and after that world-wide fame.

Joey Deacon and friends
From left - Tom Blackburn, Ernie Roberts, Joey Deaon, Michael Sangster

Their great wish, which they had expressed in the interview with the press at the end of the film, was 'to have a home of their own'. A Dutch TV channel took up this idea and used the film for their annual Christmas appeal, which brought in nearly £60,000 for the Bungalow Fund. Soon afterwards BBC's *Blue Peter* raised money with a nationwide appeal and St. Lawrence's received one of the resulting bungalows. There are now twelve bungalows in the grounds, where residents have considerable freedom in what they do and yet have the benefit of the care and supervision of nursing and medical staff always at hand.

St. Lawrence's has been recognised as an important centre of research – local people probably did not realise how much went on in parts of the building away from those two wings of wards that were so visible to the man in the street. Biochemistry, pathology, physiotherapy psychology, and the whole business of education for people with 'learning disabilities' have all benefited from experience at St. Lawrence's. New ideas were tried and tested willingly, and the gradual change from a large institution to Lifecare NHS Trust looking after people in smaller units has gone smoothly.

Special Open Day at St. Lawrence's Hospital - The Year of the Disabled, 1981
Pool Hoist provided by The League of Friends

Chapter 15

Schools

by Nigel Harris

AUDLEY COUNTY PRIMARY SCHOOL - See St. Francis R.C. School.

AVONDALE COLLEGE for girls, also preparatory for boys, from *c.*1928 to 1939, occupied several acres at 264 Croydon Road. On the site was a rose garden, tennis courts, netball, hockey and cricket lawns, an orchard and paddock. The Principal was Mrs. O. Howe-Heineman.

BOARDING SCHOOLS, CATERHAM VALLEY IN THE 19TH CENTURY –
The *Half Moon* Inn near Wapses Lodge was converted into a boarding school for 13 young ladies in 1861.
Miss Emma Bennett ran a ladies' boarding school, 'Churchills', Church Hill, recorded in 1899.
John Bosomwith had a boys' boarding and day school at Beulah House, Mount Pleasant, from 1874 to *c.*1886.
The Villas, Godstone Road. In 1881 Nos. 1 and 2 were a girls' boarding school and No. 3 a boys school opened by Henry Grinstead, who was the first Board School headmaster and later High Street postmaster. The buildings were turned into the Hydro Sanatorium in 1898.
Miss Rose Stanford had a school at 'The Priory' in 1881. In 1884 she moved to 1 West View, Harestone Hill.

CATERHAM ADULT SCHOOL founded in 1931 for the purposes of education through fellowship. In 1939 it met at Eothen School on Monday evenings. President: H.H. Daily, 150 Croydon Road.

CATERHAM HILL BOARD SCHOOL (Now Hillcroft Primary School). The land and house for Caterham's first school was given by Thomas Clarke to the parish rent free to the schoolmaster – together with the produce of the orchard – subject to free education of not less than six children. Management of the school was by the resident clergyman, the acting overseer of the poor and the owner of the manor. This must have been about 1805

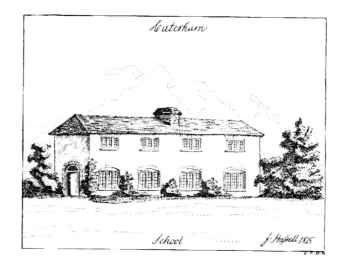

Caterham's first school, founded *c.*1805
Drawing by E.F. Bishop (1970) after J Hassell (1825)

when John Brooke was chosen as schoolmaster. He was then 65 and he continued until his death at 81 in 1821. He was succeeded by George Pratt for 29 years and on his death William Brough was appointed on 20th August

A woodwork class at (probably) Caterham Hill Board School *c.* 1921

Display of Christmas cakes remade after the first batch were burnt - Christmas 1948
Caterham Valley Secondary School

Sitting, from left: Mary Chisholm, ... , Valerie May, Ivy Skilton, Pat Dawson, Shirley Webb, Joan Sargeant, ... , Maria Beaman, ...

Standing: Jean Williams, Jean Robinson, June Williams, Gillian Watts, ...

1850 (he was also parish clerk). After the 1870 Education Act the school became the Caterham on the Hill Board School.

In 1874 Henry T. Grinstead was headmaster, Miss Mary Morris, mistress and Miss Zenobia Robinson, infants' mistress. In 1884 Miss Mills was infants' teacher and in 1885 Miss Nelson was sacked because she was too severe. She was followed by Miss Frankling. In 1899 George H. Rose was boys' master and Miss Frankling still the girls' mistress. They both lived in School Houses, Chaldon Road, designed by Richard Martin, School Board Architect. Miss M. Barrett was infants' mistress.

From 1908-1912 H.J. Davis was boys' head and in 1923 A.G. Lay was head; he was still head of the Junior Mixed School in 1937. In 1926 Miss G.A. Ellis was infants' mistress. In 1937 older children were transferred to the new Central School in the Valley near Wapses Lodge, where the headmaster was Mr.J.W. Richardson. It became known as Hillcroft in about 1979.

CATERHAM VALLEY BOARD SCHOOL, Beechwood Road. The school buildings, designed by Richard Martin, opened on 10th January 1876 with 150 pupils. By 1886 the mistress Mrs. Sarah Higgins was assisted by an infants' mistress and four young pupil teachers. In 1899 the boys' and girls' head teacher was John Perry and the infants' was Miss Miles. From 1901-1912 the head was G.W. Crane.

1923 Head: H.J. Pleydell (until 1939) who taught Standards 6, 7 and 8. Headmistress: Mrs. Allbrook, Standard 5; Mr. Persaud, 4; Miss Merton, 3; and Miss Parker 1 and 2. In 1937 older children moved to the new Central School and it continued until 1979. It is now an Adult Education Centre.

CATERHAM VALLEY CENTRAL SCHOOL. Wapses Lodge. Opened 22nd October 1937. The service was conducted by Canon J.C. Morris, MA, RD. Chairman: A.E. Hammond, CC, of Whyteleafe House, Chairman of School Managers. The address was given by Sir Philip Henriques, KBE, DL, JP of Normandy Park, Guildford, Chairman of Surrey County Council. School Managers. Headmaster: Richard V. Howell (Butch). In 1967 pupils moved to the new de Stafford School.

CATERHAM SCHOOL. Founded in 1811 for the sons of Congregational Ministers in Newington and Lewisham, it moved to Caterham in 1884 when the formal opening of the Caterham Congregational School was

Caterham School.

held on 10th October. In 1894 Revd. Thomas Rudd, headmaster since 1859, retired. There was then a total of 140 boys, boarders and day pupils. In 1912 the name was changed to Caterham School. In 1934 the Old Boys presented the Foxburrow Estate to the school in memory of Allan Mottram, Headmaster 1910 to 1934.

1935 saw the opening of the Preparatory School. In 1981 there were 669 pupils, 11 of whom were girls, recently introduced into the Sixth Form. In 1995 Eothen School for Girls was merged with Caterham School.

CATERHAM SCHOOL OF MUSIC, Croydon Road. 1899 Principal: Miss G. Rolls. In 1912 it was at *Domremy*, 1 Harestone Valley Road. Miss Rolls was a member of the famed Rolls family (of Rolls-Royce motor cars).

CONVENT OF NOTRE DAME HIGH SCHOOL FOR GIRLS, opened in 1938 with 8 pupils at *The Beeches*, Church Hill. Numbers increased rapidly but in 1942 it changed to preparatory for girls and small boys and closed in 1945.

DAME SCHOOL. c. 1880 in Croydon Road where the Co-op had its bakery about No. 37.

DAWSON SCHOOL OF DOMESTIC SCIENCE (OR ECONOMY), *Linton*, Harestone Hill. Principal: Miss S.E. Dawson. A residential school equipped with oil, gas, electric and *Aga* cookers and an up-to-date laundry. Facilities for all games and riding. Closed in 1939.

DENE SCHOOL. Founded in 1876 at 'The Dean', Underwood Road, (now 'Trundle') with F.J.C. Fenton as head. In 1898 Revd. R. Morgan Watkins became principal. 20 pupils were being prepared for Eton or similar establishments. At his instigation the school moved to Church Road in 1905. He was assisted by two masters. Sergeant-Major Clark from the Guards' Depot drilled boys twice a week.

In 1923 L.W. Paul was headmaster and from 1934 H.W. Luce was the last head as the school closed on the outbreak of war.

The Dene School 1923

SCHOOLS

DE STAFFORD COLLEGE. This school in Burntwood Lane opened in 1967 and was for the older boys and girls from Hill and Valley. In 1984 it received an award under the National Curriculum Award Scheme. In 1992 the school achieved Grant Maintained status and in 1995 it became a college of technology and the arts.

EOTHEN SCHOOL. The Misses Catherine and Winifred Pye opened their school at 2, West View, Harestone Hill, on 18th January 1892 with eight girls aged 8 to 15. The Misses Pye were sole owners until 1923 when the Eothen School Company Ltd. was established. They retired in 1938. In 1970 the school was taken over by the Church Schools Company. In 1982 there were almost 400 girls, aged 3 to 18 and over 40 staff with Miss Diana Raine as head. The school merged with Caterham School in 1995.

ESSENDENE LODGE SCHOOL, in the old St. Francis RC school buildings in Essendene Road, was opened by Mrs. Haydock as Chaldon Nursery School in June 1967 in Chaldon Village Hall and later combined with three other nursery schools and moved to the old Parish Room between the RC church and Presbytery. Moved to its present address in 1985.

ESSENDENE NAUTICAL SCHOOL, Essendene House, Whyteleafe Road. Principal: Honorary Lieutenant-Commander Soames. Closed a few years before the outbreak of World War II.

FAIRBANK SCHOOL FOR YOUNG LADIES. 1908. Principals: Misses Allen and Didier in Harestone Valley Road, just past Devon House (possibly Pelham House).

HILLCROFT PRIMARY SCHOOL. See Caterham Hill Board School.

HILLSIDE SCHOOL. 8 Tupwood Lane. The Church Army Girls' Residential School in 1957.

LINKSIDE SCHOOL OF DANCING at St. John's Hall, Stafford Road in 1958. Principal: Daphne Freebury.

Farningham Road School 1963-65 (Head Teacher Mr Sutton)
Later incorporated into Marden Lodge School (see overleaf)

MARDEN LODGE COUNTY PRIMARY SCHOOL, Wapses Lodge, opened as a combined nursery, First and Middle School in September 1989 as a result of the amalgamation of Farningham Road Schools and the existing Junior School at Wapses Lodge. In September 1993 became a Primary School, ages from 3 to 11 years. Headteacher (1995) Mrs. M.L. Kelly BEd.

OAKHYRST GRANGE SCHOOL, 154-60 Stanstead Road. For boys 4 to 12 years. Headmistress: Mrs. R.G. Allen (1961). Principal: Mrs. E.S. Cameron, MA (1964). Originally founded by Colin Cameron in 1950 at Hillside, Tupwood Lane and moved to Stanstead Road in 1957 to a house built *c.*1870 and owned by Sir Thomas Lipton, the tea merchant. The school took its name from this house.

PORTLEY HOUSE SCHOOL for the Deaf (SCC),Whyteleafe Road. This boarding school was established in Portley House in 1950 for 60 children. When John Melhuish became headmaster in 1980, numbers had fallen and the school closed in July 1983.

REST HARROW SCHOOL, 'Bairnscroft', 10 Underwood Road. A school for the treatment and education of boys and girls whose nervous disabilities rendered them unsuitable for the ordinary school. The principal was Dr. Ida Saxby. Closed in 1939.

ROCKLANDS SCHOOL, 141 Croydon Road. A boarding and day school for girls and preparatory for boys from 1908-1939 The principals were the Misses Wilson – Gertrude and Mary taught, while May looked after the domestic affairs.

Physical drill at Rocklands School, early 1930s

ROSEVILLE. A small dame school run by Mrs. Elliff at 55 Croydon Road until 1885.

ST. ANDREWS SCHOOL, 47 Chaldon Road, was run by Miss M. Christie until she was 75 in 1971. It taught children from 4½ to 10 years old.

SCHOOLS

ST. FRANCIS R.C. SCHOOL (Now Audley County Primary School). Opened October 1880 by Father Roe with fourteen children in a small building opposite the *Golden Lion* in Town End. The headmistress was Miss Pierce. In 1883 the school moved into a building between the Church and Presbytery. The teacher was Miss Hussey until December 1896, followed by Miss Murray and in August 1902 Miss Austin. The school moved into a new building in Essendene Road in 1909-10 with 80 children. In the 1920s Miss Austin was succeeded by Miss Beasley until the war years. During World War II it was staffed by Sisters from Notre Dame and the school was evacuated to Yeovil during the 'flying bomb' period. After the end of the war Miss Bold became Headmistress and Miss Agnes Walsh retired after many years teaching the infants. It was re-named **Audley County Primary School** on moving to Whyteleafe Road in the grounds of Portley House in 1972. The present headmaster is R. Gandolfo.

ST. JOHN'S NATIONAL SCHOOL. Was near the temporary St. John's Church in 1875 when it was inspected by a government inspector, who told the church that better accommodation was required for the school to continue. It was not until 1883 that the PCC decided to purchase a plot of land opposite the new Church and the

St. John's School, Godstone Road, Caterham Valley, 1940s.

old temporary church was moved across the road and built by Mr. Scrivener to become the new school in Godstone Road.

In 1875 the mistress was Miss Jane Holeyman, assisted by Mrs. Phoebe Eliff, Miss Elizabeth Eliff and pupil teacher Miss Jane Eliff. In 1899 the master was J. Croucher assisted by Miss Quixley. Subsequent heads included in 1908 C.W. Clark., 1912 A.T. Hedger, 1923 R. O'Nions, 1928 F.E. Faulkner and in 1937 B.J. Gay.

The junior school moved to Markfield Road in 1969 and the infants followed in 1975. Headmistress: Mrs. L.F. Bishop.The old school building became the Miller Centre.

SALVATION ARMY ran a school at its citadel prior to World War I.

THE SHAW SCHOOL, 'Ninehams Gables', Ninehams Road. Kindergarten and preparatory. Principal: Mrs. G.R. Howell (1957, 1961). Later moved to a house in Chaldon.

SOUTHBANK SCHOOL. Albany House, Church Hill. Preparatory and kindergarten. Principal: Mrs. F.M. McDowell, from1938. Lessons included dancing of all types. Moved to 8 Tupwood Lane in 1953. From 1946 the principal was Mrs. Edwards until its closure in 1972.

STRATHMORE NURSERY SCHOOL. 107 Whyteleafe Road. Principal: Miss Stark, run on Montessori lines for twelve children between 3 and 6 years. Post World War II.

SUNNYDOWN. Since autumn 1983 the premises at Portley House have accommodated up to 50 boys with special health problems.

UPWOOD PARK SCHOOL. Tupwood Lane, now *The Oaks*. *c.*1908-1915. The principal was H. LeGrew Harrison, assisted by his brother E. Donald Harrison. There were 16 boarders. The school occupied seven acres with tennis and cricket areas; it had a carpenter's workshop and 200 volume library. Staff Sergeant-Major Clark of the Grenadier Guards was the drill instructor .

THE WINNATS SCHOOL, 158 Burntwood Lane. Principal: Miss Smith assisted by her sister. (Pre World -War II until 1970s)

SOURCES

Blomfield, Ernest de C. *A Century at Caterham School 1884-1984*

Bourne Society Bulletin **167**Kelly's Directories

Bourne Society *Local History Records* **28**

Pye, Winifred *History of Eothen School 1892-1942*

Roffey, Miss M. Bourne Society *Local History Records* **2**

Schools and local residents

Tooke, J. *Bygone Caterham*

Tutt, Dorothy – research material

Chapter 16

The Utilities and Light Industry

I. ELECTRICITY

Extracted from *Electricity Supply in Caterham & District from 1900 to 1992* by John Pipe, published by the Bourne Society 1997.

The generation of electricity for lighting started at about the time of the Crimean War but the dynamos were always at the place of need, eg country mansions. There is no record of such early plants in Caterham but at about the turn of the century there was one owned by Mr. Louskin of 'The Mound' in War Coppice Road.

In the late 19th and early 20th centuries each community desiring a public supply of electricity needed to persuade the local authority either to provide it or to find a private company willing to do so. The Caterham Electric Lighting Order 1900 under the Electric Lighting Acts 1882 and 1888 authorised the Urban Electric Supply Co. Ltd. to supply electricity in Caterham, Warlingham and, implicitly, Whyteleafe. It placed strict requirements on the maximum price to be charged and specified the roads to which a supply must be provided by June 1902, but it was not until February 1903 that UESCL entered into a contract with Edmundsons for engineering and operating the system. A piece of land at 85 Croydon Road was purchased and Caterham Power Station was built at a cost of £8000, which included an 100 ft. high brick chimney (dismantling the machinery 22 years later cost £11,900.12.6d – the present day value of the two amounts is £340,000 and £430,000 respectively). Generation commenced at the end of October 1903.

Early power stations were not good neighbours. Many of them exhausted their steam through their chimneys in the manner of a steam railway locomotive, with all the consequent noise. Their engines with their heavy reciprocating parts caused considerable vibration in the surrounding properties. There is no evidence that the Caterham plant was particularly bad but Mr. H.H. Rivers recalled that, whilst he was living at 91 Croydon Road in the early years of the century, 'the electric light works was built and how the running of the engines used to worry us at night; we could not sleep for them but it was not long before we had to listen intently to know whether they were running or not.'

Sales of electricity at first were minute; 31,716 units in 1904 which would be just about enough for seven homes at the present time. However, there was great activity in cable laying and by 1906 sales were 68,728 units consumed almost entirely by 10,058 eight-candle power lamps. By 1913 sales had increased to 146,961 units, perhaps sufficient for 30 modern homes.

In 1922 the directors of UESCL decided to take a bulk supply of electricity for their Caterham undertaking from the County of London Electric Supply Co. Ltd. and to change the supply from direct current to alternating current. The agreement for an 11 kV bulk supply was sealed in 1924 and the power station was closed later the same year. The machinery was removed in the following year although the buildings were not demolished until 1988 having been used for a variety of purposes including that of the local electricity showroom from the mid-thirties until 1978. The bulk supply came through 14 miles of cable from CLESCO's 27,500 kW power station at Wandsworth into two substations which were on the power station site at 85 Croydon Road and at Wapses Lodge and an extension was laid to a substation built on the north side of Park Road.

The worst failure of the 11kV feeder from Wandsworth was on the afternoon of 26th August 1925 and in the absence of any alternative the whole of the Caterham area was without power for twenty-four hours until 5pm on 27th August.

The days of CLESCO were numbered and the Electricity Act 1947 resulted in the assets of CLESCO being vested in the London Electricity Board from 1st April 1948. The South Eastern Electricity Board managed the Caterham part of the inherited CLESCO undertaking until 1963 when it was formally transferred to them from LEB.

Before this took place the supply to Caterham was reinforced by the laying of twin 33kV cables from Purley and the installation of 33kV/11kV transformers at 85 Croydon Road. Responsibility for electricity supply in south east England passed from SEEB to Seeboard plc in 1990. In spite of the changes Caterham pavements still display a considerable number of joint box covers bearing the mark CLESCO.

The electricity showroom at 63a Croydon Road was closed in 1992 and the last electricity supply industry employee left Caterham.

**Caterham Power Station
in 1905**

II.   GAS

Based on a paper presented by Muriel Huitson to Croydon Natural History & Scientific Society on 4th October 1973 by Margaret Duck.

In May 1869 a small group of Caterham businessmen met in Kenley House, the home of Mr. Young, to discuss the possibility of setting up a gas company for Caterham after having waited several years for the Croydon Gas Company to extend its gas main to Caterham.

The works were to be built near the *Rose & Crown* Inn at Riddlesdown on land offered by Mr. Young. The company was to be called the Caterham & Kenley Gas Company and 1,000 shares issued at £10 each of which the directors, Messrs. Cook and Asprey, both of Caterham, were to have 20 shares each.

Gas mains were to be laid to 'Beechlands' in Stafford Road, the home of Charles Asprey, and during 1870-71 other large houses in the area were to be supplied with gas. It was hoped that the new gas company could supply gas to the new Asylum (St. Lawrence's Hospital) being built on Caterham Hill, but when the directors learned

**Changing the gas lamp
in the Asprey Fountain**

that the new institution was to produce its own gas, they were not deterred and decided to go ahead with their plans for a gas company for Caterham and Kenley. The company met regularly and comfortably in the Guildhall Tavern, London, to discuss its plans.

The company had bought old gas machinery from Croydon Gas Company, including a small gasholder, all of which quickly became useless and inadequate. The Caterham Gas Company then decided to build its own gasholder near the *Rose & Crown* Inn and put up the price of gas to pay for it.

The Guards' Depot recently built at this time at Caterham Hill was another likely customer, and was supplied with gas, which kept the company going.

In 1889 the first gas stoves were installed in Caterham. They could be hired for 1s.6d - 3s. a quarter, or could be purchased for £1 - £20.

The drinking fountain provided by Charles Asprey and erected in the middle of The Square in Caterham in November 1890 had a gas lamp over it. The lamp had three burners and in 1892 was lit all night for £8 from 16th September to 14th April excluding five nights of the full moon each month. It was the only street light in the middle of Caterham for some time.

In 1896 the prepayment gas meter was introduced into 20 houses in Caterham. Pipes, fittings and a small cooker were provided for about £4. Gas was charged at 4s.3d a thousand cubic foot. The number of houses supplied with gas gradually increased but the constant digging up of roads, before proper roads and pavements were made in Caterham, caused widespread havoc.

The company next considered building a gasholder in Caterham, in an old lime pit at the back of the Public Halls in Godstone Road, but for various reasons the plans did not go ahead.

The last meeting of the Caterham & District Gas Company, the 37th was held at the Guildhall Tavern in February 1905, when the shareholders were told that the Gas Company property was to be transferred to Croydon.

In 1974 Caterham was converted to natural gas, about 100 years or so after a small group of business men first met to discuss the possibilities of setting up a gas company.

III. CATERHAM'S POSTAL SERVICES

by Judith Faulkner

In 1857 a GPO minute stated that 'under the present post from Sanderstead to Caterham, letters are not delivered until 10.15 a.m. and the post left at 12.40 p.m.' and it was proposed to withdraw Caterham from the Sanderstead post which was processed through Croydon and to establish a post from Godstone under Reigate, when delivery would be made at 7 a.m. and despatched at 6 p.m.. During 1859/60 mail was being received in Caterham by Mrs. Jane Lock with letters arriving at 7.30 a.m. and being despatched at 12.45 and 5.45 p.m..

This was satisfactory until 1869 when a further minute stated that 'The present arrangements for serving Caterham and its neighbourhood do not afford satisfaction. This place is less than 20 miles from London and is on a branch line'. It was agreed that there would be 'three mails daily in each direction with two complete deliveries of letters'. This ended the practice of mail deliveries arriving from Redhill via Godstone. At the time the Caterham Valley post office was being run by Walter Payne and that on the Hill by James Balch who was also a tailor, butcher and a grocer. The Hill post office appears to have been on its present site since the 1870s.

By 1874 Michael King, grocer, had taken over the Valley post office and in 1876 it was being run by Mr. Phillips followed in 1880 by Eward Pollard, house and estate agent who had premises at the corner of Timber

Hill Road, 14 The Square. In the 1881 census his occupation is given as 'clothier master' and he lived there with his wife Cordelia, one son and two daughters.

In 1889/90 the post office moved to 10 Godstone Road, where it remained for about fourteen years, the Postmaster being W.R. Roalfe; the office was open every weekday from 8 a.m. until 10 p.m. and on Sundays from 8 to 10 a.m. for telegrams, stamps and letters to callers.

Caterham Valley Post Office, 10 Godstone Road, from c.1889 to 1904

In February 1904 the first purpose-built post office was opened in the Grand Parade at 1 Station Avenue where it remained until the present building was erected by J. Quittenton of Warlingham at a cost of £2,000 and opened in October 1910, the Postmaster being a A. Hahn. Opening hours in 1910 were from 8 a.m. until 8 p.m. weekdays and from 8.30 to 10 a.m. on Sundays.

By 1905 sub-post offices had opened in Croydon Road and Coulsdon Road with Banstead Road, Marden Parade and Westway sub-offices appearing during the 1930s. From 1893 the Caterham Barracks received deliveries in a locked box; their own sub post office which was not open to the public, began in the late 1930s and closed during the 1970s.

SOURCE

Moyle, Arthur, pers. comm.

IV.   LIGHT INDUSTRY

By Nigel Harris

Before the coming of the railway, Caterham was a sleepy downland village and any industry in the village was devoted to the needs of the local farming community such as the wheelwright William Reading in the High Street and Dennis the blacksmith. Lime burning was carried out by the Atkins family in the chalkpits in Godstone Road. The nearest substantial industrial activity was quarrying in Godstone and Merstham. There were only a few cottages on the Hill and fewer in the Valley until the coming of the railway in 1856, and the large houses – such as 'Portley', 'Essendene', 'Burntwood' and 'Woodlands' – that followed.

Until the turn of the century most of the local population was involved in ministering to those houses in one way or another. Local utility companies – water and gas, followed a little later by electricity – had been started. The Caterham & Kenley Gas Company, which was set up by local residents hoping to supply the newly-erected Asylum on the Hill, built its works at Whyteleafe in 1868. Beset by money problems, it was taken over by the Croydon Gas Company in 1905. The Caterham Spring Water Company was founded in 1862 but was soon absorbed by the East Surrey Water Company. The Urban Electricity Supply Company built its power station in Croydon Road – opposite *The Commonwealth* – in 1903, close to the railway and served by a siding running from the goods yard. It was later taken over by the County of London Electric Supply Co. Ltd. until it was nationalised.

By 1900 a few manufacturers had arrived, including beehive constructor Edward Bontoft of Beechwood Road, and Arthur Rich who made saddles and harnesses at 12 Godstone Road. Horses, which required regular shoeing, were the main means of local transport. This required four forges in the town. R. Vigar set up business in 1869, his forge being behind Woodland Cottages, Reigate Road (now Chaldon Road). He moved to Town End in 1883, and on his death in 1923 the business passed to George Ibbotson, his son-in-law. The building is still standing in 1997, but not as a forge. Bridgeland & Son were in the High Street, next door to the *Blacksmiths Arms,* and J. Tremain had a forge in the Valley in Godstone Road, close to St. John's Church. Mr. Vigar also opened a branch – to be run by George Ibbotson, who later became a local councillor – close to Kilby's stables in Croydon Road.

Livingstone's timber yard and saw mill occupied the area where first the *Greyhound* was built and years later the *Capitol* cinema, which was renamed the *Florida* for its last few years but is now redeveloped as Hammond House.

The scattered large houses and horse transport meant that there was a call for coach builders – Russell in the High Street and John Rivers in Croydon Road, one of the oldest businesses in the Valley started in 1871. John was one of eight sons of Thomas Rivers, who was a wheelwright and coach builder on Coulsdon Common and whose family trade can be traced back to the early part of the 18th century. Of course not everyone could afford the upkeep of a horse, and cycle makers were busy with Abbott & Co. in Croydon Road, Kilby running a depot alongside his cab business next to the station and a cycle works at 14 Godstone Road. On the hill, at 21 Park Road, Mr. C.W. Cox – maker of the 'Winner' brand – combined cycle making with being a plumber.

An early industry was that of dressmaking, and in about 1885 Mrs. Tidy employed apprentices in her business next to *Ye Olde King & Queen* in the High Street .

The large houses also meant a demand for laundry services, and at the turn of the century there was the Hurst Laundry in Beechwood Road, Mrs. Donmall in Colin Road, and another laundry in the Lime Pit run by Mr. R. Wright. On the Hill there was the Caterham Laundry in Banstead Road and the Albert Laundry in Coulsdon Road.

Oliver Taylor, General Carrier, A Taylor, Secondhand Furniture, and W.J. Kick, Hand-sewn Bootmaker, in Banstead Road. Early 20th century.

Robert Vigar and staff at the Forge

A HISTORY OF CATERHAM

Another service industry was that of printing and publishing. The *Caterham Free Press* was started in 1890 by John Abbott in Croydon Road and was bought by F.J. Holbrook in 1898 with the young Alec Braid as Editor. It moved into no. 47 a year later and published local directories between 1900 and 1908. In 1908 Alec Braid published his *Guide to Caterham* at Excelsior Works, 47 Croydon Road, the firm now being Braid & Relfe, which printed six local church magazines at this address until the death of E.J. Huggins in about 1950.

Mr. Browning combined being a tobacconist and a printer also in Croydon Road, while F.S. Cotney printed in Asylum Road (now Westway). Banstead Road was the address for J. Burns, who combined being a confectioner with that of a picture frame maker. There was another picture frame business at 41 Croydon Road opened by Mrs. Manser in 1880.

Another vital trade was that of the baker, one of the earliest being Thomas Whiffen of 37 Croydon Road established in 1886. Demand for milk was catered for by the Warren Dairy in the Valley with milk coming from Place Farm, Bletchingley and White Knobs Farm. Later it became the Caterham Model Dairy, proprietor S.H. Pocock until taken over by the Express Dairy in the '60s.

By 1902 a monumental works was at 'Ashdene', Croydon Road (the house later owned by Richard Kearton, FZS, FRPS) opposite the Board School, run by G. Cane. W.H. Price had set up as a china riveter and restorer in Banstead Road. Trevor & Co. were now upholsterers and cabinet-makers in Regent House.

When cars began to appear Waghorn & Miles opened their Victoria Carriage Works which advertised motor bodies and limousines built to order. Mr. Kilby of Kilby's Cabs also branched out into motor and motor cycle repairs in Godstone Road and Tom Vigar, son of the farrier in Town End, advertised himself as the maker of *Trusty* cycles in the High Street where the newsagent is now next to the *Royal Oak*. After the end of World War I, the Caterham Motor Company and Mr. Murrin of the Central Motor Works had joined the Victoria Motor Works in the Valley and the County Garage had opened up at the north end of Croydon Road. The Caterham Motor Company also opened the Station Garage at the corner of Stafford Road and further premises in Godstone Road (branches were also in Oxted, Purley and Woldingham). On the Hill George Ibbotson had taken over the Vigar forge and Mr. Jenner was now an undertaker, carpenter and smith behind the *Caterham Arms*.

On the Hill in 1912 Mr. Jenner had set-up as a coachbuilder with premises in Francis Road, while R. Kemp combined grocery with ironmongery and cycle making at 32 Asylum Road (Westway) and F.T. Sparrow was a printer at 149 Coulsdon Road, who later moved to Chaldon Road next to Greenslade Butchers (now Raglan Precinct). The forge in the High Street had become the *Electric* theatre next to the *Blacksmith's Arms*.

By 1912 The Holmesdale Press of Redhill had taken over the publication of the local directory and we see that another two laundries had opened in the Valley – the Caterham Sanitary Laundry, proprietor F.W. Sales at 187 Croydon Road and another one at 1 Mount Pleasant Road. There were three more on the Hill, Mrs. Smith at 7 Hawarden Road, Mrs. Smith at Elm Cottage and the Town End Laundry as well as the Caterham Laundry which later became the Beaumont Laundry and which continued in Banstead Road until the outbreak of World War II.

There was a little industry starting at the north end of Croydon Road, more or less where the *Half Moon* coaching inn had stood. W. Fuller had started a contractor's business at no.373, which previously had been C.E. Kenworthy, builders and tea rooms. Later a garage business was to be started here.

W.T. Cook started at 15 High Street as a photographer, then moved to 29 where he started a business producing covers for gramophone records and later moved to the corner of Heath Road and Chaldon Road where his factory remained until receiving a hit from one of the first flying bombs that fell on Caterham in the later part of World War II. This site was rebuilt as the printing works of Garrod & Lofthouse who specialised in printing long-playing record sleeves. Rebuilt again to house the insurance company of Bain Clarkson (now Bain Hogg).

One name forever connected with photography and Caterham is that of the Bunce Brothers. George started his business in 1902 in Asylum Road at his parents' home and was joined by his brother a year later. The backbone of the business was always the Guards' Depot and girls were employed in tinting and finishing the many

Page 120

Laundresses outside the laundry at 83-89 Godstone Road

83-89 Godstone Road, at one time a laundry run by Mr. R. Wright, in 1961
Photo courtesy of caterham Library

photographs of Guardsmen.

The 1920s brought a garage to the High Street, Cheeseman & Edwards at 37, where the Electric theatre had been and later at 49, Mr. Hewer at 36 Town End and Oliver Taylor in Banstead Road, later to be known for his coaches. F. Marden had started Layham's Engineering Company at 363 Croydon Road and further north was the British Metallising Company at 373-5, later to become BMC Silverware, but it shut down prior to World War II.

There were more than a few changes after the end of World War II. At the north end of Croydon Road the factory at 409-11, which had been the Council Waste Paper depot, was leased by Norman Plethean Ltd. who had been running a small engineering works in the shopping centre in the Valley. It made hypodermic syringes for the medical and veterinary professions and small electric heaters made from asbestos tubes. The next firm here was a knitwear company, Mill Bridge Manufacturing, which moved here from Pembrokeshire. It produced, with the help of local girls, cardigans, jumpers, etc. for Marks & Spencer amongst other firms. This company gave way after a few years to the Kenley Engineering Company, which had to move from South Croydon owing to redevelopment of its site. As principal plastic injection moulders, the company did a lot of work for GPO Telephones but also did vacuum forming as well, producing a range of model car bodies and, through an associated company, *Rareplanes*, scale model aircraft kits. This plastics company moved its expertise to the United States.

At the same address Scarab Press started in part of the old stables once occupied by a silver-plating company. There had been a toy manufacturer there for a brief period making *Atomic ducks*! Scarab was there from 1947 until the late 1970s. It took on the production of the local parish magazines after the demise of Mr. Huggins combining these with its daily work for the London Stock Exchange. A sponge importer and processor, Aegean Sponges, also worked from this address as did a firm of private investigators for a short time in the main factory where it had a side-line in making football pin-tables in between detection cases.

After World War II Layhams Engineering expanded its premises and where Caterham Transport had been, a watchmaker George White had a small workshop. Melody House (later Frank Knowles) established its television servicing department and Weber & Hudson turned the garage part into a stationery warehouse specialising in greetings cards.

On the Whyleleafe side of Wapses Lodge roundabout there had been the research laboratories of Moore & George and immediately after World War II L.M. Bellamy Ltd. built superchargers and other motor parts until the building of the Givaudans factory, which specialised in supplying aromatic chemicals, perfumes and flavours. Further north on the site of the Mountain Pools which was once the local Civil Defence mortuary, Smedley's built its headquarters and Mullard's built a factory to make radio valves.

SOURCES

Local directories

Bourne Society *Local History Records*

Personal recollections

1851 Census

Chapter 17

Caterham Valley Shops

by Margaret Duck

The rural way of life in Caterham Valley changed rapidly and dramatically after the railway from London was built in 1856. Prosperous business men and merchants left London and chose to live in the cleaner, healthier air and at the same time less affluent families came from far and wide to work in the large houses, estates and institutions, or to set up small shops to serve the rapidly increasing population. An early print of Caterham Valley shows a few buildings near the *Railway Hotel*.

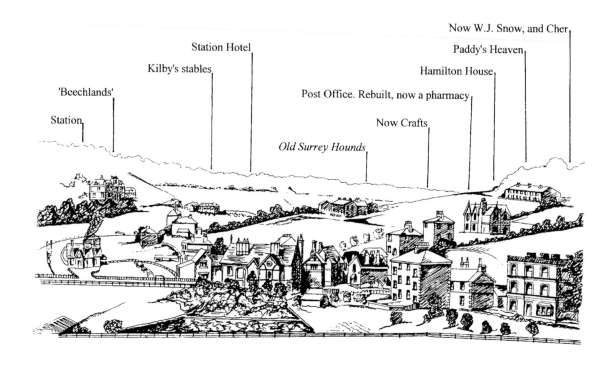

Now W.J. Snow, and Cher,

Paddy's Heaven,

Station Hotel

Hamilton House,

Kilby's stables

Post Office. Rebuilt, now a pharmacy,

'Beechlands'

Now Crafts

Station,

Old Surrey Hounds

Part of Caterham Valley in c.1868, viewed from what is now Clareville Road.

Redrawn from an illustration reproduced in the *Caterham Chronicle* at the turn of the century (copy in Caterham Library)

Many of the early shops were independent wherein all the family worked long hours and lived over the shop often in cramped conditions. The lot of the shopkeeper was not easy, although only a small capital and very basic shopfittings were required and not a great deal of expertise. Private houses had the front rooms turned into shops and, with sales strictly for cash, families could supplement their incomes.

The corner of Croydon Road next to the station became known as Kilby's Corner, where Mr. Kilby set up his stables soon after the railway was built. Horses and carriages were kept in the yard outside the station to meet passengers from the trains. There was a wall round Mr. Kilby's yard onto Croydon Road, where there were some small lock-up shops. One of these was used by M.J. Harris, a family butcher, who displayed his wares on open counters. Beadle Bros, coal merchants, had a large yard, and Mr. Fairall owned a large barn, store and stables for his heavy draught horses. Mr. Fairall was also licensee of *The Greyhound* public house, opened in 1872, so named because he kept greyhounds. For a short time this section of the Croydon Road was known as the High Street. Gradually more shops were built along Croydon Road mainly on the side backing onto the railway where there was ample space for stables and yards to house horses and carts.

At 15-19 Station Avenue, Mr. Woollett a nurseryman owned a shop selling seeds and flowers. He also owned the land and nursery behind his premises which extended behind the first *Railway Hotel*.

The first shops on The Square were built in the early 1870s. Thomas Lovegrove a draper first occupied No. 8 in 1876 followed by George Uridge a grocer. Mr. Crowe another draper traded from No. 10 until he opened a larger shop on the corner of Station Avenue. Walter Smith a high class grocer occupied No. 14. Today Mika photocopier specialists occupy these premises, one of the few businesses to have retained the original shop front and much of the interior. The basement still houses the winding gear used for lowering barrels and groceries from the pavement, where the original pavement flaps can be seen. From the back of his clothier's shop on the corner of The Square and Timber Hill, Edward Pollard ran a sub post-office This became George Ashby corn dealer, followed by Bromley Hall corn and seed merchant for about 60 years, until it was demolished in 1960.

The Square, Caterham Valley in the early 20th century

CATERHAM VALLEY SHOPS

One of the earliest company shops in Caterham was the Co-op Stores opened at 49 Croydon Road in about 1880. Matthew Harden was the manager. Over the years the departments were extended to a butcher's shop and a greengrocer's at 51 and 53. The Co-op remained in these premises until demolished in 1964 to make way for Hammond House. Many Caterham residents recall shopping at the Co-op and queuing to collect the dividend every year.

Mr. Bashford opened a large butcher's shop with a wide side entrance at 8 Croydon Road in 1880. He was followed by Robins Cooke and then R. Knight, who became well known for his Christmas displays of poultry. The Coffee Tavern adjoined in 1880, opening from 5.30 a.m. to 11.30.p.m. Eventually the top floor housed the Caterham Temperance Club. Further along Croydon Road is a block of three shops built in 1887, the year of Queen Victoria's Jubilee. To commemorate this event the builder put in a row of red, white and blue bricks across the fronts of the shops; only those over No. 20 can be seen today. Guy Hewett traded as a greengrocer from No. 20 in 1919, having moved from 103 Croydon Road. His was the oldest surviving family business in Caterham Valley until it closed in October 1996.

64 Croydon Road was Atkey's Dairy, then Pocock's and finally the Express Dairy. Some Caterham residents can remember the milk being delivered from this dairy – twice a day. The milkman had a horse and cart and the milk was ladled out of a churn with a measure. Atkey's kept four horses and carts in the stables at the back, hay was kept in the loft above. The premises were demolished in 1969.

8 Godstone Road seems to have been a greengrocer's and a tailor's alternately from about 1876 until about 1930 when it became J. Sainsbury's and remembered by so many residents. Sainsbury's closed in the early 1970s and it became an extension of Latham's Dairy from next door, which was closed in the 1980s.

R. Austin & Sons
Greengrocers and Fishmongers
72 Croydon Road   *c.*1920

10 Godstone Road, owned by Andrew Browne, Jeweller, retains many of its original features and is probably the least changed shop. The entrance is up a small step and through a solid wide door. Inside there are high ceilings and glass display cabinets. The display windows to the shop front have original decorated etchings.

Page 125

66-68 Croydon Road   (1997)
Robert Perry's family moved into No.68 in 1926

91-99 Croydon Road   (1988)
Built *c.*1880 of local stone. Demolished 1990. The archway led through to stables.

Croydon Road looking north   *c.*1948

Croydon Road 1997 looking south, showing traffic calming measures

Photo: Norman Allin

26 Godstone Road, built in 1888, was from 1900 a draper's shop owned by Mr. Scoggins, who used to travel with his pony and trap round the outlying villages selling small clothing items and haberdashery. His wife looked after the shop and a boy came in on Saturdays to clean the stables and horse and cart.

1 Godstone Road is one of the original shops and retains many of those features. Owned at first by A. Hill a bootmaker and shoemender, it became the Pelican bookshop in December 1935 with Charles Pizzey as manager from 1940. In 1955 it was owned by Mr. Pizzey until he retired in the 1978. MD Motor Sports were the next occupants until 1992 when the shop was closed and reopened in September 1994 as an art shop and picture gallery. Crafts, next door, opened in 1881 is also one of the Valley's oldest shops and since 1889 has been a stationer's.

10 Godstone Road, with its 19th century façade. 1997

J.J. Browne & Son (Jewellers) Ltd

According to the 1910 Caterham Directory the Urban District Council offices were at 13, later 15 Godstone Road prior to the opening of the Soper Hall. The last shop on this side of Godstone Road, 19 has been an eating house since 1880. In 1910 Mr. Horwell was the proprietor of Caterham Valley Refreshment Rooms followed by J. Weller, and in 1931 J.W. Morgan. Lewis & Clarke the catering firm have offices there. A restaurant named the *Hungry Toad* was there from 1986-1995 and now it is a wine bar and restaurant.

Percy Broad, a baker, opened a shop in Station Avenue in 1904 with a small tea room at the back. An elderly resident recalls going to the bakehouse very early in the morning to get hot bread. Others recall taking their Christmas poultry there to be roasted. In 1934 the bakery business was taken over by Addison's who had other bakeries in the district. The bakehouse in Station Avenue was closed in 1946 and the shop in 1990 following a fire at their bakehouse in Westway. *Graduates,* hairdressers moved from Godstone Road and reopened the premises in 1992.

Many Caterham residents have memories of shops and shopping in the 1920s and 30s. Saturday was pay day when the wages were brought home, so that became the busiest shopping day. Many families walked into Caterham where the shop windows were full of goods for sale and goods out on the pavement to lure the customers. Shops were open very late on Saturdays often until 10 p.m. or 11 p.m, especially butchers and greengrocers who had to clear their stock since there was no refrigeration. The Silver Band played in the centre round the fountain with its gas light shining on the crowd; there was much to see and talk about. The pubs were crowded. Children played outside eating crisps and drinking lemonade. The soldiers, the girls, the laughter, the dances at the Stafford Hall after the shops were closed added to the excitement.

By the early 1930s buses and cars had replaced the horse and cart and pony and trap. The Asprey fountain was taken apart and moved to White Knobs Recreation Ground, and a traffic island replaced it. Mr. Kilby's stables were demolished and in 1932 replaced by the National Provincial Bank, which was extended in 1960 and modernised in 1996.

22 Godstone Road. 1997
The low-roofed section was originally a garage owned by Mr. Kilby. Later it became part of Caterham Motor Company. During World War II it was a British Restaurant. The whole building is now occupied by William Hill, Furnishers.

The old shops 31 - 57 Croydon Road together with Caterham's cinema, latterly *the Florida*, opened in 1928, and *The Greyhound* pub, opened in 1872, were demolished in 1964 to make way for Hammond House offices with shops below. Also demolished were Mr. Ramm's hairdressing establishment where haircuts cost 4d and the jeweller's shop at No. 39 which was opened in 1921 by J. Browne followed by his son, William. He closed the old shop at 5 p.m. on Saturday, March 27th 1965 and opened his new business two days later at 9 a.m. on March 29th 1965 in spite of all the demolition and rebuilding.

59-67 Croydon Road were vacated in June 1994 by Rose & Young, motor engineers. The showrooms had been built in the 1930s with curved windows. During the war air raid sirens were made there and as well as being a food storage depot, there was a British Restaurant with cheap meals for 6d and 9d. Three vacated original shop buildings remain on this side of Croydon Road, Nos. 71-73.

A HISTORY OF CATERHAM

The most remembered shop, No. 79, was run by Polly Waters, known to everyone in Caterham in the 1920s and 30s. She was a little lady, slightly deaf and taken advantage of by her young customers. Sweets were sold in values of ¼d, ½d and 1d served in paper cones. Boys liked to ask for sweets from jars that were on high shelves so that Polly had to ascend a ladder to get them. Meanwhile the youngsters helped themselves to biscuits from the glass topped tins in front of the counter. Broken biscuits were also a favourite purchase served in blue paper cones for 1d. Gobstoppers, bullseyes, jelly babies, aniseed balls and boiled sweets all cost 1d for 4 ozs. Polly Waters also sold china and people saved 1d or 2d at a time to buy it.

At 101 Croydon Road was Mr. Duncton the chimney sweep and lamplighter who went out about 4 p.m. during winter to light the street lights. A block of retirement flats were built there in 1994.

Local independent shopkeepers provided quality service to their customers, personal undivided attention, friendly chat, orders taken in triplicate and often on credit. Serving a customer was a ritual, offering a chair to sit on, or taking the order from the carriage, usually by the manager. Items were carefully wrapped in brown paper parcels, tied and knotted with string and delivered. A shop representative could also call at the household to collect an order often travelling miles with the shop's pony and trap. Many elderly gentlemen recall starting their working lives as delivery boys, on bicycles with large baskets on the front. The boys delivered everything and anything, from half a box of cress from Sandiford's to a roll of lino from Ennor's, often cycling many miles.

High class grocers had sets of drawers to hold dry goods, tea was kept in large canisters and weighed out as required, glass topped tins held biscuits at the shop counter. Marble slabs were provided for the casks of butter and margarine which the assistant used to weigh as required using wooden 'hands'; cheeses and bacon kept under muslin were also sliced and cut to order. Goods came in bulk in sacks to the grocers – sugar, rice, lentils, oats, raisins and tapioca were some. These were weighed and packeted into blue paper sugar cones, usually in front of the customer. In quiet times in the shop raisins were stoned by hand and currants washed before packing and assistants would spend time making up cones from large sheets of blue paper.

In the greengrocer's fruits were only provided in season. Shop boys used to saw blocks of salt which was sold in 1d or 2d lumps. Shop owners were very knowledgeable about their stock and could give advice to the customers. There had to be a strict control on the perishable foods until large scale refrigeration changed this. Bookkeeping in shops was an important job. Ledgers, order books, sale records, time sheets, petty cash, invoices and balance sheets were all part of this. In many shops there was a cash railway on an overhead wire. This sent the customer's cash to a central desk, where it was checked with the sales docket, entered in a ledger, receipted and returned.

Today there are two large supermarkets. Waitrose opened in November 1982. A small brick inserted into the wall by the entrance records the birth of Prince William on 21st June 1982. It was built on the site of the British Rail carpark and land at the rear of 31-63 Croydon Road. R. Amos, the manager, has been at this store since it opened.

On the opposite side of Station Avenue the *Valley Hotel* was demolished in 1988 to make way for the entrance to a new shopping precinct named Church Walk where long before there used to be a tennis court, croquet lawn, rose garden, fountain and Mr. Woollet's nursery. Safeway's Supermarket opened with a great flourish in the Precinct on January 23rd 1990, making it possible to buy all one's provisions at one time. Stock is delivered by articulated lorries which back into the unloading bay day and night. A multi-storey car-park with lifts is provided for shoppers. Current retailing methods have led to changes in diet, for the food we can buy is often pre-prepared and ready to cook.

Common to supermarkets is the strongly-made wire shopping trolley, which can be loaded, pushed to the checkout, where goods are paid for at computerised tills. Supermarkets are now open for long hours seven days a week, in the same way as the small family run shops which were in Caterham from the mid 19th century.

THE CHANGING PATTERN OF SHOPS IN CATERHAM VALLEY SINCE THE 1890s

[1]   1889/90 was taken from named shops in directories which gave a shop's principal business.

[2]   1930 was taken from directories that gave shops' principal businesses.

[3]   *c.*1970 list provided from a school project by a girl who is now a doctor.

[4]   The 1990 list made from a walk **before** the opening of the Church Walk precinct.

[5]   Estate agents sometimes include building societies.

[6]   Postage stamps can now be bought in several shops.

[7]   Restaurants include sandwich bars, take-aways, fish & chips.

	1889/90 [1]	1930 [2]	*c.*1970 [3]	1990 [4]	1994
Baker	3	3	2	2	1
Bank	1	4	5	5	5
Beauty shop	-	-	-	2	1
Bookmaker	-	-	1	1	1
Bootmaker	3	-	-	-	-
Builder	5	1	-	-	-
Book	-	1	1	-	-
Building society	-	-	1	3	3
Butchers	3	3	3	1	-
Charity shop	-	-	2	3	4
Chemist	1	3	3	4	3
Clothes shop, Women's & Children's	1	6	9	8	7
Coal merchant	2	1	-	-	-
Coachbuilder	1	-	-	-	-
Corn dealer	2	1	-	-	-
Cycle shop	-	1	-	-	1
Dairy	1	2	1	-	-
Draper/milliner	4	1	1	1	1
Dressmaker	1	-	-	-	-
Dry cleaner	-	1	1	2	2
Estate agent [5]	1	4	4	5	5
Electrical goods	-	3	-	2	2
Fishmonger	2	2	2	-	-
Greengrocer	3	5	4	1	1
Grocer	5	6	4	-	-
Hairdresser, Women's	1	4	4	4	4

THE CHANGING PATTERN OF SHOPS IN CATERHAM VALLEY SINCE THE 1890s *(Cont'd)*

	1889/90[1]	1930[2]	c.1970[3]	1990[4]	1994
Home furnishings	-	1	3	3	3
Ironmonger	2	2	1	1	1
Jeweller	-	2	2	3	3
Newsagent/sweets	-	3	1	2	2
Nurseryman	1	1	1	-	-
Oilman	1	1	-	-	-
Optician	-	1	1	2	2
Photographer	-	1	2	1	1
Plumber	4	-	-	-	-
Post office[6]	1	1	1	1	1
Printer	1	-	-	-	-
Public house	4	4	3	2	2
Restaurant/food/tea shop[7]	-	6	5	12	12
Saddler	1	-	-	-	-
Shoes, boots	1	4	5	3	1
Smith	1	-	-	-	-
Stables	2	1	-	-	-
Stationer/office supplies	2	1	4	4	4
Supermarket	-	-	-	1	2
Sweep	1	-	-	-	-
Tailor	2	2	2	-	-
Toys	-	2	1	-	-
Tools, tool hire	-	1	-	2	2
Travel agent	-	-	1	2	2
TV, radio	-	1	2	1	2
Upholsterer	1	-	-	-	-
Watchmaker	1	-	-	-	-

SOURCES
Directories
Personal reminiscences.

Chapter 18

Clubs and Pubs

by Daphne Woosnam and Joan Cadle

1736 The Henry Rowed Map of Caterham shows plots numbered 24 and 25 as Further Butts and Hither Butts on Wilderness Farm. So it may be safe to assume that archery is the first recorded sport in Caterham.

1767-70 Caterham has an honoured place in cricket history because of its matches with the celebrated Hambledon Club of Hampshire. Repeat fixtures were played to celebrate the 200th anniversaries. The present club dates from 1873 when it was formed as Caterham Park and it has used Queen's Park since 1900. Squire Henry Rowed (1743-1803) was the driving force in those early days, and other famous cricketers from Caterham include James Bryant (Surrey & Victoria); Alfred Atfield (Gloucestershire & Natal); B.H. Lyon (Gloucestershire); M.D. Lyon (Somerset), Ernest Wilson (Surrey) and B.H. Valentine (Kent & England).

There were thriving cricket clubs attached to St. Lawrence's Hospital and Caterham Guards' Depot. Two current county cricketers, Alistair Brown and David Sales, are products of Caterham School.

1850s Clubs and societies played an important part in Victorian life. In the 1850s the public house consolidated its hold as leisure time increased through shortening of working hours and many pubs had special areas for games. These were at the landlord's discretion, and dominated by bye-laws. Among

The Greyhound, Croydon Road – one of the demolished public houses in the Valley – is shown here *c.*1925 on the occasion of a summer charabanc outing. Note the variety of fashionable headgear!

the few allowed were cribbage, skittle alleys, dominoes, darts, billiards and shove ha'penny. In Victorian days Caterham was well known for its number of public houses, four in the Valley and eight on the Hill *[The Commonwealth* (now the *Fountain), The Greyhound, The Half Moon* and *The Old Surrey Hounds* in the Valley and *The Blacksmith's Arms, The Caterham Arms, The Clifton Arms, The Golden Lion, Ye Olde King & Queen, The Royal Oak, The Tally Ho* and *The Harrow* on the Hill], most built to quench the thirst of the workmen labouring to build the Asylum (on the Hill) and the railway (in the Valley). In 1997 there are still eight pubs on the Hill but only two in the Valley.

Every now and then a stage was erected at *The Golden Lion* and prizes given to anyone who could sing a good song, and huge crowds gathered. On Saturdays in the fields off the High Street there would be coconut shies, swings etc. and there was a big wooden shed where the men played quoits, a game using heavy iron rings. The Foresters' Fete was also held in the same field, belonging to Mr. Snelling, on 22nd July. It was a red letter holiday for all. Village sports were popular and Sunday school outings to the sea became an annual event.

Caterham and the surrounding area – Portley Woods, the Common, Old Park, Upwood, Stanstead and Chaldon Woods – was considered fine hunting country. In the early 1900s it was reported that foxes bred freely in the woods ('not bought in Leadenhall Market and turned down. Hares and rabbits literally swarmed'). Deer were uncarted at the top of Church Hill and the hounds laid on. It has been recorded that there were four packs of hounds and that 'there was not a day but that one or other of the packs were in this neighbourhood'.

The Miller Centre. 1997 *(see 1886)*

CLUBS AND PUBS

1871   12 young men played in the Caterham United Minstrels, the local inhabitants providing good instruments and free rehearsal time in the lecture hall. By 1908 the Caterham Silver Band, the Caterham Brass Band and the Valley Reed & Brass Band were in existence, and amalgamated to form the Caterham United Silver Band. By 1911 this band was winning challenge cups at important competitions.

1878   Caterham Horticultural Society was founded. An annual show was held each year with prizewinners in the flower section mainly being the gardeners of the large houses. There was a separate section for the cottagers' vegetables. There is now an annual flower show at Hillcroft School.

1886   The Drill Hall (originally known as the Public Hall) in Godstone Road was built, and for many years was the focal point of interest where all local activities went on until it was bought for use as a military centre. Since 1965 it has been used as the Caterham Youth and Community Centre providing opportunities for basketball, football, archery, rifle shooting, darts, pool, table football, trips, trampolining, board games, weight training, computer club and cookery.

Warlingham Golf Club in the 1930s. *(see 1898)*
Now Manor Park

1886   The first Dramatic Club was formed; Secretary J. Rolls. Regular performances were held at the Public Hall until 1892, and the last play was presented in 1900. In 1974 Caterham Community Stage Club is on record. In 1977 the Miller Centre was founded. It occupies the site of the old St. John's School in Godstone Road. In the daytime retired people meet, and in the evening it is an entertainment centre for the whole community. The Caterham Players – themselves founded in 1945 – present five productions a year, and five are staged by other companies. Dorothy Miller was a founder member of the Players. The Junior Section was formed in 1957. The Miller Centre Workshop was also founded in 1977 to tackle modern plays and experimental work.

1890   O.J. Trinder inaugurated a tennis club on land owned by G. Asprey in Stafford Road. By 1916 it was known as the Caterham Valley Lawn Tennis & Croquet Club.

1892   Caterham & District Fanciers Club. The ninth annual show in October 1901 produced 1266 entries – poultry, pigeons, rabbits, cats, cavies, mice and cage birds. Much later, in 1936, the Caterham & District Cage Bird Society was founded.

1894   Caterham Cycling Club was founded; President Henry Poland. Race meetings were held on the Dene Field.

1898   The Surrey Hills Hydropathic and Turkish Baths Establishment for Residents and Visitors was opened. Known as 'The Hydro', 'taking the waters', Turkish, brine and mustard baths were on offer, as were billiards, tennis and croquet.

1898   Warlingham Golf Club opened on Caterham Manor Estate, Burntwood Lane. During the 1930s the annual subscription was £5 and the caddies earned 9d or 10d per round, plus a glass of fizzy lemonade. It closed after the clubhouse was bombed in 1940 and later became a public park. In 1900 Caterham Golf Club had a nine-hole course adjoining Queen's Park. Green fees for visitors were 2s.6d a round and 4s.0d a day during the week and 5s.0d a round and 8s.0d a day at weekends. It survived until after 1939. In 1910 there was still a nine-hole golf course on Kenley Common, called the Caterham & Kenley Golf Club.

1900   The Caterham Park Football Club was on record. Mr. Roger Love was a founder member. Games were played on the Common near *The Fox* public house. In 1911 it won the Redhill League. After the war it only survived for two seasons. By 1939, a number of football teams had been formed – St. Lawrence's FC, the Mental Hospital FC, St. John's FC, St. Lawrence's Lads Club FC, Caterham CV F.C., Caterham Hill Board School FC, Oak Hall FC, Guards' Depot FC, Invicta FC and Caterham Old Boys' FC, Caterham Municipal FC, Harestone Social Club FC, Caterham LCC Hospital FC, Caterham Motor Co. FC.

1900   The President of the Caterham Institute was Percy Clarke. In December 1902 the Institute was using the upper rooms in what was then known as the Coffee Tavern, Croydon Road. The facilities included billiards, chess, draughts and a ladies' room. By 1916 it was known as the Caterham Club, with membership for men only and women as invited guests. In 1996 under pressure the Committee changed the rules to allow women members.

1900   Caterham Choral Society was on record, president J.E. Street The chorus numbered over 100 voices and there were well-reviewed concerts at the Public Hall. The Caterham Community Choir was founded in 1949 by Harry Kerridge. Its present conductor is Ian Cornwell. In 1961 the East Surrey Choral Society was founded under Arthur Toms. From 1975 until 1995 Michael Pilkington was conductor.

1900   Queen's Park opened on 23rd May. 18 acres were purchased by the Parish Council in 1898 for £1800 to commemorate Queen Victoria's Diamond Jubilee. The pavilions were donated by Harry Lloyd & W.G. Soper. Clubs using the park then were Caterham Bowling Club, the Hockey Club, Caterham Cricket Club and Spartans Cricket Club. A children's playground was opened in the late 1980s. Caterham Bowling Club joined Surrey County BA in May 1911, the greens opening on 5th June 1911 with grand ceremony. In 1997 members still use the greens in Queen's Park, and with money left by the late Mrs. Wilson a new clubhouse has been built.

Bowling at Queen's Park, Caterham.   The original pavilion stands in the background.

1902   The Village Club, Town End, opened on 10th October to provide healthy amusement for men who did not wish to frequent pubs. It was equipped with gymnasium, reading, recreation and billiard rooms. It is now the Royal British Legion, formed in 1921.

1902   A Hockey Club was formed with a membership of 30. Clubhouse – Cedar Grange. The Hill Tradesmen's Sports Association, president H. Niblett, held an annual popular tradesmen's event on August Bank Holiday. By 1910 it was known as 'Ye Olde Village Sports Club'. In 1905 the Girls' Gymnasium Club was sponsored and trained by Miss Iolanthe Morgan-Thomas. It held annual displays at the Congregational Church Hall; all participants dressed in white with white shoes and coloured sashes. In 1939 Caterham LCC Hospital Athletic Club and Caterham Asylum Athletic Club were on record. In 1948 Mr. Cowie of the Surrey Beagles (Athletic Club) ran with the Olympic Torch from Godstone to Oxted. In 1952 its juniors were winners of the East Surrey League Challenge Cup.

1904   Caterham Institute Camera Club. Alec Braid was awarded medals in 1904/05 which were donated by his son in 1973 to be awarded to future competition winners.

1907   Caterham & District Rifle Club was formed on 4th October. The Clubroom and range were built in Waller Lane. It was opened with grand celebration, the Minister of War paid a visit, and a military parade was held in Queen's Park followed by a torchlight tattoo.

Surrey Beagles Athletic Club (Juniors) 1952.
Winners of East Surrey Athletic League Challenge Cup (Junior Division)

A. Glover,   C. A. Chapman,   J. Staples.   S. Copland,   D. K. Coomber,   J. H. Gridley

R. W. Rowlinson,   F. Payne,   D. E. Bone
(Club Captain)

Surrey Beagles Athletic Club (Juniors)   1952

St. Mary's Girl Guides   *(see 1908)*

CLUBS AND PUBS

1908   Boy Scouts – 1st Caterham troop was formed and run by Eric Cooper until 1912. The troop had started as 5th Croydon. During World War I scouts collected waste paper, fire watched and acted as orderlies at the Burntwood Hospital for wounded soldiers. In 1924 scouts from 1st Caterham troop assisted the Fire Brigade in quelling a serious heath fire on White Hill. In 1941 Lord Baden-Powell and over 200 scouts and guides were at a memorial service at St. Mary's. There are now troops at Caterham School, 2nd Caterham; St. John's, 3rd Caterham; St. Francis, 5th Caterham and Mottrams, 6th Caterham; with associated Venture Scouts, Cub Scouts and Beavers.

    1st Caterham (St. Mary's) Girl Guide company was formed before World War I, and there are at present three others – 2nd Caterham Valley, St. John's; 3rd Caterham Hill and 4th Caterham Hill, St. Francis; with associated Brownies and Rainbows. For many years the highlight of the guide calendar was the Campcraft Competition held in Manor Park.

1909   Caterham Land Club was formed to secure gardens for working men. By 1916 it had taken over the council allotments on Tillingdown Hill.

1909   Electric Theatre, Caterham's first cinema, had wooden seats with no backs, and music was provided by a horn gramophone. In 1913 George Gammon transformed the assembly rooms behind *The Commonwealth* into a 220 seater cinema. It was renovated in 1923 as the 'Valley Cinema and Varieties' but by 1928 it was advertised 'To let'. In 1928 the Capitol Cinema, Croydon Road was built. In 1955 it was refurbished and renamed *The Florida*. It closed on 12th August 1960 and was demolished in 1964.

The Florida cinema in 1960

1910   Congregational Literary Association was on record with lectures, whist drives, dances etc. at Soper Hall.

1921   Caterham Valley Women's Institute was formed (closed 1995). A Caterham Hill WI was founded in 1988. Not until 1953 is there a record of the Caterham Hill Afternoon Townswomen's Guild (also now closed). Beechwood Women's Club met at the Caterham Valley Adult Education Centre from 1960 until 1993, and is now at St. Mary's Church Hall. In 1978 Barbara Nurse was organiser of a Caterham group of the National Housewives' Register.

1938   Caterham Library, 53 High Street, was on record. In 1945 it moved to a disused ARP hut in Westway and to its present site in 1966. In 1952 the Valley branch was officially opened at the rear of *The Commonwealth*. In 1964 it moved to its present building.

1942   The Caterham Unit of the Sea Cadet Corps was commissioned under the Admiralty's wartime expansion programme. It was open to boys between 13 and 16 and started at Caterham Hill School, then met at the Fire Engine House and later at the Barracks.

1942   Caterham & District Youth Movement founded, fostered by the Education Authority & UDC. It met at the Youth Centre at St. John's School, and had a wide programme of activities for its membership of over 200 young people from the age of 13½.

1945   The Caterham Group of Artists was founded, meeting in a tiny garden shed. There were fewer than 20 members when it held its first exhibition. Its name changed to 'Caterham Art Group' in 1951 and it now meets at the Red Cross Hut on the Hill. In 1975 the Tandridge Art Society was formed to hold exhibitions, inviting artists from outside the district as well as those within to show their work.

**A Bourne Society *(see 1956)* visit to Streete Court School
just before the school's closure in 1994**

1946   The Caterham Community Association was created in January by representatives of local voluntary societies.

1946   The Caterham Philatelic Society was formed. It has regular meetings in members' homes.

1956   The Bourne Society was founded. Its aims are to extend knowledge of local history and ensure the preservation of records and objects of historical interest.

1956   The Caterham Group of the English Folk Dance & Song Society was meeting at the Community Centre on the Hill and in 1960 the North Downs Morris Men are on record as being in urgent need of either a fiddler or accordian player.

1958   The first Carnival was held with 53 entries for the procession and a full sized fete on Westway Common. Attractions included displays of trampolining, dancing and dog training.

Carnival procession at Caterham High Street 1969
Photo courtesy of East Surrey Museum

1962   Demonstrating the level of local leisure activity, in the Residents' Association Caterham Diary the following associations were mentioned —

Caterham & District Foreign Travel Club

Caterham Old Time Dancing Club

Caterham Open Forum

Caterham Players

Discussion Group of the National Adult School Union

> Old Contemptibles Association
> St. John's Nursing Cadets
> Caterham Valley Institute
> Caterham & Whyteleafe Girl Crusaders
> Motor Cycle Club.

1966   Probus, a club for retired businessmen, was founded in Caterham and is now international.

1977   The East Surrey Family History Society was formed and members are actively involved in the transcribing and indexing of local records.

1978   The Aquarius Swimming Club was on record as a non-competitive club at de Stafford School.

1980   The East Surrey Museum at 1 Stafford Road was opened. During the first year there were over 6000 paying visitors. Some 45 displays were organised by the first curator, Lesley Ketteringham. She was succeeded by John Bushby. Friends of the Museum were formed in the same year.

Christmas exhibition at East Surrey Museum   1981/82

c.1985   Caterham Embroiderers' Guild was formed by Janice Lawrence and Barbara Cooper.

A number of institutes have been developed in Caterham to encourage adult education —

> The Caterham Adult School
> The National Adult School Union
> The University of the Third Age
> Workers' Educational Association

CLUBS AND PUBS

There have over the years been many organisations created to give voluntary help whenever and wherever the need arose. The impressive list includes —

Bluebirds Concert Party

Caterham Volunteers, formed in 1885, which became 1st company 2nd Batt. Surrey Volunteers

Caterham Division of the St. John Ambulance Brigade, formed in 1896

Caterham and surrounding area branches of the RSPCA and the NSPCA

Caterham & District Benefit Nursing Association

Caterham Band of Mercy, founded in 1906 to promote kindness to animals

Caterham Voluntary Detachment, affiliated to the British Red Cross in 1914

Caterham Committee for the Welfare of the Unemployed, formed in 1932

Caterham Hill Voluntary Workers – from 1937-87 – for the welfare of mothers and children

Caterham Good Neighbours Scheme

Caterham Overseas Aid Trust – tackles projects in the Third World

Caterham & District Old People's Welfare Association

Caterham, Oxted & Godstone Lions Club

League of Friends of Caterham & District Hospital

League & Friends of St. Lawrence's Hospital

Masonic Lodges

Tandridge Phab Club – furthers integration of the physically handicapped into the community.

Women's Royal Voluntary Service

There have been many church and political groups not listed individually and there will almost certainly be a number of clubs, associations and activities that have not been recorded in the pages above, some no doubt because of unfortunate omission, others because no precise dates or other information is available.

SOURCES

Caterham Diary

Bourne Society Local History Records

Tooke, J. (1988) *Bygone Caterham*, Phillimore

Tooke, J. & Packham, R. (1986) *Caterham in old Picture Postcards*

Official guides

Old newspapers

Personal communications

Trade directories

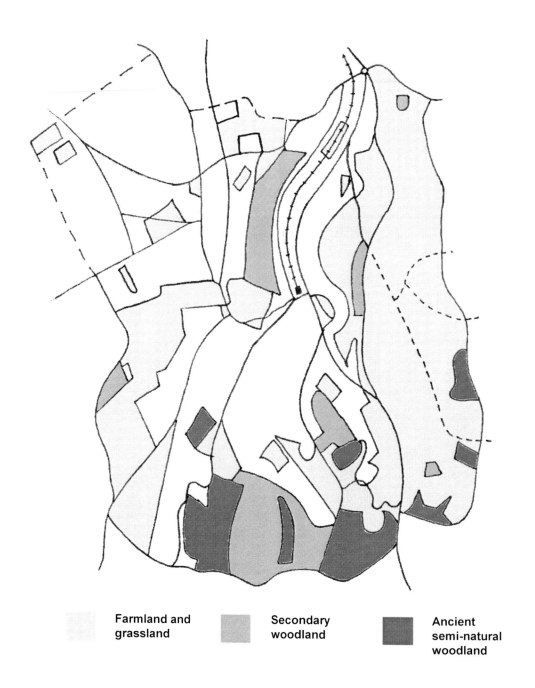

Farmland and grassland   Secondary woodland   Ancient semi-natural woodland

Open Spaces in Caterham

Chapter 19

The Countryside

by Gwyneth Fookes

The downland scenes around us that are so admired were all man-made, farmed and managed through the centuries. The original settlement was set on the plateau on the gentle north facing slopes of the North Downs, where the clay with flints soil provided frugal crops. The steep hillsides of the dissecting valleys are alkaline chalk with very thin topsoils only suitable for sheep grazing. Until last century the marshy valley bottoms were avoided. Towards the summit of the Downs, wooded Blackheath pebble beds cap the clay with flints. This variety of soils provides a variety of habitats for wildlife and, even today, when Caterham is a commuter town, it is perhaps surprising to find that some 60% of the parish is still *country*, which is protected by Green Belt legislation.

To the east of the A22 Tillingdown Farm and Paddock Barn are still farmed. To the south Old Park is high quality downland and ancient woodland, which has been at risk of development. Fosterdown Wood and Tupwood Scrubs are still attractive woodland. To the west there are quite large areas of grazing, mostly by horses, and to the north there is woodland along the steep slopes above Stafford Road. The only remnant of the former extensive Caterham Common is Westway Common. There is nothing left of other early commons at Tupwood, Platts Green and Stanstead. Several public parks preserve open spaces. Throughout the parish there is a network of public footpaths and bridleways, lined with hedgerows, most of them many centuries old. Since the development of the area and consequent vast increase in water abstraction and lowering of the water table, there are neither waterways nor marshy areas and almost all the ponds, which were once so important in every community, have gone.

FARMS & FARMLAND

Table 1a - Open Spaces in Caterham - 1997 - Farms and Farmland

(inclusion in this table does not imply public access)

Aldercombe Farm
Burntwood Lane
Former Caterham Golf Course
Further Lunch etc. west of A22
Above Timber Hill
Greenhill Avenue
Harestone Hill
Rear of *The Harrow*
Paddock Barn Farm
Roffes Lane
Tillingdown Farm
Between Timber Hill & Tillingdown Hill
Woldingham Road

A HISTORY OF CATERHAM

It can be seen that there are still a number of areas in and around Caterham that are farmed. Sheep and cattle are found on Tillingdown, Paddock Barn and Woldingham Road but mostly the grassland is horse grazed. In recent years a number of arable areas are being allowed to go untended, such as between Timber Hill and Tillingdown Hill, which is resulting in the encroachment of scrub and woodland. Where farmed, modern farming methods often restrict the wildlife value of the land, but when the land is left to its own devices and with 'set aside' policies, restoration in terms of recolonisation of wildlife is proving to be quite a speedy process.

WOODLAND

Table 1b Open Spaces in Caterham – 1997 – Woodland	
(A = Ancient Semi-natural woodland S = Secondary woodland)	
A22 roadside Shaw	S
Old Park Wood (Abbots Wood)	A
Beechhanger	A
Clarks Croft	A
Eight acre	A
Essendene Woods	S
Fosterdown Wood	A
Harestone Lane	S
Markfield Wood	S
Ockley Wood	S
Paddock Wood	A
Round Shaw	S
Ten Acre Shaw (Cassock Wood)	A
Tupwood Scrubs	S
Winders Hill	A

Ancient semi-natural woodland is the term used to describe woodland that has been known to exist since at least 1600. It is not wildwood, which is the term used to refer to woodland that has never been managed by man. It has been managed by man over the centuries, usually by coppicing. Woodland was a vital requisite in days gone by. Not only were construction and fencing materials, charcoal and firewood obtained, but pigs were allowed to scour the woods in autumn. Deer and other animals lived there. Old Park backing the summit of the North Downs and surrounded by Old Park Wood and Ten Acre Shaw, was an old deer park incorporated into North Park, Bletchingley in the 13th century. The original earth embankment boundaries can still be followed.

The woods on the chalk slopes are predominantly beech (beechhangers), and those on the clay with flints and Blackheath pebble beds are dominated by oak. They support very different flora, the former being alkaline and the latter acid soils. Plenty of ash is to be found with sycamore frequent in some woods. Hazel, hawthorn and holly form the shrub layer. Whitebeam, which occurs occasionally in most woodland is the dominant species in some areas of Old Park. A number of wild plants are indicative of the ancient semi-natural woodland, such as bluebells, ramsons, wood spurge, sanicle, sweet woodruff and golden scale fern and all of these and many more occur in Caterham woodlands. Dog's mercury, which is found abundantly, is termed a 'weak indicator'.

Such a tree as the magnificent cedar of Lebanon outside the old Rectory on the Hill is one of the most wellknown features of Caterham, estimated to be about 200 years old.. There is a fine beech opposite St. John's Church in the valley and an enormous beech pollard in Abbotts Wood, which is between 350 and 400 years old. A number of fine beeches at View Point were felled in one night in 1987 during the great storm along with many other trees in the district, but natural regeneration is rapidly filling the gaps created with saplings. Deer, foxes, badgers and rabbits find cover in the woodland.

Richard Kearton, a nationally well-known figure at the turn of the century, lived in Caterham Valley and photographed and filmed a wide range of birds in the chalk valleys. He photographed predominantly in the fields behind Greenhill Avenue where he saw such species as butcherbirds (Red-backed shrikes) frequently, a species not seen now in the Caterham area for a number of years. The Caterham Valley is on a bird migration route, so a wide range of birds can be seen from the tiny goldcrest and wren, to chiffchaffs and warblers, and to the large tawny owl and woodcock.

The woodlands on the acid Blackheath pebble beds support a wide range of fungi from the well-known red spotted fly-agaric, the death cap and the rare *Amanita echinocephala,* to the edible boletes, blewits and chanterelles. Tiny yellow waxcaps are to be found on the close-mown lawns of Queen's Park and the slender black fingers of *Geoglossum cookeianum* in St. John's Churchyard.

PARKS, PUBLIC OPEN SPACES, PLAYING FIELDS & PRIVATE GROUNDS

Table 1c - Open spaces in Caterham - 1997 - Parks, open spaces, Playing Fields and Private grounds

(P = public areas   Pr = Privately owned   I = Improved grassland   U = Unimproved grassland)

Allotment areas		Pr	I
Dene Field		Pr	I
Harestone Hill		Pr	U
Westway		P	U
View Point		P	U
Public parks:	Queen's Park	P	I
	White Knobs	P	U
	Town End	P	I
	Stafford Road	P	I
School grounds:	de Stafford	Pr	I
	Caterham	Pr	U
	Hillcroft	Pr	I
	St. John's	Pr	I
	Marden Lodge	Pr	I
Churchyards:	St. John's	P	U
	St. Lawrence's	P	U
	St. Mary's	P	U
	Sacred Heart	P	I
	United Reform	P	I
Caterham Barracks		Pr	I
Vipers' Hollow		Pr	U
Waterworks		Pr	U

While there is a great deal of grassland in Caterham, leaving some wide open spaces, its value as wildlife habitat is often affected by intensive management. The diversity of plant and animal becomes very restricted. Parks and playing fields are often 'improved' with weedkillers and other chemicals. Unimproved grassland is valuable and decreasing nationally in quantity at an alarming rate.

Looking over St. Mary's Churchyard towards Paddock Barn Farm   1997

View Point, Caterham in the early 1920s

Above left: Flower-rich grassland with spotted orchids and bird's foot trefoil.

Above right: Whitebeam leaves opening in Spring, showing the white undersides. Good examples occur in Old Park.

Left: Sweet woodruff, a good indicator of ancient woodland, frequent in Caterham's woods.

Unimproved grassland on the chalk soils supports a wide range of wild flowers from the tiny, perfumed wild thyme and pink striped squinancywort through to purple knapweeds and blue scabious. A number of wild orchids, including the greater butterfly orchid, the bird's nest orchid, the bee and fly orchids, will flourish where the grass is allowed to grow in the flowering season. Gardens can often support a good chalk flora - a number of orchids have been reported from private lawns. One rarity, the tiny blue Kentish milkwort, *Polygala austriaca,* was found last century on the grassy banks along Stafford Road. It was the only site in Surrey but was assumed to have been lost long ago, presumably when houses were built along the road – it is just possible that it survives on an unsuspecting resident's lawns. The slender bedstraw, *Galium pumilum,* was found on the lawns of St. John's churchyard some ten years ago and is preserved each summer by low fencing to keep the lawn mower at bay during its flowering season. Bushes and small trees will soon colonize unmanaged grassland and in time woodland will take over.

A number of butterflies occur on chalk grassland, especially the blues. Small tortoiseshells, peacocks, brimstones and many other butterflies will visit gardens. Several species of ladybird are often seen in our gardens. The commonest is the 7-spot, but they are found with up to 22 spots in reds, yellows, browns and blacks. Glow-worms occur occasionally. Adders and grass snakes are found on the Downs and slow-worms are frequent around Caterham, even in gardens. Lizards are still occasionally seen.

Snails may not be high on most people's list of popular wildlife, but the large Roman snail is only found in the southern areas of the British Isles and is often found in Caterham, again on unimproved grassland, along with humbug-striped *Helicella sp.* and small hairy snails that are noticeably hairy! In woodland, a number of interesting species can be found, such as the disc snail, the garlic glass snail that does smell of garlic, and the door snails that look like inch-long cigars. Chalky areas are particularly rich in species.

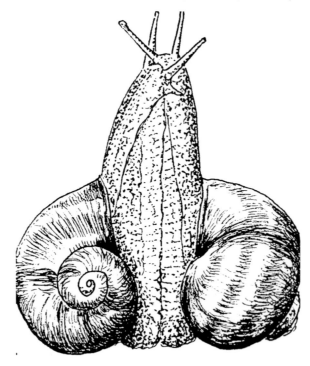

Roman snails 'courting'

OTHER HABITATS

Table 1d - Open Spaces in Caterham – 1997 – Other habitats	
Hedgerows	Some ancient
Verges	Often unimproved
Railway embankments	
Walls	
Roman Road	Ancient
Waller Lane	Ancient
Ponds	
The Bourne	
Restored land	

Hedgerows – provide shelter for a wide range of species, for birds, mammals, large and small, butterflies and moths. It is very probable that a number of the hedgerows in and around Caterham are very old. Certainly some have been aged and proved to be several hundred years old, using Hooper's rule which calculates that for each tree species occurring in a 30 yard stretch, add 100 years to the age of the hedge, so that say several 30 yard stretches with 4 species would prove that the hedge was 400 years old. This rule has been hotly debated, but there can be little doubt that hedges with a variety of native tree species are old and should be checked against other available sources to confirm. Bearing this in mind in referring to the 1736 Rowed map, it is certainly possible to trace a number of the land boundaries shown on that map and some of those boundaries are hedged. One example can be demonstrated – the hedge on the east side of the Godstone Road opposite White Knobs Way has an average of six species, which would suggest an age of 600 years which is perfectly possible.

Verges – can often prove to be a valuable habitat. A number of unusual species are found on the verges along the A22, including orchids and the dark green mouse-ear, *Cerastium semidecandrum*.

Railway embankment - provides a linear habitat, which over the past 150 years has been recognised as the enabling factor in the distribution of a number of wild plant species. One that has arrived in Caterham in this way is the sticky groundsel, *Senecio viscosus*. The ballast, uninviting though it may seem, supports other plants.

Walls – old walls will support small ferns, and on the Barracks walls, there is wall rue in plenty, black spleenwort and hartstongue. In other crevices you will find buddleia, a species introduced from China at the end of last century, willowherbs and ragworts.

Roman Road – along the eastern skyline seen from the Valley there is a deep bank along the Roman road which is topped by a line of oak trees. The bank itself has hawthorn, blackthorn, cow parsley, ivy and other plants.

Waller Lane – the narrow road linking the Valley and the Hill is lined with fine beech trees on high banks. Such banks are themselves indicative of age – of roads worn down year upon year, summer and winter, by the treading of feet of man and hoof of beast before the days of asphalt surfacing. White Hill just outside Caterham parish towards Bletchingley along Stanstead Road is a more dramatic example.

Waller Lane, showing steep beech-topped banks

Ponds – The number of remaining historic ponds in Caterham can be counted on the fingers of one hand. Nearly all ponds are man-made and ponds in the parish once supplied drinking water for man and beast. It is not obvious which was the main village pond that would also have been used for other purposes such as perhaps the ducking stool!

There was one in Money Road, another where the Council tip is now in Chaldon Road, one by St. Lawrence's church, two by Tillingdown Farm, one of which is still extant. There were two by Paddock Barn Farm and no doubt in the yards of other farms in the area. The ornamental garden and school educational ponds have taken the place of these and they support frogs, toads, newts, dragonflies and water plants in Caterham.

The Bourne – There are virtually no remnants of the damp marshy land that once made the Caterham Valley so inhospitable that even the Romans skirted it. There is the occasional pendulous sedge that has persisted from the Victorian garden and for some years fools' watercress was to be found in the United Reform Church grounds. From the geological formation of the district it would seem obvious that at least one bourne stream once rose somewhere along Harestone Valley Road and the water flowed northwards to join the Bourne that now rises near the Woldingham viaduct and then to the Wandle, in the past causing havoc traditionally every seven years. The Bourne waters were often called the 'woe waters', and were reputed to foretell national disasters.

Restored ground – Gravel workings in Stanstead Road and Upper Greensand workings at Fosterdown are both areas restored, the latter with power station ash. They have been recolonising with flora and fauna naturally over a number of years and have proved most interesting. Disturbed soil supports a wide range of ephemeral plants, those that become crowded out by vigorous species and unexpected plants can often be found in the early years after disturbance.

Pond provided in school grounds by school governors for St. John's Infants and Junior Schools.   Opened in July 1996

SOURCES

Margary, I., 1948 *Roman Ways in the Weald*

Rackham, O., 1989 *The History of the Countryside* Dent

Regimental Sergeant Major Ronald Brittain, MBE
Photo courtesy of Caterham Library

Chapter 20

Personalities

by Joan Cadle, Sue Beach & Marie Barnes

Many residents have contributed to the development of Caterham, supporting local institutions, churches, hospitals and societies over many years. Some figures have been of national significance, others familiar in day to day life. No doubt many have been omitted, but as many have been included as space allows.

ABBOTT, JOHN de LACY
Founder in 1890 of Caterham's first weekly newspaper, the *Caterham Free Press*, from his premises in Croydon Road.

AGLIONBY, HENRY AGLIONBY 1790-1853
Member of Parliament for Cockermouth, he lived at Manor Cottage for at least 15 years.

ASPREY, CHARLES 1813-1892
Charles Asprey of the celebrated jewellery company came during the mid 1860s and built 'Beechlands' in Stafford Road. He purchased considerable land in the area and with others in 1869 he formed the Caterham & Kenley Gas Co. He donated the drinking fountain that has recently been returned to the centre of the town.

BALCH, JAMES 1815-1871
Born at Downing Street, Westminster. Enumerator of the 1851 Census, living in High Street, where he ran the Post Office and was a tailor, butcher and grocer. In 1859 he bought Box Cottage and had 'Caterham House' built in 1873 on the corner of High Street and Park Road.

BATLEY, JAMES 1915-1982.
Prominent in local history – a dynamic founder member of the Bourne Society and East Surrey Museum.

BORER, HENRY JAMES – 1878-1900
Aged 22, he died in Portland Hospital, Bloemfontein. One of the earliest and youngest members of local St. John Ambulance Brigade. A memorial was erected in Queens Park.

BRAID, ALEC 1871-1936
A Cornishman, he came to Caterham in 1891 to edit the new *Caterham Free Press*, staying 11 months. During this time he married local baker's daughter, Minnie Whiffen. In 1898 he returned with Mr. Holbrook and stayed for 11 years as editor. He produced many guides and postcards of the area. He left in 1909 to further his career with national newspapers and then in films.

BRIGHT, REVD. F.A. 1842-1907
Ordained a deacon in 1867, he became a priest the following year. He came first as curate to Revd. Heard in 1882 and became rector in 1892. Elected to UD Council representing West Ward.

BRITTAIN, RSM RONALD, MBE 1900-1981
Joined the army in 1917. Re-enlisted at end of World War I in the Coldstream Guards, coming to Caterham in 1919. Married local girl, Mildred Charlton in 1921. By 1935, now Regimental Sergeant Major, he trained cadets at Sandhurst and Aldershot. The Two Cities Film Co. shot some scenes for the film *They were not Divided* at Caterham Barracks. He took part and earned title of the loudest mouth in Britain.

BROOKER, NAPKIN   ? -1780
From 1770 he leased land from Henry Rowed for a term of 21 years. He also rented *Half Moon Inn* (Wapses Lodge) from Joseph Hodgkins at rent of £9. 6s. 4d a year.

BROUGH, WILLIAM   1824-1913
Born in Staffordshire. Headmaster of the National School of Caterham Hill from 1850 until 1870, when he became first clerk to School Board. He also became parish clerk and overseer until his death. He was the last person to be buried in St. Lawrence's graveyard.

BUNCE, GEORGE & HERBERT.
Well known for their postcards, photographs and portraits taken at their studio in Westway. They were official photographers to Guards' Depot. Flourished during Edwardian times and between the wars.

The Bunce brothers

PERSONALITIES

CHRISTIE, Miss MARION ? -1976
The niece of local artist, Ernest Christie (1863-1937) who had lived in the area from 1910 to 1921. Trained as a governess and in 1920 she opened a school for girls, 'St. Andrews', Chaldon Road.

CLARKE, JAMES 1824-1888
A Suffolk man, he came to Caterham in the mid 1870s. Became editor of *Christian World*, eventually becoming owner. He bought 'Beechhanger' in Harestone Valley Road and soon became involved with the Congregational School.

COBB, GEORGE 1844-1924
Spent his early life in Chelsea and came to Caterham between 1878-9 when he bought a decorator's business in Croydon Road. He was prominent in local affairs and later became Caterham Valley funeral director.

COOKSEY, Canon 1871-1955
Born in Basingstoke, he became a catholic and was ordained at St. George's Cathedral on 8th April 1901. During World War I he served as army chaplain on Western Front and soon after was appointed priest to Caterham Church until his death.

CRICHTON, ROBERT 1812-1914
When he died he had earned the title of oldest bachelor in Britain. Born in Alythe, Perthshire. He worked a cattle ranch for 20 years in New South Wales, then returned to England, settling first in Horsham, then at 'The Mardens', Tupwood Lane after checking the cemetery to find out if people of Caterham were long-lived.

Robert Crichton in 1912, after his 100th birthday
Photo courtesy of Caterham Library

CROUDACE, OLIVER REDMAYNE ? -1970s
Caterham born, lived in Chaldon Road. He set up business with J.B. Ratcliffe after World War II, first general building repairs, then contract home building.

DANVERS, Sir JULAND, KCSI 1826-1902
Came to Caterham prior to 1861, living with his family at 'Woodlands', Stanstead Road. He was a civil engineer and Director of Indian Railway Co.

DAVIS, FRED
Well known by locals in area for the many miles he would tramp doing his *Evening Standard* paper round, never missing whatever weather. He lived in Oak Road.

DAY, CHARLES 1784-1836
Bought Manors of Salmons, Portley and Caterham. Elected overseer of parish. He shared with Rector the cost of building a Vestry room and other major work at St. Lawrence's church.

DREW, GEORGE, Snr. 1789- ?
Born at Bermondsey. A solicitor by profession he acquired the estate of Charles Day, moving into 'Burntwood House'. He had many interests including local housing, railway and road building. George Henry Drew, his son, was also influential in local community.

ELLIFFE, FREDERICK 1858- ?
Lived in Waller Lane in 1891. He was a local architect and surveyor with his office in Station Avenue.

FARR, PHILLIP, FSAA 1869-1935
Came to Caterham in 1929, living at 'Bassishaw' in Burntwood Lane. Elected to Church Council of St. Mary's. He was treasurer to building fund for St. Paul's Church and was prominent in local affairs.

GASSON, MARY
Lady tramp. Family home in Nelson Road. It was said she had been jilted. Would bathe in horse trough on Westway Common. Sold firewood. Befriended by Mrs. Wilde of Clifton Hill and spent last years at St. Anne's, Redhill.

GOLD, Major R.J. 1879-1948
Born at Exeter, educated at Cranleigh, joined engineering branch of GPO. Came to Caterham in 1921. His home, 'Bedrutam' in Harestone Hill was totally destroyed by a night raid in March 1944. A leading figure at beginning of local Toc H and Caterham Philatelic Club.

GUIMARAENS, FREDERICK A. 1851-1923
First lived at 'Orchard Leigh', Harestone Valley Road, then at 'Sunnyside', Whyteleafe Road. He was prominent in local affairs and senior Grand Master for Surrey Masons.

GWYNNE, WILLIAM J. 1802-1896
Born at Battersea. A major local property owner – of Caterham Railway, Railway Hotel, surrounding shops, cottages and land. Between 1896 and 1901 both his sons died and his daughter sold his property in 1901.

HALL, Mrs. AGNES 1860-1944
Lived at 'Shortfurrows', Whyteleafe Road. Widow of Percy Hall, solicitor and was prominent in local affairs.

HEALEY, F.C. 1876-1955
Came to Caterham in 1929. With his wife he started Caterham Adult School. Working for unemployed in 1933 and later had Community Centre erected. He was associated with founding of Community Association and served on UD Council.

PERSONALITIES

HEARD, Revd. J.B. 1849-1909
First minister of St. John's Church. He had a distinguished Art career at Cambridge University. Through his hard work the church was built in 1882.

HEWETT, GUY 1887-1978
Greengrocery business started in 1870s by his mother, Hannah and continued by him and later his sons and grandsons. The business in Caterham closed in October 1996, although they still trade in Old Coulsdon.

JOHNSTON, C.P. 1866-1947
His home was 'Annadale', Harestone Hill, where he lived for 50 years. He was prominent in local affairs and was one of the promoters when acquiring White Knobs Sports ground.

KEARTON, RICHARD 1862-1928
Well known as an author, teacher, zoologistand ornithologist, he first came to Caterham for his health in 1898. Travelled extensively. Lectured locally when time allowed. President of local Photographic Society. A development has been named after him on site of his home 'Ashdene' in Croydon Road.

Richard Kearton

KEPPEL, Hon. VIOLET 1881-1959
Relative of the famous Alice Keppel. An active worker for the RSPCA. Devoting her life to animals, she opened a successful clinic at St. Paul's Church. Her home was 'Tryon House' on Church Hill.

LE PERSONNE, Mrs. HENRIETTA ? -1925
First woman member of Surrey County Council. The Le Personne Homes in Banstead Road were built in her memory.

LIVERSIDGE, HOWARD, JP 1869-1934
Lived in Whyteleafe Road. Elected to first Urban District Council in 1899, becoming Chairman in 1911. He was also a member of Surrey County Council.

LOVEGROVE, ADA 1863-1949
Long standing member of Salvation Army. Every week – wet or fine – 'Sec', as she was known, sold the Army's *War Cry*. She ran *Sunbeams* and *Guards* clubs for local girls.

MARCUSE, GERALD 1886-1961
With an interest in amateur wireless, he began transmitting in 1921. Lived at 'Coombe Dingle', Queen's Park Road, where he converted attic for his work with radio signals, transmitting the sound of 'Big Ben' to the country in 1929. Later President of Radio Society of Great Britain.

Gerald Marcuse 1924
Photo courtesy of Caterham Library

MARTIN, HENRY RICHARD 1864-1944
Was appointed Surveyor and Architect to the Council in 1899 and held position for 32 years. He designed Soper Hall. He worked at the Barracks during World War I, taking care of sanitary arrangements – with 14,000 men expected, this was a vital duty.

MEDWIN, MATTHIAS ENGLAND 1893-1940
Had a small general provision shop in Chaldon Road. During a wartime raid he was killed by machine gun fire whilst saving the lives of several children on their way home from school.

PERSONALITIES

MOTTRAM, ALLAN 1875-1934
Educated at Caterham School and returned in 1902 as science master. In 1907 he visited America & Canada to study methods of education. Promoted to headmaster until his unfortunate death. Former home of Countess Lindon was bought as boarders' accommodation and re-named 'Mottrams' in his memory.

OLSEN, Dr. J.B.
On 25th March 1903 he purchased 'Cambrian House', 1 The Villas, Godstone Rd., and took a lease on the field at rear on behalf of the Good Health Association. These were converted and opened as the Good Health Sanatorium.

PATON, Sir GEORGE WILLIAM ? -1930
Made Knight Bachelor for his public work. He was Chairman and Director of Bryant & May Match Co. President of the Horticultural Society in 1927. He lived at 'Portley'.

POLAND, HENRY
Lived at 'Greenland', Buxton Lane (now 'Buxton Lodge'). He was a Lloyds underwriter and financed the Village Club, Town End (now the British Legion) He was founder of the Caterham Cycling Club and involved in other local sports.

POOK, CHARLES 1831-1907
Founder member of Caterham Valley Methodists and played the organ there. He was an early photographer in the Valley area.

PURSSORD, PERCY 1893-1969
Came as teacher to the Valley Board School in 1913. Served in Egypt during World War I, when he was injured. In March 1919 he resumed teaching until his retirement in 1957-43 years. At some time a child called him Mr. Pur*dagger*, not Purs*sord*, and he became known as 'Dagger'.

PYE, Misses CATHERINE & WINIFRED
Opened private school on 18th January 1892, which in 1923 was transferred to Eothen School Co.Ltd. The school was later enlarged and offered accommodation for boarders. They retired in 1938.

ROWED, HENRY and family
The earliest dated map of Caterham –1736 – shows that a Henry Rowed owned most of the land in Caterham. The parish registers show that Richard Rowed married Mary Frisby on 22nd June 1691. A son, Henry, was baptized on 10th January 1694 – he could be the Henry Rowed, landowner. The family fortunes appear to have changed for they disappear to return 15 years later as carpenters and husbandmen.

ROE, Father FRANCIS RAMSDEN 1850-1918
Son of infantry officer, educated at Oratory School, first taught by Cardinal Newman. He came to Caterham in 1879 before the Roman Catholic church and presbytery were completed. Died on last day of World War I.

SARGEANT, CHARLES 1911-1994
Born in Caterham. Put up posters for cinema (silent films). Worked for Guy Hewett's, World Stores and then during World War II for Addison's the bakers. Member of the Land & Poultry Club.

SCARBOROUGH, Father CYRIL 1905-1985
Roman Catholic priest at Caterham from 1955 to 1979. Held as POW during World War II - spent some of his years in captivity at Colditz.

SETH-SMITH, ELSIE 1883-1969
Youngest daughter of William Seth Smith. Moved to 'Alleyne', Harestone Valley Road in 1900. First book published in 1904 *To the Shrine of Truth*. She continued to have adult and children's books published in England and the United States. Married 1921 to Arthur Murrell and had three daughters.

Left: Father Francis Ramsden Roe (on right)   1911

Photo courtesy of Caterham Library

Below: Jeoffry Spence on the occasion of the unveiling of the Bourne Society's plaque at Purley Station   1988

PERSONALITIES

SIBLEY, Major-General 1827-1915
India Mutiny veteran. Served in Delhi and Afghan war. He had 'Shirley Goss' built in Harestone Valley Road. Committee member of Cottage Hospital, JP on Godstone bench. A keen gardener, he had great success at summer shows.

SOPER, WILLIAM GARLAND 1837-1908
Married in 1860, he settled at 'The Priory', Stafford Road. Became a partner in his father-in-law's firm. Founder member of Congregational Church. Later had 'Harestone House' built in 1879. Prominent local benefactor. The land for Queen's Park was bought through his efforts and the park was opened in 1900. Soper Hall was built in his memory in 1912. He was the first chairman of Caterham Urban District Council.

SPENCE, JEOFFRY 1915-1992
Founder member of the Bourne Society, later President. He wrote several books on railway history.

TOMES, Sir JOHN 1815-1895
He was an eminent dental surgeon and encouraged establishment of professional qualifications. Retiring in 1876 he moved to 'Upwood Gorse', Tupwood Lane. His tomb has been restored by a Dutch College of Dentistry.

Robert Vigar
Photo courtesy of
Caterham Library

Frederick Bradbury Winter and his wife Fanny (née Mason)

PERSONALITIES

THOMAS, MORGAN JP 1841-1916
First lived at 'Beechwood' in 1875, later 'Hampton Mount'. He had several houses built in Clareville Road and was prominent in local affairs.

VALENTINE, BRIAN HERBERT 1908-1983
At one time his home was 'Woodside', Stanstead Road. A cricketer of distinction, he played for Kent from 1927-48 and for England in seven test matches; President of Kent in 1967. An excellent tennis player and a soccer blue.

VIGAR, ROBERT 1844-1923
Came to Caterham in1869, setting up as farrier and blacksmith. He formed the Caterham Silver Band and was Chief Officer in the newly formed Fire Brigade. Hunted with the Surrey Hounds. He earned the freedom of the City of London.

WEATHERLY, Madame 1836-1914
A Court milliner, lived in France, retiring to 'Iviza', Croydon Road. During 1906 she formed the Caterham Valley Band of Mercy in connection with the RSPCA. She started the Grand Horse Parade, presenting a cup for the best kept working horse in the haulage business.

WILSON, Mrs. E.M. ?-1993
Presented the clock tower in Queen's Park on 5th May 1954 as a memorial to late husband. She left money to Caterham Bowling Club which was used for a new clubhouse.

WINTER, FREDERICK BRADBURY 1826-1902
A marine engineer, he came to Caterham in 1864 for his health. With others he established the Congregational Church in Caterham. An overseer of the parish and guardian to the authoress, Edna Lyall (Ada Bayley) who stayed at his home, 'Broomfield', for six years.

WOOD, Revd. Fergus ? -1949
Minister of St. John's Church from 1894-1919, leaving to become minister of Tandridge. One of the governors of Eothen School. He was an authority on English history.

SOURCES

Bourne Society publications

Local newspapers

Bolger, Pat - pers. comm.

One of the earliest roads that has left its mark on our landscape is part of the Roman London to Brighton Way. From the Wapses Lodge roundabout it leaves the A22 and follows Tillingdown Hill towards Tillingdown Farm. It can be seen as a bank in a playground before it rejoins the A22 at the southern end of the Caterham by-pass.

The photograph shows the Roman road on the hill behind Crescent Road.

Chapter 21

Caterham's Roads

by Elaine Williams

Road names are in bold print the first time they are mentioned.

Most of Caterham's history can be followed by studying its road names. In the Iron Age there was a hill-fort at War Coppice, but in more modern times the area was coppiced woodland. **WAR COPPICE ROAD** runs through it now. In 1907 two new roads were built there forming a new garden village. One was called **WOODLAND WAY** and the other **WEALD WAY**, probably because the nearby extensive views lead to the Weald of Sussex. The Roman London to Brighton Road passes through Caterham. From the Wapses Lodge roundabout it leaves the A22 and follows **TILLINGDOWN HILL** where it can be seen as a bank in the playground before it follows the side of the hill and rejoins the A22 at the southern end of the **CATERHAM BYPASS.**

Jumping a few centuries, in the 13th century Caterham was held by Waltham Abbey. The *Victoria County History* states 'In the reign of King John, Roger son of Everard de Gaist gave the church to the monastery of Waltham Holy Cross'. When, in the mid 1940s the Tillingdown Hill estate was built, all the road names were centred round this theme. Thus we have **ABBOTS WALK, EVERARD LANE, GAIST AVENUE, MONKS PLACE, ROGERS CLOSE** and **WALTHAM ROAD.** The Earls of Stafford also held land in and around Caterham between the 14th and 16th centuries. This period is remembered in the name of **STAFFORD ROAD** which formed part of the Caterham Park estate in 1870. It was to all intents and purposes a private road and had gates at each end, which were closed one day a year to keep the road private.

Whilst some of our old roads have disappeared, the majority are extant and provide the framework for today's road system. One such road is the old turnpike road which runs along the Caterham Valley. The Rocque map of 1762 named it as **STONEHAM LANE**, but it has had several name changes since then. It first changed to **GODSTONE ROAD**, then became known as **GODSTONE ROAD NORTH** and **GODSTONE ROAD SOUTH** or even just **MAIN ROAD.** It was not until the 1880s that the road became known by its two names of GODSTONE ROAD and **CROYDON ROAD**, with even the name **HIGH STREET** appearing for a short time.

BURNTWOOD LANE, often written on maps as **BURNT WOOD LANE**, was drawn on the undated map of the Mannor *(sic)* of Portley in Surrey showing a field on its north side called Burnt Wood Field and an area on the south side named Burnt Wood Hill. In 1907 the upper part of the road was described as being 'very narrow and overgrown with trees'.

BUXTON LANE has had several names in the course of its long history. It is unnamed on a map of 1793 but *c.*1820 it appears as **TAYLOR LANE.** By the time of the 1851 census the name had changed to **BUCKSTONE LANE** and later the 1871 and 1879 Ordnance Survey maps showed it as **BUXTON'S LANE.** A Miss Buckstone held land there in the 19th century. However, in the 1880s the rate books call the road **GREENLANDS LANE** after the house of that name which is now the Buxton Lodge Nursing Home, but maps of 1913 and 1933 continued to name it Buxton's Lane.

The 1736 Rowed map was entitled *A map of the Court Lodge and Red-Hall Farms in the Parish of Catterham in the County of Surrey belonging unto Henry Rowed.* **STANSTEAD ROAD, ROFFES LANE, WALLER LANE,** HIGH STREET and **TUPWOOD LANE** can be identified from this map plus GODSTONE ROAD as described above. These, therefore, are among Caterham's oldest surviving roads.

Stanstead Road at the beginning of the 20th century

The name STANSTEAD is probably derived from the ancient word for stone, i.e. *stan*, indicating the stony surface of the roadway before it was made up. To reinforce this assumption the stretch of road running near *The Harrow* inn appears on an 1839 map, and in later census returns, as **STONE STREET**. It also appears in various deeds under the names **STANE STREET** and **STONY STREET**. Part of STANSTEAD ROAD was diverted in the 1860s when Mr. Winter had his new house 'Broomfield' built and used part of the old road for the drive up to the house.

The road joining STANSTEAD ROAD and **CHALDON ROAD** used to have two names. The 1828 parish map showed the southern section as **ROFFES LANE** but the northern end which joined CHALDON ROAD rejoiced in the name **HOLLIDAY'S BOTTOM**, bottom indicating that it lay at the foot of a hill. In 1909 James Balch junior wrote in his reminiscences of Caterham that his grandmother's ancestors, the Roff (Roffey) family had the lane made, hence its name. It appears from the rate book that the whole road officially became ROFFES LANE in 1928.

We can see from the Rowed map that **CHURCH HILL** was the name of a field. Originally the road of that name started at this field and formed an L-shaped junction with STANSTEAD ROAD, there being no route at that point down to the valley. However, by 1805 there was a private road called **CHURCH HILL ROAD** which belonged to John Hitchin. The Caterham Park Estate map of 1870 showed this road as **GREAT HILL ROAD**. The crown of the hill was very steep and was lowered in 1894. It was made up in 1922 and was used by the bus service that started in the same year.

WALLER LANE was the main route which connected the hill village of Caterham to the valley before CHURCH HILL was opened for public use. The Rowed map refers to it as **WALLOM LANE**, an 1839 map called it **WATTER LANE**, while at one time it was known as **WALWAYE LANE**. Even in the 1990s it is very much a country lane.

The **HIGH STREET**, on the Hill, seems to have acquired this name only in the 1870s. Before then no name appeared on maps, the area being generally known as 'the village'. 'High' meant important and therefore indicated that the road was a highway as opposed to a byway.

Church Road, showing the ancient St. Lawrence's Church

TUPWOOD LANE is shown on the Rowed map as leaving the Godstone Road almost as it does today and leading to Tup Wood Common. Sometimes – as in the 1841 census returns – the T is omitted, giving us Up Wood. Where the lane left GODSTONE ROAD it crossed a piece of land called Colliers Down. When part of this area was built on in 1961 the road was called **COLLIERS**, and so the name lives on. Again, when flats were being built off **WHYTELEAFE ROAD** and with the same idea in mind the new road was called **FURROWS PLACE** because here the fields on the Rowed map were known as 'Furrows'.

From 1801 a population census has been held every decade, but it was not until 1841 that road names were included in the returns. Caterham's returns for that year, however, do not include many road names. Instead areas like Plat Green, Village and Common are entered or well-known buildings such as *The Harrow* and White Nobs which was the farm remembered in **WHITE KNOBS WAY**. However, the delightfully named **PEPPER ALLEY** is entered. It must have been Caterham's shortest road for it was tucked away between STANSTEAD ROAD and **HARESTONE LANE** and contained just three agricultural labourers' cottages. HARESTONE LANE was known as **DREWS LANE** in the 1850s. It was probably named by, or after George Drew who owned a great part of Caterham at the time.

During the 120 years following the draughting of the Rowed map, very little seems to have changed. However, in November 1855 the vestry of St. John's, Old Coulsdon, resolved 'That a road nearly as straight as possible be made over Coulsdon Common from the Signpost by the Church Lane to unite with the Caterham Road'. Thus **COULSDON ROAD** was built.

The arrival in the valley of the railway in 1856 heralded the beginning of Caterham as we know it today, i.e. the two centres of Caterham on the Hill and Caterham Valley. New houses were built for the railway construction workers, such as those at the top of **MOUNT PLEASANT ROAD** which the local population nicknamed 'Paddy's Heaven'. MOUNT PLEASANT ROAD also had its sobriquets. It was either referred to as **JONES' HILL**, after the fishmonger on one corner, or **COFFEE TAVERN HILL**, after the tavern on the other. The

The Hare Stone, now in the grounds of Caterham School

name **COMMONWEALTH ROAD** derives from the Commonwealth Land Building and Investment Society. **FARNINGHAM ROAD** was built a few years later – across the hillside, which is perhaps why it was also called **CROSS ROAD.** Professional and business men from London had grand houses built, mostly in the valley, which gave rise to the construction of **HARESTONE VALLEY ROAD** (where the hare stone can still be seen today in the grounds of Caterham School) and **UPWOOD NEW ROAD** or **TUPWOOD NEW ROAD** as it was also called; today it is known as **HARESTONE HILL.** These roads formed part of the Caterham Park Estate.

It is clear from the estate map that the road now called **CRESCENT ROAD** was originally meant to be called **TIMBER HILL ROAD.** The naming of this road once more takes us back to the Rowed map which showed land called Timbers Hill and Timbers Hill Bottom where the road was later built. The road was crescent-shaped and so took the name CRESCENT ROAD instead, and the original name was transferred to the road which linked it to GODSTONE ROAD.

One major new road appeared on the hill in the 1860s. George Henry Drew, son of George Drew, proposed in 1860 to pay for a road 'Commencing at the west end of Waller Lane ... continuing thence in a northerly direction and crossing Burntwood Lane ... terminating at the boundary of the said Parish of Caterham near a house called Whiteleaf House'. The length of the road was to be 3198 yards and called **WHITELEAF ROAD.** It was later changed to WHYTELEAFE when the owner of Whiteleaf House changed the spelling of his house name.

ESSENDENE ROAD was also constructed in the 1860s. It linked the grounds of Essendene to the HIGH STREET. Like STAFFORD ROAD it was closed one day a year to keep it private.

Crescent Road in the 1980s

Essendene Road before World War I

Major changes came to Caterham Hill in the 1870s with the building of the Metropolitan District Asylum in 1870, and the Guards Depot seven years later. Both were built in COULSDON ROAD. A link road was cut across Caterham Common from the village so that building materials could be transported more easily. This road was for many years called **ASYLUM ROAD** but was changed to **WESTWAY** in about 1912, mainly due to the representations of the Bunce Brothers.

Towards the end of the 19th century large estates began to sell some of their land for housing developments. The Oaks Estate was started in the late 1870s and an indenture of 1879 told of a new road to be known as **OAK ROAD**. **BANSTEAD ROAD** originally ran diagonally across the Town End Recreation Ground. It was diverted to its present line in 1908. Another, later, road which was part of the Oaks estate was **AUCKLAND ROAD**. In spite of a slight variation in spelling, it seems probable that it was named after John Loxley Aukland who owned land nearby.

The 1890s saw the beginning of the Ninhams (sic) Estate. A large part of Ninham's land was sold and **ADDISON, CAMPBELL, CROMWELL, ELDON, GORDON, MILTON** and **SPENCER ROADS** were created. In the 1893 rate book **a HILDON ROAD** is listed as being on the new housing estate. However, in 1894 the name ELDON ROAD appeared instead. More confusion arises over the naming of SPENCER ROAD. Caterham already had a SPENCER ROAD, next to **LONDON ROAD**. It was renamed **NELSON ROAD** sometime between 1904 and 1910; in 1963 it was extended to form the present cul-de-sac.

CHALDON ROAD also had two names which appear to have been used concurrently, at least until 1904, i.e. CHALDON ROAD and **REIGATE ROAD.**

Another road with dual names is **TOWN END**, formerly called **TOWNS END**. The road runs through the former Townsend Farm, of which part of the 17th century farmhouse still stands. The road in front of the farm up to Tewksbury's shoe shop was liable to flood, which was probably why this section of TOWN END was known locally as **THE CAUSEWAY** at least from the 1880s.

The development of Greenhill Avenue before World War II

THE ROADS OF CATERHAM

As the 20th century progressed the rate of development in Caterham increased rapidly. 19th century roads such as **BEECHWOOD GARDENS** and **PARK ROAD** began to be filled with houses.

The Queen's Park Estate was started and plans for the building of **HOMESTEAD ROAD** were submitted in 1902, Homestead being the name of the nearby farm. In 1903 the Council approved plans for the construction of **COURT ROAD**, although there had been plans for this road since 1870. It was built by a local builder, Mr. Bramham, and the road was eventually made up in 1925, as was **QUEENS PARK ROAD**.

Property began springing up on Caterham Common between ASYLUM ROAD and BANSTEAD ROAD. The area around Money Pit was developed and gave rise to **MONEY ROAD**, at first called **MONEY PIT ROAD**, and **ELIZABETH ROAD**. However, in 1909 the rate book shows that another name change had been made, for ELIZABETH ROAD had now become **LIVINGSTONE ROAD** – perhaps to complement **STANLEY STREET**.

Some of our roads have been named after either national heroes, such as **NELSON ROAD** and **WELLINGTON ROAD**, or local people. In 1895 Thomas Bourne of Ninhams Farm bought land off **NINHAMS LANE** (later renamed **FOXON LANE**) from a Mr. Field. When Thomas Bourne's children inherited the land, they sold it in 1936 and when the area was built on the right-of-way became **BOURNE LANE**. **REID AVENUE**, built in 1953 by the military authorities, was named after General Reid.

Road names are nowadays decided by the local council, in conjunction with developers. One of the few instances where the UDC minutes record the reason why a road is given a certain name occurred in 1949. Here we learn that **GARLAND WAY** was named in memory of the first chairman of the Council, William Garland Soper. This road leads off **LE PERSONNE ROAD** which was named after another local worthy. Louis Antoine Georges le Personne, a Belgian, lived in the house called the Oaks in NINHAMS LANE. He founded the Le Personne homes.

Burntwood Lane at its junction with Stafford Road before road widening in the 1960s

MILNER ROAD was probably named after Richard John Neville Milner, who lived in nearby 'Burntwood House' in BURNTWOOD LANE in the 1920s. An indenture dated 1876 explained that John Glenny of Loxford House, Highbury, Middlesex and James Mathias of Harestone House, Caterham owned land either side of **LOXFORD ROAD.** They agreed to share the expense of the maintenance and repair of the road but it seems that John Glenny must have wielded more influence as the road bears the name of his house.

Building continued apace in Caterham in the 1930s. After the demolition of the former manor house, Caterham Court, in the late 1920s, the land was developed under the name of the Caterham Court Park Estate. **MANOR AVENUE** still retains two pillars marking the entrance to Caterham Court. **PARK AVENUE**, part of the same development, was once the location of the Caterham Hill Lawn Tennis Club.

Probably the most important road to be constructed in Caterham in the first half of the 20th century was the CATERHAM BYPASS with its innovative roundabout at Wapses Lodges. Burntwood Lane and the other roads coming off the roundabout had to be realigned and the levels raised to combat the threat of flooding from the Bourne. The bypass opened on 7th April 1939.

Throughout the post-war years, new roads have continued to be built. Since building land is at a premium often the only course open to developers is to demolish a large old house and thereby make land available. This is not a new idea but has been practised throughout the century. Roads named after big houses include **ELGIN CRESCENT, RYELANDS CLOSE, ST. KATHERINE'S ROAD, STONEHOUSE GARDENS, UNDERWOOD ROAD** and **WOODVILLE PLACE** to name but a few. Although some of the houses have gone their names live on. **ALDERCOMBE LANE** is an example of a road being named after a former farm and also of a road name change – the 1939 directory says that the lane was originally called **THE GLADE.**

In the 1990s the demolition and sale of the site of St. Lawrence's Hospital has freed acres of land for developments and has thereby created many new roads. One area was built on by Admiral Homes and all their roads have been named after admirals, e.g. **CORNWALLIS CLOSE, DRAKE AVENUE, FAIRBOURNE LANE** and **MONTAGUE DRIVE.** Another area developed by Bellway Homes in 1997 has road names using local personalities suggested by the Bourne Society. More such developments are awaited on the sites of Eothen School and possibly Caterham Barracks.

SOURCES

Bourne Society *Local History Records*

Caterham UDC minutes

Directories

Estate Maps

Rowed Map